IIS 4
The Cram Sheet

This Cram Sheet contains the distilled, key facts about IIS 4. Review this information last thing before you enter the test room, paying special attention to those areas where you feel you need the most review. You can transfer any of these facts from your head onto a blank sheet of paper before beginning the exam.

PLANNING

1. The IIS 4.0 components are: WWW service, FTP service, Transaction Server, SMTP service, NNTP service, Index Server, and Certificate Server.

2. HTTP 1.1 provides support for pipelining, persistent connections, chunked transfers, and proxy.

INSTALLATION AND CONFIGURATION

3. IIS requires:
   - NT Server 4.0
   - Service Pack 3
   - IE 4.01
   Personal Web Server requires:
   - NT Workstation 4.0
   - Service Pack 3
   - IE 4.01 or Windows 95 and IE 4.01.

4. TCP Port defaults: Web is 80; FTP is 21

5. HTTP keep-alives sustain communication links between the client and server.

6. HTTP headers are used to host multiple Web sites over a single IP address.

7. Both NTFS- and site-level security must match for users to read, execute (Web), and write (FTP).

8. MMC snap-in configurations saved in .MSC can be used during later sessions.

9. Individual operators are able to remotely administer their Web and FTP sites using HTMLA.

CONFIGURATION AND MANAGING RESOURCE ACCESS

10. Directory Security: allow/restrict anonymous access; Basic Authentication (clear text passwords) (Web); Windows NT Challenge/Response.

11. Secure Web Communications: SSL digital certificates, 40-bit/128-bit, required/enabled, https://, SSL port: 443, client certificates.

12. IP Address And Domain Name Restrictions: grant or deny all, fine-tune with exceptions (single IP, IP and subnet mask, or domain name).

13. Content for a resource URL can be hosted on IIS, over a network share, or redirected to an alternate URL (Web only).

14. Sites can be assigned to specific IP address or to (All Unassigned).

INTEGRATION AND INTEROPERABILITY

15. An Index Server catalog can be up to 40 percent of corpus.

16. Index Server files:
    - **.HTM** Query form
    - **.IDQ** Query parameters
    - **.HTX** Results formatting
17. IIS communicates with ODBC via IDC (Internet Database Connector).

RUNNING APPLICATIONS

18. IIS supports server-side includes (**#INCLUDE** only).
19. ASP is used to enable server-side scripting.
20. ISAPI filters are used on a per-site basis to enable application customization.
21. The SMTP service is used to send out email messages from a site and accept all mail sent to a hosted domain.
22. The SMTP service uses port 25 for normal transmissions.
23. The SMTP service can hide source domains by using a masquerade domain on all outbound messages.
24. Increased security can be employed by requiring reverse DNS lookup on incoming messages.
25. The NNTP service is used to host threaded discussion groups.
26. The NNTP service uses port 119 for normal transmissions and port 563 for SLL transmission
27. Moderated group messages are sent to the moderator by email.
28. NNTP service discussion groups can be indexed and searched via Index Server.
29. Both the SMTP and NNTP services of IIS are respectively SMTP and NNTP standards compliant. SMTP service does not support POP3 and NNTP service does not support newsfeeds.

MONITORING AND OPTIMIZATION

30. Bandwidth throttling can be done on by server and by site; a site setting overrides the server setting.

31. Performance Tuning: <10,000, <100,000, >100,000 match traffic patterns to optimize memory.
32. HTTP keep-alives sustain communications across multiple requests.
33. Limit connections to improve per-user performance.
34. Reduce connection timeout to terminate inactive sessions more quickly.
35. The Site Server Express Content Analyzer is used to generate statistics verify links.
36. Usage Import And Report Writer uses IIS log files to generate site reports.
37. The installation of IIS adds the Internet Information Services Global, Web service, FTP service, and Active Server Pages to Performance Monitor.

TROUBLESHOOTING

38. Most CGIs only require Execute access, but some(.IDX and .HTX files) may also require Read.
39. 400-series HTTP error messages are related to the client; 500 series HTTP error messages are related to the server.

The following table lists pertinent HTTP error messages:

400 Bad Request	Request could not be understood by the server.
401 Unauthorized: Logon Failed	The credentials passed to the server do not match the credentials required to log on to the server.
403 Forbidden: Execute Access Forbidden	Execution attempted from a directory that does not allow programs to be executed.
404 Not Found	Cannot find the file or script asked for.
500 Internal Server Error	Server is incapable of performing the request.
501 Not Implemented	Server does not support the functionality required to fulfill the request.
502 Bad Gateway	The server received an invalid response from an upstream server.

Are You Certifiable?

That's the question that's probably on your mind. The answer is: You bet! But if you've tried and failed or you've been frustrated by the complexity of the MCSE program and the maze of study materials available, you've come to the right place. We've created our new publishing and training program, *Certification Insider Press*, to help you accomplish one important goal: to ace an MCSE exam without having to spend the rest of your life studying for it.

The book you have in your hands is part of our *Exam Cram* series. Each book is especially designed not only to help you study for an exam but also to help you understand what the exam is all about. Inside these covers you'll find hundreds of test-taking tips, insights, and strategies that simply cannot be found anyplace else. In creating our guides, we've assembled the very best team of certified trainers, MCSE professionals, and networking course developers.

Our commitment is to ensure that the *Exam Cram* guides offer proven training and active-learning techniques not found in other study guides. We provide unique study tips and techniques, memory joggers, custom quizzes, insights about trick questions, a sample test, and much more. In a nutshell, each *Exam Cram* guide is closely organized like the exam it is tied to.

To help us continue to provide the very best certification study materials, we'd like to hear from you. Write or email us (**craminfo@coriolis.com**) and let us know how our *Exam Cram* guides have helped you study, or tell us about new features you'd like us to add. If you send us a story about how an *Exam Cram* guide has helped you ace an exam and we use it in one of our guides, we'll send you an official *Exam Cram* shirt for your efforts.

Good luck with your certification exam, and thanks for allowing us to help you achieve your goals.

Keith Weiskamp
Publisher, Certification Insider Press

IIS 4

Exam # 70-087

Microsoft
Certified
Systems
Engineer

The Coriolis Group, Inc.
An International Thomson Publishing Company
14455 N. Hayden Road, Suite 220
Scottsdale, Arizona 85260

602/483-0192
FAX 602/483-0193
http://www.coriolis.com

Library of Congress Cataloging-in-Publication Data
Stewart, J. Michael
    MCSE IIS 4 exam cram/by J. Michael Stewart and Ramesh Chandak
      p.   cm.
    Includes index.
    ISBN 1-57610-194-0
    1. Electronic data processing personnel--Certification.   2. Microsoft
software--Examinations--Study guides.   3. Microsoft Internet information
server.   I. Chandak, Ramesh
QA76.3.T574   1998
005.7'13769--dc21   98-3699
                                   CIP

Printed in the United States of America
10 9 8 7 6 5 4 3 2 1

Publisher
Keith Weiskamp

Acquisitions
Shari Jo Hehr

Project Editor
Jeff Kellum

Production Coordinator
Kim Eoff

Cover Design
Anthony Stock

Layout Design
April Nielsen

Marketing Specialist
Cynthia Caldwell

an International Thomson Publishing company

Albany, NY • Belmont, CA • Bonn • Boston • Cincinnati • Detroit • Johannesburg • London • Madrid
Melbourne • Mexico City • New York • Paris • Singapore • Tokyo • Toronto • Washington

About The Authors

James Michael Stewart

James Michael Stewart is a full-time writer focusing on Windows NT and Internet topics. Most recently, he has worked on several titles in the *Exam Cram* series, including *MCSE NT Server 4 Exam Cram*, *MCSE NT Workstation 4 Exam Cram*, *MCSE NT Server 4 in the Enterprise Exam Cram*, and *MCSE Windows 95 Exam Cram*. Additionally, he has coauthored the *Hip Pocket Guide to HTML 4.0* (IDG Books Worldwide, 1998) and the *Intranet Bible* (IDG Books Worldwide, 1997), plus made contributions to *Windows NT Networking for Dummies* (IDG Books Worldwide, 1997), *Building Windows NT Web Servers* (IDG Books Worldwide, 1997), and *Windows NT, Step by Step* (Microsoft Press, 1995). Michael has written articles for numerous print and online publications, including *C\Net*, *InfoWorld*, *Windows NT* magazine, and *Datamation*. He's also a regular speaker at Networld+Interop, has taught at WNTIS and NT SANS, and is a former leader of an NT study group at the Central Texas LAN Association.

Michael has been developing Windows NT 4 MCSE-level courseware and training materials for several years, including both print and online publications as well as classroom presentation NT training materials. He has been an MCSE since 1997, with a focus on Windows NT 4.0. He's currently pursuing MCSE + Internet certification, with his sights set on MCT.

Michael has been active on the Internet for quite some time, where most people know him by his *nom de wire*, McIntyre. He spends his spare time reading, two-stepping, and remodeling his condo. You can reach Michael by email at michael@lanw.com, or through his Web pages at http://www.lanw.com/jmsbio.htm or http://www.impactonline.com/.

Ramesh Chandak

Ramesh Chandak is a graduate with a Fellowship in Advanced Engineering Study from MIT (Cambridge, MA). Ramesh has a total of eight years of work experience in the IT industry. Ramesh has worked extensively with Internet,

Microsoft, Sybase, PowerSoft, and Java technologies. In addition, Ramesh has authored 14 books, tech edited 13 books, and published 25+ technical articles for several leading publishers on client/server, databases, multimedia, and Internet technologies.

Acknowledgments

James Michael Stewart

Thanks to my boss, Ed Tittel, for including me in this book series. Thanks to all my co-workers, whose efforts in the trenches have enabled this series to grow to fruition. To my parents, Dave and Sue, thanks for your consistent love, evident pride, and ongoing encouragement. To Mark, through all my hills and valleys, knowing you are my friend doesn't help one bit because you're in the wrong state—COME HOME SOON! To John Paul "The Pope" Henry—when it absolutely, positively, has to get there... and your point? To HERbert, your feline company is more comforting than you'll probably ever be able to understand. And finally, as always, to Elvis: I find myself sneering my lip, strumming an air guitar, and humming "Hound Dog"... then I realize people are watching me.

Ramesh Chandak

Thanks, The Big B (Amitabh Bachchan), for being my inspiration and role model throughout my life. Thanks, Dad, for your love, care, blessings, and more. Thanks, Mom, for being the *best* mom in this world.

Table Of Contents

Introduction

Welcome to *MCSE IIS 4 Exam Cram*. This book aims to help you get ready to take—and pass—the Microsoft certification test numbered Exam 70-087, titled "Implementing and Supporting Microsoft Internet Information Server 4.0." In this introduction, we introduce Microsoft's certification programs in general and talk about how the *Exam Cram* series can help you prepare for Microsoft's certification exams.

Exam Cram books help you understand and appreciate the subjects and materials you need to pass Microsoft certification exams. The books are aimed strictly at test preparation and review. They do not teach you everything you need to know about a topic. Instead, we (the authors) present and dissect the questions and problems that you're likely to encounter on a test. Our aim is to bring together as much information as possible about Microsoft certification exams.

Nevertheless, to completely prepare yourself for any Microsoft test, we recommend that you begin your studies with some classroom training or that you pick up and read one of the many study guides available from Microsoft and third-party vendors, including the *Exam Prep* book by Certification Insider Press. We also strongly recommend that you install, configure, and explore the software or environment that you'll be tested on, because nothing beats hands-on experience and familiarity when it comes to understanding the questions you're likely to encounter on a certification test. Book learning is essential, but hands-on experience is the best teacher of all.

The Microsoft Certified Professional (MCP) Program

The MCP Program currently includes five separate tracks, each of which boasts its own special acronym (as a would-be certified professional, you need to have a high tolerance for alphabet soup of all kinds):

➤ **MCP (Microsoft Certified Professional)** This is the least prestigious of all the certification tracks from Microsoft. Attaining MCP status requires an individual to pass at least one core operating system exam. Passing any of the major Microsoft operating system exams—including those for Windows 95, Windows NT Workstation, or Windows NT Server—qualifies an individual for MCP credentials. Individuals can demonstrate proficiency with additional Microsoft products by passing additional certification exams.

➤ **MCSD (Microsoft Certified Solution Developer)** This track is aimed primarily at developers. This credential indicates that those who hold it are able to design and implement custom business solutions around particular Microsoft development tools, technologies, and operating systems. To obtain an MCSD, an individual must demonstrate the ability to analyze and interpret user requirements; select and integrate products, platforms, tools, and technologies; design and implement code and customize applications; and perform necessary software tests and quality assurance operations.

To become an MCSD, an individual must pass a total of four exams: two core exams plus two elective exams. The two core exams are the Microsoft Windows Operating Systems And Services Architecture I and II (WOSSA I and WOSSA II, numbered 70-150 and 70-151). Elective exams cover specific Microsoft applications and languages, including Visual Basic, C++, the Microsoft Foundation Classes, Access, SQL Server, Excel, and more.

➤ **MCT (Microsoft Certified Trainer)** Microsoft Certified Trainers are individuals who are considered competent to deliver elements of the official Microsoft training curriculum, based on technical knowledge and instructional ability. Therefore, It is necessary for an individual seeking MCT credentials (which are granted on a course-by-course basis) to pass the related certification exam for a course and successfully complete the official Microsoft training in the subject area, as well as to demonstrate teaching ability.

This latter criterion may be satisfied by proving that one has already attained training certification from Novell, Banyan, Lotus, the Santa Cruz Operation, or Cisco, or by taking a Microsoft-sanctioned work-shop on instruction. Microsoft makes it clear that MCTs are an important cog in the Microsoft training channels. Instructors must be MCTs to teach in any of Microsoft's official training channels, including its affiliated Authorized Technical Education Centers (ATECs), Authorized Academic Training Programs (AATPs), and the Microsoft Online Institute (MOLI).

➤ **MCSE (Microsoft Certified Systems Engineer)** Anyone who possesses a current MCSE is warranted to possess a high level of expertise with

Windows NT (either version 3.51 or 4) and other Microsoft operating systems and products. This credential is designed to prepare individuals to plan, implement, maintain, and support information systems and networks built around Microsoft Windows NT and its BackOffice family of products.

To obtain an MCSE, an individual must pass four core operating system exams plus two elective exams. The operating system exams require individuals to demonstrate competence with desktop and server operating systems and with networking components.

At least two Windows NT-related exams must be passed to obtain an MCSE: "Implementing and Supporting Windows NT Server" (version 3.51 or 4) and "Implementing and Supporting Windows NT Server in the Enterprise" (version 3.51 or 4). These tests are intended to indicate an individual's knowledge of Windows NT in smaller, simpler networks and in larger, more complex, and heterogeneous networks, respectively.

Two more tests must be passed: These tests are related to networking and desktop operating system. At present, the networking requirement can be satisfied only by passing the Networking Essentials test. The desktop operating system test can be satisfied by passing a Windows 3.1, Windows for Workgroups 3.11, Windows NT Workstation (the version must match whichever core curriculum is pursued), or Windows 95 test (and soon Windows 98).

The two remaining exams are elective exams. The elective exams can be in any number of subject or product areas, primarily BackOffice components. These include tests on SQL Server, SNA Server, Exchange Server, Systems Management Server, and the like. However, it is also possible to test out on electives by taking advanced networking topics such as "Internetworking with Microsoft TCP/IP." (Again, the version of Windows NT involved must match the version for the core requirements taken.)

Whatever the mix of tests, individuals must pass six tests to meet the MCSE requirements. It's not uncommon for the entire process to take a year or so, and many individuals find that they must take a test more than once to pass. Our primary goal with the *Exam Cram* series is to make it possible, given proper study and preparation, to pass all the MCSE tests on the first try.

➤ **MCSE + I (Microsoft Certified Systems Engineer + Internet)** This is the newest certification level developed by Microsoft. MCSE + I is designed to certify MCSE-level experts in the topical fields commonly associated with the Internet. This level of certification requires the completion of 7 core exams and 2 electives. The core exams are Networking Essentials, TCP/IP, a client (Windows 95, Windows 98, Windows NT Workstation), Windows NT Server, Windows NT Server in the Enterprise, Internet Information Server, and Internet Explorer Administration Kit. There are five tests that can be used as the two required electives: System Administration with SQL Server, Implementing Database Design with SQL Server, Exchange Server, Proxy Server, and SNA Server. Needless to say, this certification level is significantly more work to achieve than the standard MCSE.

A related certification is that of MCP + I (Microsoft Certified Professional plus Internet). This mid-level MCSE certification is attained by completing 3 core exams: Windows NT Server, TCP/IP, and Internet Information Server.

Ongoing Certification

Certification is an ongoing activity. Once a Microsoft product becomes obsolete, MCSEs (and other MCPs) typically have a 12- to 18-month time frame in which they can become recertified on current product versions (if individuals do not get recertified within the specified time period, their certification is no longer valid). Because technology keeps changing and new products continually supplant old ones, this should come as no surprise.

The best place to keep tabs on the MCP program and its various certifications is on the Microsoft Web site. The current root URL for the MCP program, titled Microsoft Certified Professional, is http://www.microsoft.com/mcp/. However, Microsoft's Web site changes frequently, so if this URL doesn't work, try using the Search tool on Microsoft's site with either MCP or the quoted phrase "Microsoft Certified Professional Program" as the search string. This will help you find the latest and most accurate information about the company's certification programs. There is also a special CD-ROM that contains a copy of the Microsoft Education and Certification Roadmap. The Roadmap covers much of the same information as the Web site and it's updated quarterly. To get your copy of the CD-ROM, call Microsoft at (800) 636-7544, Monday through Friday, 6:30 A.M. through 7:30 P.M. Pacific Time.

Taking A Certification Exam

Alas, testing is not free. You'll be charged $100 for each test you take, whether you pass or fail. In the United States and Canada, tests are administered by Sylvan Prometric. Sylvan Prometric can be reached at (800) 755-3926 or (800)

755-EXAM, any time from 7 A.M. to 6 P.M., Central Time, Monday through Friday. If you can't get through on this number, try (612) 896-7000 or (612) 820-5707.

To schedule an exam, call at least one day in advance. To cancel or reschedule an exam, you must call at least 12 hours before the scheduled test time (or you may be charged). When calling Sylvan Prometric, have the following information ready for the telesales staffer who handles your call:

➤ Your name, organization, and mailing address.

➤ Your Microsoft Test ID. (For most U.S. citizens, this is your social security number. Citizens of other nations can use their taxpayer IDs or make other arrangements with the order taker.)

➤ The number and name of the exam you wish to take. (For this book, the exam number is 70-087 and the exam name is "Implementing and Supporting Microsoft Internet Information Server 4.0.")

➤ A method of payment. (The most convenient approach is to supply a valid credit card number with sufficient available credit. Otherwise, payments by check, money order, or purchase order must be received before a test can be scheduled. If the latter methods are required, ask your order taker for more details.)

On the day of the test, try to arrive at least 15 minutes before the scheduled time slot. You must bring and supply two forms of identification, one of which one must be a photo ID.

All exams are completely closed book. In fact, you will not be permitted to take anything with you into the testing area; you will be furnished with a blank sheet of paper and a pen. We suggest that you immediately write down the most critical information about the test you're taking on the sheet of paper. *Exam Cram* books provide a brief reference—The Cram Sheet, located in the front of each book—that lists the essential information from the book in distilled form. You will have some time to compose yourself, to record this information, and even to take a sample orientation exam before you must begin the real thing. We suggest you take the orientation test before taking your first exam; they're all more or less identical in layout, behavior, and controls, so you probably won't need to do this more than once.

When you complete a Microsoft certification exam, the software will tell you whether you've passed or failed. All tests are scored on a basis of 1,000 points, and results are broken into several topical areas. Even if you fail, we suggest you ask for—and keep—the detailed report that the test administrator should print out for you. You can use the report to help you prepare for another go-round, if necessary. If you need to retake an exam, you'll have to call Sylvan Prometric, schedule a new test date, and pay another $100.

Tracking MCP Status

As soon as you pass any Microsoft operating system exam, you'll attain MCP status. Microsoft also generates transcripts that indicate the exams you have passed and your corresponding test scores. You can order a transcript by email at any time by sending an email addressed to mcp@msprograms.com. You can also obtain a copy of your transcript by transcript tool on the secure private MCP Web area. This is accessed by clicking the "For MCPs Only" link on the MCP page. You'll need to provide your unique MCP ID number and password to gain entry. Your password will be included in your MCP welcome message from Microsoft. This welcome will be sent two to six weeks after you have completed your first operating system exam.

Once you pass the necessary set of six exams, you'll be certified as an MCSE. Official certification normally takes anywhere from four to six weeks, so don't expect to get your credentials overnight. When the package arrives, it will include a Welcome Kit that contains a number of elements, including:

➤ An MCSE certificate, suitable for framing, along with an MCSE Professional Program membership card and lapel pin.

➤ A license to use the MCP logo, thereby allowing you to use the logo in advertisements, promotions, documents, on letterhead, business cards, and so on. An MCP logo sheet, which includes camera-ready artwork, comes with the license. (Note: Before using any of the artwork, individuals must sign and return a licensing agreement that indicates they'll abide by its terms and conditions.)

➤ A one-year subscription to TechNet, a collection of CDs that includes software, documentation, service packs, databases, and more technical information than you can possibly ever read. In our minds, this is the best and most tangible benefit of attaining MCSE status.

➤ A subscription to *Microsoft Certified Professional Magazine*, which provides ongoing data about testing and certification activities, requirements, and changes to the program.

➤ A free Priority Comprehensive 10-pack with Microsoft Product Support, and a 25 percent discount on additional Priority Comprehensive 10-packs. This lets you place up to 10 free calls to Microsoft's technical support operation at a higher-than-normal priority level.

➤ A one-year subscription to the Microsoft Beta Evaluation program. This subscription will get you all beta products from Microsoft for the next year. (This does not include developer products. You must join the MSDN program or become an MCSD to qualify for developer beta products.)

Many people believe that the benefits of MCSE certification go well beyond the perks that Microsoft provides to newly anointed members of this elite group. We're starting to see more job listings that request or require applicants to have an MCSE, and many individuals who complete the program can qualify for increases in pay and/or responsibility. As an official recognition of hard work and broad knowledge, MCSE certification is a badge of honor in many IT organizations.

How To Prepare For An Exam

At a minimum, preparing for a Windows NT Server-related test requires that you obtain and study the following materials:

➤ The Microsoft Windows NT Server 4 manuals (or online documentation and Help files, which ship on the CD-ROM with the product and also appear on the TechNet CD-ROMs).

➤ The *Microsoft Internet Information Server Resource Kit*, published by Microsoft Press, Redmond, WA, 1996. ISBN 1-57231-638-1.

➤ The exam prep materials, practice tests, and self-assessment exams on the Microsoft Training And Certification Download page (http://www.microsoft.com/mcp/). Find the materials, download them, and use them!

➤ This *Exam Cram* book! It's the first and last thing you should read before taking the exam.

In addition, you'll probably find any or all of the following materials useful in your quest for Internet Information Server expertise:

➤ **The Exam Prep Series** These comprehensive study guides, also published by Certification Insider Press, are designed to teach you everything you need to know from an exam perspective. *MCSE IIS 4 Exam Prep* is the perfect learning companion to prepare you for Exam 70-087, "Implementing and Supporting Microsoft Internet Information Server 4.0." Look for this book in bookstores soon.

➤ **Classroom training** ATECs, AATPs, MOLI, and unlicensed third-party training companies (such as Wave Technologies, American Research Group, Learning Tree, Data-Tech, and others) all offer

assroom training on Internet Information Server. These companies
aim to help prepare network administrators to understand Internet
Information Server concepts and pass the MCSE tests. Although such
training runs upward of $350 per day in class, most of the individuals
lucky enough to partake (including your humble authors, who've even
taught such courses) find them to be quite worthwhile.

➤ **Other publications** You'll find direct references to other publications
and resources in this book, but there's no shortage of materials available
about Internet Information Server. To help you sift through some of the
publications out there, we end each chapter with a "Need To Know
More?" section that provides pointers to more complete and exhaustive
resources covering the chapter's information. This should give you an
idea of where we suggest you should look for further discussion.

➤ **The TechNet CD-ROM** TechNet is a monthly CD-ROM subscription available from Microsoft. TechNet includes all the Windows NT
BackOffice Resource Kits and their product documentation. In addition,
TechNet provides the contents of the Microsoft Knowledge Base and
many kinds of software, white papers, training materials, as well as other
good stuff. TechNet also contains all service packs, interim release
patches, and supplemental driver software released since the last major
version for most Microsoft programs and all Microsoft operating
systems. A one-year subscription costs $299—worth every penny, if only
for the download time it saves.

Microsoft periodically offers a free trial issue of TechNet as part of a
special promotion. Keep your eyes on the TechNet CD Web site (http://
www.microsoft.com/technet/) for these promotions. As of April of
1998, a free issue of TechNet was available by registering on the IT
Home Web site (http://www.microsoft.com/ithome/).

This set of required and recommend materials represents a nonpareil collection of sources and resources for Internet Information Server topics and software. In the section that follows, we explain how this book works, and give you
some good reasons why this book should also be in your required and recommended materials list.

About This Book

Each topical *Exam Cram* chapter follows a regular structure, along with graphical
cues about especially important or useful material. Here's the structure of a
typical chapter:

➤ **Opening hotlists** Each chapter begins with lists of the terms, tools, and techniques that you must learn and understand before you can be fully conversant with the chapter's subject matter. We follow the hotlists with one or two introductory paragraphs to set the stage for the rest of the chapter.

➤ **Topical coverage** After the opening hotlists, each chapter covers a series of at least four topics related to the chapter's subject. Throughout this section, we highlight material most likely to appear on a test using a special Study Alert layout, like this:

This is what a Study Alert looks like. Any information found offset in Study Alert format is worthy of unusual attentiveness on your part. Indeed, most of the facts appearing in The Cram Sheet appear as Study Alerts within the text.

Occasionally in *Exam Cram* books, you'll see tables called "Vital Statistics." The contents of vital statistics tables are worthy of an extra once-over. These tables contain informational tidbits that might well show up in a test question.

Pay close attention to material flagged as a Study Alert or included in a Vital Statistics table. Although all of the information in this book pertains to what you need to study, we flag certain items that are really important. That's one reason why this book is less than half the size of a typical study guide devoted to IIS. It's also why, as we've said before, this book alone is probably not enough to carry you through the exam process in a single try.

In addition to the Study Alerts and Vital Statistics tables, we have provided tips that will help build a better foundation for IIS knowledge. Even if the information is not on the exam, it is certainly related and will help you become a better test taker.

This is how tips are formatted. Keep your eyes open for these, and you'll become an IIS guru in no time.

➤ **Exam Prep Questions** This section presents a series of mock test questions and explanations of both correct and incorrect answers. We also try to point out especially tricky questions by using a special icon, like this:

Ordinarily, this icon flags the presence of an especially devious question, if not an outright trick question. Trick questions are calculated to "trap" you if you don't read them carefully and more than once, at that. Although they're not ubiquitous, such questions make regular appearances in the Microsoft exams. That's why we say exam questions are as much about reading comprehension as they are about knowing Internet Information Server material inside out and backward.

➤ **Details and resources** Every chapter ends with a section titled "Need To Know More?" This section provides direct pointers to Microsoft and third-party resources that offer further details on the chapter's subject. In addition, this section tries to rate the quality and thoroughness of the topic's coverage by each resource. If you find a resource you like in this collection, use it; but don't feel compelled to use all the resources. On the other hand, we recommend only resources we use on a regular basis, so none of our recommendations will be a waste of your time or money.

The bulk of the book follows this chapter structure slavishly, but there are a few other elements that we'd like to point out: the answer key (Chapter 14) to the sample test that appears in Chapter 13 and a reasonably exhaustive glossary of IIS-specific and general Microsoft terminology. Finally, look for The Cram Sheet. This is a valuable tool that represents a condensed and compiled collection of facts, figures, and tips that we think you should memorize before taking the test. Because you can dump this information out of your head and onto a piece of paper before answering any exam questions, you can master this information by brute force—you need to remember it only long enough to write it down when you walk into the test room. You might even want to look at it in the car or in the lobby of the testing center just before you walk in to take the test.

How To Use This Book

If you're prepping for a first-time test, we've structured the topics in this book to build on one another. Therefore, some topics in later chapters make more sense after you've read earlier chapters. That's why we suggest you read this book from front to back for your initial test preparation. If you need to brush up on a topic or you have to bone up for a second try, use the index or table of contents to go straight to the topics and questions that you need to study. Beyond the tests, we think you'll find this book useful as a tightly focused reference to some of the most important aspects of this operating system.

Given all the book's elements and its specialized focus, we've tried to create a tool that you can use to prepare for—and pass—Microsoft certification exam

70-087, "Implementing and Supporting Microsoft Internet Information Server 4.0." Please share your feedback on the book with us, especially if you have ideas about how we can improve it for future test takers. We'll consider everything you say carefully, and we'll respond to all suggestions. You can reach us via email at examcram@lanw.com. Please remember to include the title of the book in your message; otherwise, we'll be forced to guess which book you're making a suggestion about. Its also a good idea to list the page number which relates to your questions or comments. And we don't like to guess—we want to *know*!

For up-to-date information, online discussion forums, sample tests, content updates, and more, visit Certification Insider Press at www. certificationinsider.com or the authors' Web site at http://www.lanw.com/ examcram/.

Thanks, and enjoy the book!

Microsoft
Certification Exams

Terms you'll need to understand:

√ Radio button

√ Checkbox

√ Exhibit

√ Multiple-choice question formats

√ Careful reading

√ Process of elimination

Techniques you'll need to master:

√ Preparing to take a certification exam

√ Practicing (to make perfect)

√ Making the best use of the testing software

√ Budgeting your time

√ Saving the hardest questions until last

√ Guessing (as a last resort)

Exam taking is not something that most people anticipate eagerly, no matter how well prepared they may be. In most cases, familiarity helps ameliorate test anxiety. In plain English, this means you probably won't be as nervous when you take your fourth or fifth Microsoft certification exam as you'll be when you take your first one.

Whether it's your first exam or your tenth, understanding the details of exam taking (how much time to spend on questions, the setting you'll be in, and so on) and the exam software will help you concentrate on the material rather than on the environment. Likewise, mastering a few basic exam-taking skills should help you recognize—and perhaps even outfox—some of the tricks and gotchas you're bound to find in some of the exam questions.

This chapter explains the exam environment and software as well as describes some proven exam-taking strategies that you should be able to use to your advantage.

The Exam Situation

When you arrive at the Sylvan Prometric Testing Center where you scheduled your exam, you'll need to sign in with an exam coordinator. He or she will ask you to produce two forms of identification, one of which must be a photo ID. Once you've signed in and your time slot arrives, you'll be asked to deposit any books, bags, or other items you brought with you, and you'll be escorted into a closed room. Typically, that room will be furnished with anywhere from one to half a dozen computers, and each workstation will be separated from the others by dividers designed to keep you from seeing what's happening on someone else's computer.

You'll be furnished with a pen or pencil and a blank sheet of paper, or, in some cases, a plastic sheet and an erasable felt-tip pen. You're allowed to write down any information you want on both sides of this sheet. You should memorize as much of the material that appears on The Cram Sheet (inside the front of this book) as you can and then write that information down on the blank sheet as soon as you're seated in front of the computer. You can refer to this sheet anytime you like during the test, but you'll have to surrender it when you leave the room.

Most test rooms feature a wall with a large picture window. This permits the exam coordinator to monitor the room, to prevent exam takers from talking to one another, and to observe anything out of the ordinary that might go on. The exam coordinator will have preloaded the Microsoft certification exam you've signed up for—for this book, that's Exam 70-087—and you'll be permitted to start as soon as you're seated in front of the computer.

All Microsoft certification exams allow a certain maximum amount of time in which to complete your work (this time is indicated on the exam by an onscreen counter/clock, so you can check the time remaining whenever you like). Exam 70-087 consists of 55 questions. You're permitted to take up to 100 minutes to complete the exam.

All Microsoft certification exams are computer generated and use a multiple-choice format. Although this may sound quite simple, the questions are constructed not only to check your mastery of basic facts and figures about Internet Information Server, they also require you to evaluate one or more sets of circumstances or requirements. Often, you'll be asked to give more than one answer to a question; likewise, you may be asked to select the best or most effective solution to a problem from a range of choices, all of which technically are correct. Taking the exam is quite an adventure, and it involves real thinking. This book will show you what to expect and how to deal with the problems, puzzles, and predicaments you're likely to encounter.

Exam Layout And Design

The following is a typical exam question. This multiple-choice question requires you to select a single correct answer. Following the question is a brief summary of each potential answer and why it was either right or wrong.

Question 1

Creating a key certificate request is an integral step of what process?

- O a. Installing IIS 4.0
- O b. Configuring a Web server to offer SSL-based secure communications
- O c. As a client, purchasing a product with a credit card over a secure link
- O d. Applying Service Pack 3 to Windows NT Server

Creating a key certificate request is an integral part of configuring a Web server to offer SSL-based secure communications. Therefore, answer b is correct. Installing IIS and applying Service Pack 3 does not require a key request. Therefore, answers a and d are incorrect. As a client, purchasing a product with a credit card over a secure link does not require a key request to be generated, but it does rely on the Web server to have already installed a certificate. Therefore, answer c is incorrect.

This sample question corresponds closely to the type you'll see on the Microsoft certification exams. The only difference on the exam is that questions are not followed by the answer key. To select the correct answer, position the cursor over the radio button next to answer b and click the mouse button to select that answer.

Let's examine a question that requires choosing multiple answers. This type of question provides checkboxes rather than radio buttons for marking all appropriate selections.

Question 2

A user performs a query using an Index Server query form on the office's intranet. The results from his query fail to list the SALES1997.DOC file, which he knows contains the words "April" and "1997". What could be the reason for this?

❑   a. The user was not authenticated.

❑   b. The user does not have read access to the file.

❑   c. Another user was accessing the document at the time the query was performed.

❑   d. The file is not included in the corpus.

A known file not appearing in a results list can be caused by the user not being authenticated, the user not having read access, or the file not being part of the corpus. Therefore, answers a, b, and d are correct. Because queries are performed against an index and not the original file, the file is not affected by the use status of the document. Therefore, answer c is incorrect.

For this type of question, one or more answers are required. For Question 2, you have to check the boxes next to items a, b, and d to obtain credit for a correct answer.

Although these two basic types of questions can appear in many forms, they constitute the foundation on which all the Microsoft certification exam questions rest. More complex questions may include so-called exhibits, which are usually screen shots of the Internet Services Manager or some other TCP/IP-related Windows NT utility. For some of these questions, you'll be asked to make a selection by clicking a checkbox or radio button on the screen shot itself; for others, you'll be expected to use the information displayed therein to guide your answer to the question. Familiarity with the underlying utility is your key to choosing the correct answer(s).

Other questions involving exhibits may use charts or network diagrams to help document a workplace scenario that you'll be asked to troubleshoot or configure. Careful attention to such exhibits is the key to success. Be prepared to toggle frequently between the picture and the question as you work.

Using Microsoft's Exam Software Effectively

A well-known principle when taking exams is to first read over the entire exam from start to finish while answering only those questions you feel absolutely sure of. On subsequent passes, you can dive into more complex questions more deeply, knowing how many such questions you have left.

Fortunately, Microsoft exam software makes this approach easy to implement. At the top-left corner of each question is a checkbox that permits you to mark that question for a later visit. (Note: Marking questions makes review easier, but you can return to any question if you're willing to click the Forward or Back button repeatedly.) As you read each question, if you answer only those you're sure of and mark for review those that you're not sure of, you can keep working through a decreasing list of questions as you answer the trickier ones in order.

There's at least one potential benefit to reading the exam over completely before answering the trickier questions: Sometimes, you can find information in later questions that sheds more light on earlier ones. Other times, information you read on later questions may jog your memory about Internet Information Server facts, figures, or behavior that also will help with earlier questions. Either way, you'll come out ahead if you defer those questions about which you're not absolutely sure.

Keep working on the questions until you're absolutely sure of all your answers or until you know you'll run out of time. If questions are still unanswered, you'll want to zip through them and guess. Not answering a question guarantees you won't receive credit for it, and a guess has at least a chance of being correct.

At the very end of your exam period, you're better off guessing than leaving questions unanswered.

Exam-Taking Basics

The most important advice about taking any exam is this: Read each question carefully. Some questions are deliberately ambiguous, some use double negatives, and others use terminology in incredibly precise ways. We have taken numerous exams—both practice and live—and in nearly every one, we've missed at least one question because we didn't read it closely or carefully enough.

Here are some suggestions on how to deal with the tendency to jump to an answer too quickly:

➤ Make sure you read every word in the question. If you find yourself jumping ahead impatiently, go back and start over.

➤ As you read, try to restate the question in your own terms. If you can do this, you should be able to pick the correct answer(s) much more easily.

➤ When returning to a question after your initial read-through, read every word again—otherwise, your mind can fall quickly into a rut. Sometimes, revisiting a question after turning your attention elsewhere lets you see something you missed, but the strong tendency is to see what you've seen before. Try to avoid that tendency at all costs.

➤ If you return to a question more than twice, try to articulate to yourself what you don't understand about the question, why the answers don't appear to make sense, or what appears to be missing. If you chew on the subject for awhile, your subconscious may provide the details that are lacking or you may notice a "trick" that will point to the right answer.

Above all, try to deal with each question by thinking through what you know about the Internet Information Server utilities, characteristics, behaviors, facts, and figures involved. By reviewing what you know (and what you've written down on your information sheet), you'll often recall or understand things sufficiently to determine the answer to the question.

Question-Handling Strategies

Based on exams the authors have taken, some interesting trends have become apparent. For those questions that take only a single answer, usually two or three of the answers will be obviously incorrect, and two of the answers will be plausible—of course, only one can be correct. Unless the answer leaps out at you (if it does, reread the question to look for a trick; sometimes those are the ones you're most likely to get wrong), begin the process of answering by eliminating those answers that are most obviously wrong.

Things to look for in obviously wrong answers include spurious menu choices or utility names, nonexistent software options, and terminology you've never seen. If you've done your homework for an exam, no valid information should be completely new to you. In that case, unfamiliar or bizarre terminology probably indicates a totally bogus answer. As long as you're sure what's right, it's easy to eliminate what's wrong.

Numerous questions assume that the default behavior of a particular utility is in effect. If you know the defaults and understand what they mean, this knowledge will help you cut through many Gordian knots.

As you work your way through the exam, another counter that Microsoft thankfully provides will come in handy—the number of questions completed and questions outstanding. Budget your time by making sure that you've completed one-quarter of the questions one-quarter of the way through the exam period (or the first 14 questions in the first 25 minutes) and three-quarters of them three-quarters of the way through (41 questions in the first 75 minutes).

If you're not finished when 95 minutes have elapsed, use the last 5 minutes to guess your way through the remaining questions. Remember, guessing is potentially more valuable than not answering, because blank answers are always wrong, but a guess may turn out to be right. If you don't have a clue about any of the remaining questions, pick answers at random or choose all a's, b's, and so on. The important thing is to submit an exam for scoring that has an answer for every question.

Mastering The Inner Game

In the final analysis, knowledge breeds confidence, and confidence breeds success. If you study the materials in this book carefully and review all the exam prep questions at the end of each chapter, you should become aware of those areas where additional learning and study are required.

Next, follow up by reading some or all of the materials recommended in the "Need To Know More?" section at the end of each chapter. The idea is to become familiar enough with the concepts and situations you find in the sample questions that you can reason your way through similar situations on a real exam. If you know the material, you have every right to be confident that you can pass the exam.

Once you've worked your way through the book, take the practice exam in Chapter 13. This will provide a reality check and help you identify areas you need to study further. Make sure you follow up and review materials related to the questions you miss before scheduling a real exam. Only when you've covered all the ground and feel comfortable with the whole scope of the practice exam should you take a real one.

TIP If you take the practice exam and don't score at least 75 percent correct, you'll want to practice further. At a minimum, download the Personal Exam Prep (PEP) exams and the self-assessment exams from the Microsoft Certification And Training Web site's download page (its location appears in the next section). (Unfortunately, at the time of this writing, the IIS PEP was not yet available.) If you're more ambitious, or better funded, you might want to purchase a practice exam from one of the third-party vendors that offers them.

Armed with the information in this book and with the determination to augment your knowledge, you should be able to pass the certification exam. You need to work at it, however, or you'll spend the exam fee more than once before you finally do pass. If you prepare seriously, the execution should go flawlessly. Good luck!

Additional Resources

A good source of information about Microsoft certification exams comes from Microsoft itself. Because its products and technologies—and the exams that go with them—change frequently, the best place to go for exam-related information is online.

If you haven't already visited the Microsoft Training And Certification pages, do so right now. The Training And Certification home page resides at www.microsoft.com/mcp/ (see Figure 1.1).

> *Note: This page may not be there by the time you read this, or it may have been replaced by something new and different, because things change regularly on the Microsoft site. Should this happen, please read the sidebar titled "Coping With Change On The Web."*

Through the menu options offered in the column on the left side of the Microsoft Certified Professional Web page, you can access information about individual tests, certification levels, training materials, and more.

Coping With Change On The Web

Sooner or later, all the information we've shared with you about the Microsoft Certified Professional Web pages and all the other Web-based resources mentioned throughout the rest of this book will go stale or be replaced by newer information. In some cases, the URLs you find here may lead you to their replacements; in other cases, the URLs will go nowhere, leaving you with the dreaded "404 File not found" error message.

Figure 1.1   The Training And Certification home page.

When that happens, don't give up. There's always a way to find what you want on the Web if you're willing to invest some time and energy. Most large or complex Web sites—and Microsoft's qualifies on both counts— offer a search engine. Looking at Figure 1.1, you'll see that a Search button appears along the top edge of the page. As long as you can get to Microsoft's site (it should stay at www.microsoft.com for a long while yet), you can use this tool to help you find what you need.

The more focused you can make a search request, the more likely the results will include information you can use. For example, you can search for the string "training and certification" to produce a lot of data about the subject in general, but if you're looking for the preparation guide for Exam 70-087, "Implementing and Supporting Microsoft Internet Information Server 4.0," you'll be more likely to get there quickly if you use a search string similar to the following:

```
"Exam 70-087" AND "preparation guide"
```

Likewise, if you want to find the training and certification downloads, try a search string such as this:

```
"training and certification" AND "download page"
```

Finally, don't be afraid to use general search tools such as www.search.com, www.altavista.com, and www.excite.com to search for related information. Although Microsoft offers the best information about its certification exams online, plenty of third-party sources of information, training, and assistance are available in this area that don't need to follow the party line like Microsoft does. The bottom line is: If you can't find something where the book says it lives, start looking around. If worse comes to worst, you can always email us! We just might have a clue.

Need More Practice?

LANWrights, Inc., the company behind this book, also offers practice tests for sale. You can order practice exam diskettes via snail mail. Because we wrote them ourselves, we don't feel comfortable telling you how great they are—but they surely are a good deal! Currently available tests include NT Server 4.0, NT Server 4.0 in the Enterprise, NT Workstation 4.0, Networking Essentials, TCP/IP, Proxy Server 2.0, IIS 4.0, and Windows 95. Please send a check or money order to the following address: LANWrights, Inc., P.O. Box 26261, Austin, TX 78755-0261.

Each diskette includes two complete practice tests. Either Netscape Navigator 3 (or higher) or Microsoft Internet Explorer 3 (or higher) is required to use the Java-based testing system on the diskettes. Single exam diskettes are $25 each. Multiple diskettes can be purchased at a discount, as follows:

$ 25 for single diskette	$115 for any six
$ 45 for any two	$130 for any seven
$ 65 for any three	$145 for any eight
$ 85 for any four	$160 for any nine
$100 for any five	$175 for all ten
All amounts are US$	

Prices include U.S. shipping and required taxes. (Mexico and Canada add $5; all other countries outside North America, add $10 for additional shipping charges.) Please be sure to include your name, shipping address, contact phone number, and the number and titles for those practice exams you wish to order.

Introduction To IIS 4.0

Terms you'll need to understand:

- √ ASPs (Active Server Pages)
- √ Certificate Server
- √ Chunked transfers
- √ Host headers
- √ HTTP (Hypertext Transfer Protocol) 1.1
- √ IIS (Internet Information Server)
- √ Index Server
- √ Internet Connection Services for MS RAS
- √ Message Queue Server
- √ MMC (Microsoft Management Console)
- √ Option Pack
- √ Persistent connections
- √ Pipelining
- √ Service Pack
- √ Site Server Express
- √ SMTP and NNTP services
- √ Transaction Server
- √ Web/FTP server

Techniques you'll need to master:

- √ Understanding Internet Information Server
- √ Examining the basic components of IIS 4.0
- √ Learning the applications distributed on the Option Pack
- √ Identifying the features of IIS 4.0

Microsoft Internet Information Server (IIS) 4.0 is the latest version of the Internet information service publication and management system. This chapter gives you an overview of the software and highlights many of the new features found in IIS 4.0.

Internet Information Server: Explored And Explained

Internet Information Server 4.0 (referred to as IIS or IIS 4.0) is the latest full-release version of the standards-based Web and FTP application server from Microsoft. It's designed to operate on the Windows NT Server 4.0 network operating system. IIS is an Internet standards-compliant HTTP (Hypertext Transfer Protocol) server that offers FTP and several other valuable Web/FTP-related services. IIS 4.0 gives you more publishing capabilities than most other Web servers. For instance, with IIS 4.0 you can perform the following tasks:

➤ Publish information over the Web or FTP quickly and easily

➤ Develop and operate Web-based applications

➤ Fully manage and administer your Web site

IIS 4.0 offers HTTP 1.1 support with full backward-compatibility with HTTP 1.0 for older browsers. HTTP 1.1 offers significant improvements in performance (50 to 100 percent), which results in a more responsive Web experience for your users. The performance improvements of HTTP 1.1 and IIS 4.0 are a result of the following:

➤ **Pipelining** HTTP 1.0 servers processed a single resource request at a time per client. In other words, the client waited for each request to be processed before the next request was sent. HTTP 1.1 uses *pipelining* to allow clients to send multiple requests without waiting for a server's response. Pipelining improves response time and Web display performance.

➤ **Persistent connections** Typically, for each item contained in a single Web document (HTML, GIFs, Java applets, and so on), a separate connection between the client and server must be established. Therefore, if eight items compose a single document, eight connections are created between the client and server. The overhead for establishing, maintaining, and tearing down these connections is high in comparison to the amount of data sent over them. IIS 4.0 uses *persistent connections* to send multiple objects over fewer connections. This reduces communication overhead and improves performance.

➤ **Chunked transfers** Active Server Pages (ASPs) vary in size due to their dynamic nature. HTTP 1.0 can have difficulty delivering data when the actual bit size of the resource is unknown at the beginning of the transfer. HTTP 1.1 is able to transmit the variable documents more efficiently through the use of *chunking*. Chunking is the process of breaking a transmission into multiple pieces of different sizes, each with its own header and size indicator. This method greatly increases the efficiency of ASP delivery.

➤ **Proxy support** HTTP 1.1 has caching information built into the protocol itself. This provides servers and proxies with sufficient information to manage cached resources. HTTP 1.1 can provide details, such as expiration dates for resources, without changing the content.

Other benefits of IIS 4.0 reach beyond performance. With new wizards to help you create Web sites and versatile administration tools, IIS 4.0 has become the premier Web server. Here are some of the highlights of IIS:

➤ Integrated setup

➤ Flexible management

➤ Complete content control

➤ Configuration backup and restoration

➤ Hosting of multiple Web sites

➤ Allocating network bandwidth

➤ Familiar Windows NT Server administration tools

Integrated Setup

IIS 4.0 is no longer distributed as an individual, separate product. It is now an integral part of the Windows NT 4.0 Option Pack. This product distribution contains IIS 4.0 (and its subcomponents), Service Pack 3, Internet Explorer 4.01, Transaction Server 2.0, Message Queue Server Standard Edition, Site Server Express, and Connection Services for Microsoft RAS.

The integrated Setup wizard for the Option Pack lets you easily install IIS and other components simultaneously. The wizard asks you which components you want to install, requests a few other parameters, and then completes the installation. The Option Pack greatly simplifies the process of configuring an entire Web publication system so that Web applications can be developed and deployed with the greatest of ease and speed.

You can download the Option Pack from www.microsoft.com/ntserver/guide/ whatisntop.asp (the Windows NT Server full version of the Option Pack is 87MB). It's included in the box with the new Windows NT Server 4.0 Enterprise Edition, or it can be purchased separately at a local reseller for under $100. The Option Pack can be installed in a fashion similar to that of Internet Explorer 4.0, where only those components selected are actually downloaded. Then, when additional components need to be installed later, only the necessary additional files are retrieved.

 If several servers are destined to host IIS 4.0, an unattended installation script can be built that installs Windows NT Server 4.0, Service Pack 3, Internet Explorer 4.01, and any or all components of the Option Pack.

Flexible Management

IIS offers a solid collection of management and administration tools to give you complete control and insight into the operation of your Web server and its related components. In addition, by using the IIS administration objects, you can create customized interfaces to meet your particular needs or work flow.

Windows-Based Administration

The most obvious change or improvement to IIS is the introduction of the Microsoft Management Console (MMC). The MMC is a Windows-based tool that provides total management of all services and applications within a single utility. The MMC is also Active Desktop-capable and will eventually be used to access management and control aspects of the entire Windows NT system. In fact, Windows NT 5.0's control mechanisms center around snap-ins for MMC.

MMC offers you control over every aspect of your Internet site through a single, unified, and standardized interface. Every component of IIS and the Option Pack is managed via an MMC snap-in; this includes WWW, FTP, SMTP, NNTP, Transaction Server, and Index Server services. MMC's Web compatibility provides remote management capabilities in addition to customized console control.

Web-Based Administration

A new and improved Web-based interface for administrative tasks has been added that incorporates ASPs and JavaScript. This interface maximizes your ability to manage your Internet site from a remote browser. This gives the single-site user the freedom to travel; plus, it allows Internet Service Providers (ISPs) or other multisite hosting centers to grant individual customers administrative control over their Web site.

IIS Administration Objects

New IIS Administration Objects (IISAOs) are used to control an entire server programmatically through automated objects. IISAOs enable command-line administration via scripts or command prompts, customized interfaces, and automation of common tasks.

Complete Content Control

With improved granular control and flexibility of object properties, IIS offers more specific control and information about an entire Web server or an individually hosted Web site. By properly defining properties on a Web server, a Web site, a virtual directory, or even individual files, you gain more control over your site. You can reduce log file sizes by choosing to log hits of HTML documents only, instead of every object of a Web document (GIFs, WAVs, Java applets, and so on). This also gives you more accurate information on site hits. Secure Sockets Layer (SSL) 3.0 security can be assigned to individual directories rather than to an entire Web site. You can reduce redundant tasks by selecting upline settings to apply to downline objects (that is, a Web site's settings can apply to virtual directories, a Web server's settings can apply to all hosted Web sites, and so on). Fine-tuning content control can also improve performance by reducing the number of metric reading tasks required by the server for each client's requested document or object.

Configuration Backup And Restoration

IIS configuration settings can be imported from and exported to a file for an entire server, individual sites, individual directories, or even single files. This enables the maintenance of accurate configuration backups, system rollback and restoration, and configuration transfers from one server to another.

Hosting Multiple Web Sites

Previous versions of IIS required each Web site hosted on a single IIS to have a unique IP address. IIS 4.0, with the use of HTTP 1.1 host headers, enables multiple Web sites to be hosted over the same IP address. A single IP address for multiple Web sites reduces administration, allows more sites to be hosted from a single installation, and reduces costs associated with IP registration and leasing. However, HTTP 1.1 is not supported by all browsers. Therefore, deployment of this feature should be limited to controlled environments until more browsers on the Internet support HTTP 1.1 host headers.

Allocating Network Bandwidth

An installation of IIS, which hosts multiple Web sites, can offer guaranteed bandwidth to each site via *bandwidth throttling*. Therefore, higher priority sites or sites with greater popularity can be allocated a larger portion of available bandwidth to ensure delivery to clients. Bandwidth throttling can improve performance for even the low-end sites restricted to the smallest portion of available bandwidth. This is done by guaranteeing pipeline size and preventing connection termination or interference due to widely fluctuating bandwidth and network response.

Familiar Windows NT Server Administration Tools

Because IIS 4.0 is tightly integrated with Windows NT Server, little additional knowledge is required to administer it. Most of the management and administration tools used by NT Server are used to manage and control aspects of IIS. User accounts, including the anonymous account, are still managed through User Manager For Domains. Performance Monitor and Network Monitor are still used to locate bottlenecks, track system performance, and isolate network communication problems.

IIS includes several service and operational-specific objects and counters that are added to Performance Monitor to provide more insight into the system's operations. IIS still logs security and application events in the Event Viewer log files. Therefore, auditing IIS-accessed objects and related events can offer additional sources of information.

IIS Components

As previously mentioned, IIS 4.0 is distributed as part of the Windows NT Option Pack. The Option Pack contains seven distinct software components, or applications, that can be installed as an integrated whole to provide Internet publishing and management capabilities. As Microsoft continues to integrate its products, the division line between one product or service and another becomes blurred. In addition to the individually named components in the Option Pack (IIS 4.0, Service Pack 3, Internet Explorer 4.01, Transaction Server 2.0, Message Queue Server Standard Edition, Site Server Express, and Connection Services for Microsoft RAS), there are several other components. These are installed along with IIS's Web and FTP services. These include Index Server 2.0, Certificate Server 1.0, several data access (database) and development (SDK) components, the SMTP service, the NNTP service, the Microsoft Management Console (MMC), and the Microsoft DNA (Distributed interNet Applications) architecture. These are not strictly components of IIS, but at the same time, IIS would not function correctly or be as flexible if they were not present.

In the following sections, the IIS and Option Pack components are discussed briefly. All of these items are dealt with on a more intimate and in-depth basis in subsequent chapters of this book.

Index Server 2.0

IIS 4.0 includes an updated and improved Index Server 2.0. Index Server brings site content indexing and searching to IIS-hosted Web sites. A set of default or customized interface query forms offers users a wide range of search options. With support for ASPs, use of SQL queries, new content filter types, multiple language support, improved performance, fine-tuned scope/range control, updated cache management, and new MMC administration, Index Server 2.0 is a full-featured content search engine.

Certificate Server 1.0

Digital certificates can have two purposes—proving the identity of a Web site and proving the identity of a site's user. Web site identity verification is still performed through a contract with a certificate authority. However, until IIS 4.0 and Certificate Server 1.0, organizations were unable to use this technology for client/server authentication. Certificate Server gives individual Web servers the ability to issue, revoke, and renew X.509 digital certificates to clients. Such certificates are used to provide the client's identity, maintain status information, and to circumvent manual user authentication. Certificate Server is also used in the standard sense by supporting SSL and Private Communication Technology (PCT) protocols for authorized secure communications.

Site Server Express 2.0

An express version of the Microsoft Site Server is included with the IIS 4.0 Option Pack. This application gives you a wide variety of analysis tools to keep tabs on your Web sites and several publishing utilities to ease content issuance. The Usage Import And Report Writer translates the cryptic IIS log files into easy-to-read documents that contain information, such as hits, user information, length of stay, and more. The Content Analysis module creates a visual representation of a Web site and can check for broken links. The Web Publishing wizard can be used by clients to easily post new documents to an IIS-hosted Web site.

Microsoft Transaction Server 2.0

The integration of Microsoft Transaction Server (MTS) into IIS 4.0 has brought new robustness, fault tolerance, and programmable extensibility to IIS and Web applications. MTS allows distributed transaction applications to be developed for IIS. MTS simplifies Web application development for multiuser environments by providing much of the basic low-level system interaction structure. Through MTS, each Web application can be launched as a separate process that can persist beyond a single client request, and its operation and system resources will not interfere with IIS or any other active Web application.

Microsoft Message Queue Server 1.0

As Web applications developed for distributed deployment become more commonplace, the reliability of applications to communicate with each other and within themselves becomes critical. The Microsoft Message Queue Server (MSMQ) enables applications to communicate via a message queue system, even when remote systems are offline. Called applications are currently nonexecuting, or on nonheterogeneous networks. The range of flexibility and the fault tolerance of distributed Web applications are widened because of MSMQ's integration of MTS, support for ActiveX, and asynchronous communication.

Internet Connection Services For Microsoft RAS 1.0

Internet Connection Services (ICS) is an extension and upgrade module for Windows NT Server's Remote Access Service (RAS). ICS adds several enhancements to RAS, including customizable client dialers, centrally controlled network phonebooks, new RADIUS authentication support, and improved administration and management tools. ICS was designed to help reduce ISP and connectivity costs, improve and simplify end-user operation, and enable new Internet business solutions. Many of the improvements found in ICS are also found in the Routing And Remote Access Service Update for Windows NT Server.

SMTP Service

IIS now includes an SMTP client service that allows Web applications to send and receive email messages. In addition, Web server events can trigger email notification to administrators. The SMTP service gives the Web server an email message box in which error messages, user feedback, or undelivered messages can be deposited for manual administrator processing.

NNTP Service

IIS, with added NNTP support, can host single-server discussion groups. These discussion groups can be accessed via a standard Web interface or any of the NNTP-compliant newsreaders. The NNTP service is designed to host private discussion forums and does not support news feeds or message replication from the global Usenet NNTP news services. To add true Usenet NNTP news services to an Internet site, you would need to purchase and deploy Microsoft Exchange Server 5.5, which has full NNTP service support (including news feeds and message replication).

Data Access And SDK Components

Because IIS supports several standardized data access models and components, Web applications have the widest communication possibilities with database and other information provisioning applications. IIS includes ActiveX Data Objects (ADO), Remote Data Service (RDS), and Open Database Connectivity (ODBC) drivers. In addition, the Software Development Kit (SDK) that comes with IIS 4.0 contains detailed documentation about developing customized methods and interfaces for existing components to expand and enhance Web applications via ASPs, custom IIS configurations, unique model and object types, logging adaptations, and server extensions. The Microsoft Script Debugger can be used to easily debug ASPs and several types of programming scripts, such as Visual Basic Scripting Edition (VBScript), JScript (Microsoft's JavaScript), and Java, to simplify Web application development.

Microsoft Management Console

As already described, the Microsoft Management Console (MMC) is the new management, administration, and control interface for Windows NT. It's added to the NT 4.0 environment via the installation of IIS 4.0, but it's going to be a standard component of NT 5.0. It replaces several other interfaces and utilities. The MMC is able to manage and control all aspects of a network environment—including those services added by IIS—through the use of programmatic controls called *snap-ins*. Every significant component of IIS has a snap-in that gives you administrative control over that component and its related objects. MMC can be accessed through a Web interface, or controlled via command-line instructions by the new Windows Scripting Host (WSH), a language-independent scripting host for 32-bit Windows platforms.

Windows DNA Architecture

In its continued effort to develop true distributed applications, Microsoft has created Distributed interNet Applications (DNA). DNA is a Windows platform architectural framework to enable the deployment of scalable, multitiered distributed computing solutions over any type of network. DNA combines Internet, communication link establishment, client/server computing, TCP/IP communications, transactions, and more, into a conglomerated whole.

Basically, DNA is the system or underlying programming structure that enables all the components and related services of IIS, NT Server, and the clients to interact reliably, efficiently, and at peek performance levels.

Service Pack 3

Service Pack 3 (SP3) for Windows NT 4.0 is included in the Option Pack. SP3 is a requirement for IIS 4.0 and its related components. Be sure to install SP3 before attempting to install IIS or any other application from the Option Pack.

Internet Explorer 4.01

Internet Explorer 4.01 for Windows NT 4.0 is included in the Option Pack. IE 4.01 is a requirement for IIS 4.0 and several of its related components. Be sure to install IE 4.01 immediately after installing SP3 and before installing IIS or any of the other applications from the Option Pack.

IIS Features

The features list of IIS 4.0 is huge. Microsoft spent considerable time and effort to improve this product, and it shows in the broad range of features, functions, support, and capabilities. In the following sections, many of these features are highlighted; however, they are also covered in more depth and detail in subsequent chapters.

Internet Standard Services

As previously mentioned, IIS 4.0 is fully HTTP 1.1 standards-compliant. This includes support for persistent connections, pipelining, chunking, host headers, and more. Some of the client/server communication features added by HTTP 1.1 include HTTP **PUT** and HTTP **DELETE** for easier Web publishing. HTTP **PUT** uses HTTP to transfer files to a Web server, and HTTP **DELETE** deletes files from a Web server. Support for HTTP 1.1 does not exclude browsers limited to HTTP 1.0. If an older browser is encountered, IIS simply responds by using the HTTP level supported by the browser.

As part of IIS's ability to host multiple Web sites off of a single IP address, IIS includes backward-compatible support for older browsers that do not support host headers natively. *Host headers* are the delivery and communication mechanisms used by IIS to distribute multiple sites using transferred session information. If host headers are not supported, IIS uses a less sophisticated method to "multiplex" Web sites. (Basically, when host headers are in use, the responsibility of tracking the location of a particular browser/client within a Web site is returned to the server instead of with the client.)

With the addition of native support for NNTP and SMTP, Web authors, administrators, and visitors are able to stay more informed, and lines of communications are broadened.

Improved Setup And Administration

IIS 4.0, distributed as a component of the Option Pack, is easier to set up than ever before. Plus, you no longer have to install each supporting component of IIS separately; they can all be installed together. This level of setup integration produces an installation of IIS that is not only more powerful, but also more likely to be properly configured right out of the box. In addition, any options not initially selected can be easily added without complicated reconfigurations.

The upgrade path from IIS 2.0, IIS 3.0, or even IIS 4.0 beta 3 is relatively painless. Microsoft has taken great pains to ensure that when you install the final release over an existing installation, as much configuration and setup information as possible is maintained. This provides easy upward migration without requiring the reconfiguration of the entire Web server.

If you're not installing from an Option Pack CD-ROM, IIS's setup utility pulls the distribution files from Microsoft over the Internet. A significant benefit of this installation method is that only those distribution files needed for the selected components are downloaded. Also, when other components are added to an existing setup, only the distribution files needed to add the new components are downloaded. This provides for a fast and efficient Internet installation of this product.

IIS installation can be automated, similar to the installation of Windows NT Server. An answer file is used to guide the setup process. This eliminates the need for a human baby-sitter. Automated installations simplify the deployment process of IIS on enterprise intranets or on mirrored or distributed Web hosts.

A new paradigm of system management, namely the MMC, is introduced to Windows NT via IIS. MCC, which is a standard feature of the upcoming NT 5.0 release, revolutionizes the administration and management tasks of IIS (and soon every other aspect of Windows NT).

A related feature of MMC is the modulation of each management utility. Most of these modular components can be launched from a command line. This gives administrators a wider range of control over their systems. The command-line administration capability can be used from any command line, including scheduled execution of batch files.

Individual site operator segregated management allows each Web site operator to have access to a wide range of administration controls for a particular site. This simplifies the overall management responsibilities for multisite hosting installations of IIS. Site administrators are given full control over their sites, but they are unable to make any security or configuration changes across sites or to the Web server itself.

IIS now supports configuration replication. This allows multiple IIS installations to act as a single logical server. All the configuration settings applied to one IIS server will be replicated to all other "slaved" IIS installations.

A wider range of flexibility is offered through the Web site–specific application of ISAPI filters. For IIS installations hosting multiple sites, maintaining separate applications of ISAPI filters grants you the ability to fine-tune each site individually.

IIS's logging capabilities have been expanded to support W3C extended logging. This industry-standard logging format grants administrators the ability to customize Web logs. Log files can be configured to record only those information fields important or relevant to the site, or exclude others. This produces a smaller log size, more focused data, and faster performance. The logging system also supports COM-designed custom logging capabilities.

Web Applications

With the tight integration of several applications from the Option Pack, IIS's ability to support distributed Web applications is greatly improved. Transactional ASPs enrich commerce and business communications by improving script management. ASPs can execute with a transaction. Therefore, if the script fails, the transaction is aborted. This provides for a more secure, reliable, and faster communication link between business customers.

IIS is more immune to failed processes than ever before. Launching each application or subprocess in a separate virtual machine isolates each Web site and application from the core IIS system. If any site or application fails or stalls, the rest of the system is not affected. Plus, when a failed application is requested again, IIS restarts the process by creating a new virtual machine. This provides IIS with a system for crash protection and recovery. Launching each process separately also enables individual components to be loaded and unloaded from memory without restarting the entire IIS system.

Programmers can now reap the benefits of the built-in Microsoft Script Debugger. This tool gives realtime interactive feedback for designing and troubleshooting Active Server Pages.

Using the clustering services of Windows NT Server Enterprise Edition, IIS can perform server failover. For example, if two sites are hosted on two separate IIS installations and one of the servers fails, the other server automatically takes over by hosting both sites.

 The Microsoft Virtual Machine, which provides Java support, has been updated to improve performance, provide more robust applications, and support server-side component execution.

Improved Security And Authentication

With the addition of the Certificate Server to IIS, organizations are able to establish their own X.509 certificate authorities. This capability improves client/customer recognition and provides for improved certificate/identity authentication.

Improved SSL protocol support grants IIS greater control over secure communications. Server Gated Crypto (SGC) is an extension to SSL, which grants IIS the ability to use 128-bit encryption.

Some firewall filtering capabilities, such as refusing service based on the domain of a client, are built into IIS. This feature can be used to block unwanted access or to simply restrict access to a limited number of users.

Content Control And Administration

IIS has several improvements in the area of managing and controlling content. Index Server 2.0 adds a greater range of index and searching capabilities. As a powerful search engine in its own right, Index Server enables HTML, text, Microsoft Office documents, Adobe PDF, and many other file formats to be searched for online. With the use of ASPs, ActiveX, and SQL, Index Server is more than just a Web search engine.

With the widespread concern for approved or age-controlled content, IIS supports the assignment of content ratings. Currently, the PICS rating labels are used to define information about a Web resource's content.

With the need for immediate, accurate, and up-to-date information, it can be critical to know the age of a document. Through a content expiration date assignment, IIS can inform you and your users when a document's content has aged significantly. The primary purpose of this feature is to inform proxy and caching systems when to refresh resources pulled from your Web server.

Redundant information, standard information, or control data can be added to documents as a header or footer by IIS. This reduces authorship time and improves consistency across an entire site.

Client-encountered error messages can be customized to provide more specific information or to route users to new locations for more information. Errors can forward users, return informational documents, or even launch an application.

As a scaled-back version of Site Server's capability, IIS can be used to replicate the content tree of an entire server to another server. This one-to-one replication feature simplifies distributed Web hosting, site management, site backup, and new site rollout.

A new system of directory and file aliasing or redirection improves the ability to send or forward users from one location to another.

Improved Documentation

One of the overlooked features of IIS is its documentation. All of IIS's documentation can be accessed through a browser, even when the IIS server is not functioning. The Web-based documentation is similar to the standard Help system found in Windows. The documentation can be perused on a content/title basis, keyword basis, or via a full-text search. With several multimedia enhancements, step-by-step walkthroughs, and interactive tutorials, the documentation for IIS is a marked improvement.

IIS And Windows

IIS 4.0 is designed for deployment on Windows NT Server 4.0 or Windows NT Server 4.0 Enterprise Edition. IIS 4.0 is unlimited in the number of simultaneous Internet/intranet Web users (please read license restrictions within the IIS documentation). However, your network and Internet communication media and hardware robustness can restrict access for high-traffic high-volume sites.

For users of Windows NT 4.0 Workstation or Windows 95, Microsoft has also released Peer Web Services (PWS) 4.0, which reflects most of the improvements found in IIS 4.0. However, it does not include Site Server Express, Index Server, or Certificate Server. Also, it isn't designed to be a high-volume, multiuser Web server; instead, it's limited by the license agreement to support only 10 simultaneous connections. Its primary purpose is to simply provide content sharing within an intranet or with friends or coworkers over the Internet.

Exam Prep Questions

Question 1

> What feature of HTTP 1.1, which is supported by IIS 4.0, allows multiple Web sites to be easily supported over a single IP address?
>
> ○ a. Chunked transfers
>
> ○ b. Pipelining
>
> ○ c. Persistent connections
>
> ○ d. Host headers

Host headers are the primary means by which IIS 4.0 hosts multiple Web sites over a single IP address to clients. Therefore, answer d is correct. A chunked transfer is a delivery method to speed and improve ASPs. Therefore, answer a is incorrect. Pipelining is the process of handling multiple client requests without requiring the client to wait for a server response. Therefore, answer b is incorrect. A persistent connection is a communication feature in which a single connection between the server and client is maintained to transfer multiple resources. Therefore, answer c is incorrect.

Question 2

> Which of the following applications are found on the Option Pack and can be installed along with IIS 4.0? [Check all correct answers]
>
> ❑ a. Transaction Server 2.0
>
> ❑ b. Site Server Express
>
> ❑ c. Message Queue Server Standard Edition
>
> ❑ d. Routing And Remote Access Service Update

Transaction Server 2.0, Site Server Express, and Message Queue Server Standard Edition are all included on the Option Pack. Therefore, answers a, b, and c are correct. The Routing And Remote Access Service Update is not part of the Option Pack. Therefore, answer d is incorrect.

Question 3

> Which of the following are requirements for the installation of IIS 4.0? [Check all correct answers]
>
> ❑ a. Service Pack 3 for Windows NT 4.0
>
> ❑ b. NetBEUI
>
> ❑ c. Internet Explorer 4.01
>
> ❑ d. Windows NT 4.0 Workstation

Service Pack 3 and Internet Explorer 4.01 are installation requirements for IIS 4.0. Therefore, answers a and c are correct. NetBEUI is not a requirement of IIS 4.0. Therefore, answer b is incorrect. Windows NT 4.0 Workstation is not a requirement of IIS 4.0. In fact, NTW cannot host IIS, and can only host Peer Web Services. Therefore, answer d is incorrect.

Question 4

> What is the new administration feature/utility installed with IIS 4.0 that will be a standard component of Windows NT 5.0?
>
> ○ a. Microsoft Management Console
>
> ○ b. Microsoft Transaction Server
>
> ○ c. Microsoft Message Queue Server
>
> ○ d. Microsoft Administration System

Microsoft Management Console is the new administration feature/utility installed with IIS 4.0 that will be a standard component of Windows NT 5.0. Therefore, answer a is correct. Microsoft Transaction Server and Microsoft Message Queue Server are not administration utilities, nor are they destined to be standard components of NT 5.0. Therefore, answers b and c are incorrect. Microsoft Administration System is fictitious. Therefore, answer d is incorrect.

Question 5

IIS 4.0 allows you to save the configuration settings of one out of three sites hosted on the same server so the configuration can be used in a rollback.

○ a. True

○ b. False

True, IIS 4.0 supports configuration export and import on a server, site, directory, and file basis for the purposes of rollback, backup, or duplication. Therefore, answer a is correct.

Question 6

Which of the following standard Internet services are new features of IIS 4.0 (meaning the service support was not native to IIS 3.0 or earlier)? [Check all correct answers]

❏ a. SMTP

❏ b. Web

❏ c. NNTP

❏ d. Gopher

SMTP and NNTP are new services of IIS 4.0. Therefore, answers a and c are correct. Web services are not new to IIS. Therefore, answer b is incorrect. Gopher was a service supported by IIS 3.0, but due to its lack of Internet popularity, it was dropped from the features list of IIS 4.0. Therefore, answer d is incorrect.

Question 7

> Which of the following are true statements about IIS 4.0 and its support services and applications? [Check all correct answers]
>
> ❑ a. HTML, text, Microsoft Office, and Adobe PDF documents can be searched.
>
> ❑ b. Client identities can be tracked and verified.
>
> ❑ c. A single Web server can be duplicated to three or more other servers simultaneously.
>
> ❑ d. Applications can communicate even if network connections are broken.

The statements in answers a, b, and d are all correct. Answer a refers to Index Server, answer b refers to Certificate Server, and answer d refers to Message Queue Server. The statement in answer c is incorrect. Site Server Express can only replicate one server to one server. Only the full Enterprise version of Site Server can replicate one server to multiple servers.

Question 8

> When IIS 4.0 is installed over an existing installation of IIS 3.0, all configurations for virtual directories must be completely redefined.
>
> ○ a. True
>
> ○ b. False

False. IIS 4.0 provides a smooth upgrade from IIS 3.0 that retains all existing configuration settings. Therefore, answer b is correct.

Question 9

> What tool is included with IIS 4.0 to simplify the troubleshooting
> process of Active Server Pages?
>
> ○ a. Java Virtual Machine
>
> ○ b. Script Debugger
>
> ○ c. W3C logging
>
> ○ d. ODBC drivers

The Script Debugger is the tool included with IIS 4.0 that simplifies the trouble-shooting process of Active Server Pages. Therefore, answer b is correct. The Java Virtual Machine is not a troubleshooting tool for ASPs. Therefore, answer a is incorrect. W3C logging is a troubleshooting tool for the Web server as a whole. Therefore, answer c is incorrect. ODBC drivers are not troubleshooting tools; they enable database application communications. Therefore, answer d is incorrect.

Question 10

> The new documentation for IIS 4.0 allows which of the following
> functions? [Check all correct answers]
>
> ❑ a. Listing by keyword
>
> ❑ b. Listing by topic
>
> ❑ c. Interactive tutorials
>
> ❑ d. Full-text searching

IIS's documentation can be listed by keyword, listed by topic, or full-text searched; plus, it contains interactive tutorials. Therefore, answers a, b, c, and d are all correct.

Need To Know More?

 The best overview information for Internet Information Server 4.0 can be found in the Reviewer's Guide for IIS 4.0. This document can be found on the TechNet CD-ROM or online via the following IIS Web area: http://www.microsoft.com/iis/.

Installing IIS

Terms you'll need to understand:

√ Computer name

√ Domain name

√ Network adapter card

√ Boot and emergency repair diskettes

√ DNS

√ DHCP server

√ TCP/IP

√ NetBIOS interface

√ NetBEUI protocol

√ RPC

Techniques you'll need to master:

√ Knowing the hardware and software requirements for installing IIS

√ Understanding the complete process of IIS installation

√ Understanding the differences between NTFS and FAT file systems

By definition, IIS is an information server that provides information-publishing services for the Internet and intranets. This chapter explores the process of installing IIS 4.0.

Note: Windows NT must be properly installed and configured to successfully install IIS 4.0.

IIS System Requirements

IIS 4.0 installs onto Windows NT Server 4.0. Therefore, most of the hardware and software requirements are automatically met if the machine satisfies the requirements for NT Server 4.0. The following sections provide a detailed list of the requirements for IIS.

Software Requirements

IIS 4.0 requires the following software to be installed on the hosting server computer:

➤ Microsoft Windows NT Server 4.0

➤ Microsoft Windows NT Server 4.0 Service Pack 3

➤ Microsoft Internet Explorer 4.01

➤ Microsoft Windows NT Server 4.0 Option Pack

Hardware Requirements

Most of the hardware requirements for IIS 4.0 are basically the same as those for Windows NT Server 4.0; however, you should modify them to meet the expected workload. The following configuration assumes you have already installed Windows NT on the server.

For Intel-based Windows NT systems up to 300 clients:

➤ Intel 486 66MHz minimum/Pentium 133MHz recommended

➤ 32MB RAM minimum/64MB RAM recommended

➤ Windows NT Server: 50MB of free hard disk space for installation

➤ Windows NT Workstation: 40MB of free hard disk space for installation

➤ 200MB minimum/2GB disk space recommended for caching

For Intel-based Windows NT systems from 300 to 1,999 clients:

➤ Intel Pentium 133MHz or greater

➤ 64MB RAM minimum

➤ From 2GB to 4GB disk space for caching

For Intel-based Windows NT systems of 2,000 or more clients:

➤ Intel Pentium 166MHz or greater

➤ 64MB of memory RAM minimum

➤ From 2GB to 4GB disk space for caching

For DEC Alpha systems:

➤ DEC Alpha 150MHz minimum

➤ 32MB RAM minimum/64MB RAM recommended

➤ Windows NT Server 4 or Windows NT Workstation 4: 50MB of free hard disk space

➤ 200MB minimum/2GB disk space recommended for caching

The hardware requirements for installing the Personal Web Server—a scaled down version of IIS—are as follows:

For Intel-based Windows 95 systems:

➤ Intel 486 33MHz minimum/Pentium 133MHz recommended

➤ For Intel-based systems: 16MB RAM minimum/32MB RAM recommended

➤ 40MB of free hard disk space for installation

➤ 200MB minimum/2GB disk space recommended for caching

Here are some items that must be ready and available before you install Windows NT and IIS 4.0:

➤ A machine that meets the minimum or recommended system requirements

➤ Windows NT CD-ROM, Windows NT Service Pack 3 CD-ROM, Internet Explorer 4.01 CD-ROM, and Windows NT 4.0 Option Pack CD-ROM.

➤ A network adapter card installed within the machine

➤ Three high-density, preformatted 3.5" 1.4MB blank diskettes

➤ One high-density 3.5" 1.4MB blank diskette (to create an emergency repair diskette)

In addition, here are some things you should do before installing Windows NT and IIS 4.0:

➤ Check all your hardware against the Windows NT Hardware Compatibility List (HCL). Obtain the updated Windows NT HCL from www.microsoft.com/ntserver/hcl/hclintro.htm.

➤ Back up all the data files from the machine on which you plan to install Windows NT.

➤ Determine a name for the machine on which you plan to install Windows NT and IIS 4.0. In addition, determine a name for the domain under which you install Windows NT.

Installing IIS On Various File Systems

In this section, we'll discuss the various file systems on which you can install IIS and how they should be configured. First, we'll examine how to choose the correct file system for your needs.

Choosing A File System: NTFS Vs. FAT

You can install Windows NT on an NTFS or a FAT file system. Here are a few major differences between the two file systems:

➤ **File size** Under NTFS, the maximum file size is 64GB. Under FAT, the maximum file size is 2GB.

➤ **Activity log** You can log the activities of IIS services, such as WWW and FTP, under an NTFS file system; you can't under a FAT file system.

➤ **Security** NTFS supports complete Windows NT security; FAT does not. As a result, you can prevent any unauthorized access to the IIS services with NTFS.

➤ **Operating system compatibility** If the machine on which you install Windows NT (NTFS) runs another operating system, such as MS-DOS, you *can't* see any of the files, including the files related to the IIS publishing services from the other operating system. This is part of NTFS's security.

If the machine on which you install Windows NT (FAT) runs another operating system, such as MS-DOS, you *can* see all the files, including the files related to the IIS publishing services from the other operating system. As such, all the files are not secure within FAT.

Installing IIS On Intel-Based Systems

To install IIS on Intel-based systems, you must follow these steps:

1. Install Windows NT Server 4.0 (approximate installation time: three hours). At the time of installation, Setup asks if you would like to install IIS 2.0. You may install IIS 2.0 because the Windows NT Service Pack upgrades IIS 2.0 to IIS 3.0. Otherwise, you may choose not to install IIS 2.0 and directly install IIS 3.0.

2. Download and install Windows NT 4.0 Service Pack 3 from the Micro-soft Web site at http://backoffice.com/downtrial/moreinfo/ne4sp3.asp (approximate installation time is 15 to 20 minutes). At the time of installation, Setup asks if you would like to install IIS 3.0. Install IIS 3.0 because the Windows NT 4.0 Option Pack then upgrades IIS 3.0 to IIS 4.0.

3. Download and install Internet Explorer 4.01 from the Microsoft Web site at http://www.microsoft.com/ie/download (approximate installation time is 20 to 30 minutes, depending on the components you choose to install).

4. Install the Windows NT 4.0 Option Pack, which includes IIS 4.0 (approximate installation time is 20 to 50 minutes, depending on the components you choose to install). You can download IIS 4.0 from the Microsoft Web site at http://www.microsoft.com/msdownload/ntoptionpack.askwiz.asp, or you can order the CD-ROM from Microsoft. A total of 52 files (74.6MB) exist within the Windows NT 4.0 Option Pack for installing IIS 4.0.

   Note: Windows NT 4.0 Service Pack 3 and Internet Explorer 4.01 must be installed before the Windows NT 4.0 Option Pack.

Installing IIS On RISC-Based Systems

To install IIS on RISC-based systems, you must follow these steps:

1. Install Windows NT Server 4.0 (approximate installation time: three hours). At the time of installation, Setup asks if you would like to install IIS 2.0. You may install IIS 2.0 because the Windows NT Service Pack upgrades IIS 2.0 to IIS 3.0. Otherwise, you may decide not to install IIS 2.0 and directly install IIS 3.0.

2. Download and install Windows NT 4.0 Service Pack 3 from the Microsoft Web site at http://backoffice.com/downtrial/moreinfo/ne4sp3.asp (approximate installation time is 15 to 20 minutes). At the time of installation, Setup asks if you would like to install IIS 3.0. Install IIS 3.0 because the Windows NT 4.0 Option Pack upgrades IIS 3.0 to IIS 4.0.

3. Download and install Internet Explorer 4.01 from the Microsoft Web site at http://www.microsoft.com/ie/download (approximate installation time is 20 to 30 minutes, depending on the components you choose to install).

4. Install the Windows NT 4.0 Option Pack, which includes IIS 4.0 (approximate installation time is 20 to 50 minutes, depending on the components you choose to install). You can download IIS 4.0 from the Microsoft Web site at http://www.microsoft.com/ntserver. Click the Option Pack link and follow the approprate steps. Or you can order the CD-ROM from Microsoft. A total of 52 files (86.9MB) exist within the Windows NT 4.0 Option Pack for installing IIS 4.0.

Installing Internet Information Server 4.0

In this section, we'll cover the installation of IIS 4.0 and all its components, including Windows NT, Windows NT Service Pack 3, Internet Explorer 4.01, and Windows NT 4.0 Option Pack.

As you've already learned, IIS 4.0 runs on Windows NT 4.0 or higher (either Server or Workstation) or on Windows 95. The steps outlined in the following sections assume that you will be installing on a Windows NT Server 4.0 that is already running IIS version 2.0. If you are installing Personal Web Server on either a Windows NT Workstation or Windows 95 computer, some of the steps may not apply. For example, installing Personal Web Server on a Windows 95 system does not require that Service Pack 3 is installed.

Some of the questions in this chapter's Exam Prep Questions test your knowledge of the NT installation process.

Installing Windows NT Service Pack 3

The Windows NT Service Pack 3 includes several components and application programming interfaces for Windows NT that are required before you can install IE 4.01 or the Windows NT 4.0 Option Pack. These include the following:

➤ Microsoft Internet Information Server 3.0

➤ Microsoft Active Server Pages 1.0b

➤ Microsoft Index Server 1.1

➤ Microsoft NetShow 1.0

➤ Microsoft FrontPage 97 Server Extensions

➤ Microsoft Crystal Reports

In addition, Service Pack 3 installs a number of security components and application programming interfaces, including the following:

➤ SMB signing

➤ Password filtering

➤ Restricting unauthorized user access

➤ Using a system key to strongly encrypt password information

➤ CryptoAPI 2.0

➤ New RPC transport for Microsoft Message Queue Server

➤ Microsoft DirectX 3.0 application programming interface (API)

➤ Microsoft Direct3D API

➤ ODBC 3.0

➤ Microsoft Win 32 APIs and SDK for Service Pack 3

Service Pack 3 also provides the necessary functionality for the Microsoft NetMeeting 2.0 conferencing software Windows NT Client as well as fixes for several bugs.

To install Windows NT Service Pack 3, follow these steps:

1. Insert the Windows NT Service Pack 3 CD-ROM.

2. Double-click NT 4.

3. Double-click NT 4 Service Pack 3.

4. Double-click NT4SP3-I.EXE.

The installation utility copies all the files. For changes to take effect, you must reboot your machine.

Installing Internet Explorer 4.01

You can download and install Internet Explorer 4.01 (IE 4.01) from the Microsoft Web site at http://www.microsoft.com/ie/download. You must install IE 4.01 because it installs various system DLLs on the server that provide functionality for the Microsoft Management Console, the Microsoft Java VM, and so on.

Installing Windows NT 4.0 Option Pack (And IIS 4.0)

The Windows NT 4.0 Option Pack adds a few new applications and communication services. It also upgrades the existing services that you have installed on your machine. Here are some of the more important components of the Option Pack:

➤ **Internet Information Server 4.0** Read more about IIS at http://www.microsoft.com/iis.

➤ **Microsoft Transaction Server 2.0** Read more about this application at http://www.microsoft.com/ntserver/guide/trans_intro.asp?A=2&B=2.

➤ **Microsoft Message Queue Server 1.0** Read more about this server application at http://www.microsoft.com/ntserver/guide/msmq.asp?A=2&B=2.

➤ **Internet Connection Services For Microsoft RAS** Read more about this option at http://www.microsoft.com/communications/RASOverview.htm.

Note: You don't have to install all the components at the same time. You can install only the components you want.

To install the Option Pack, follow these steps:

1. Insert the Option Pack CD-ROM.

2. Double-click SETUP.EXE.

3. Setup indicates it will remove the existing Gopher publishing service on your machine (IIS 4.0 does not support Gopher).

4. Setup displays the licensing agreement.

5. Upon accepting the agreement, Setup displays the two installation options: Upgrade Only and Upgrade Plus (as shown in Figure 3.1). The Upgrade Only option simply upgrades IIS. The Upgrade Plus option upgrades IIS as well as installs a few new components.

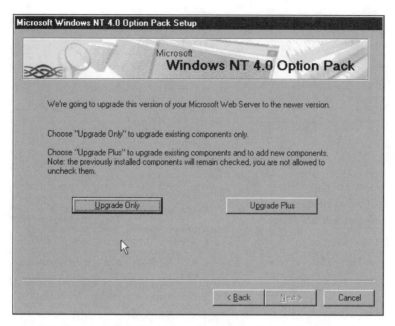

Figure 3.1 The two installation options for IIS.

6. After choosing an installation option, Setup asks you to choose from the list of components to install (see Figure 3.2).

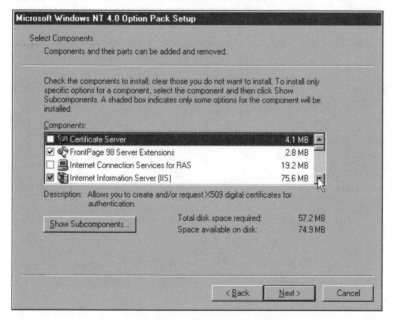

Figure 3.2 Choosing the components you want to install.

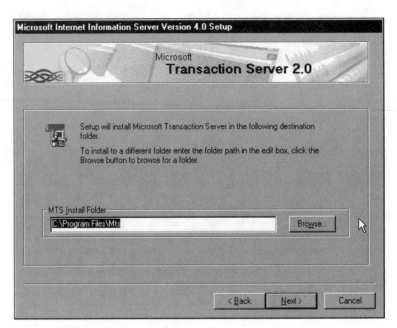

Figure 3.3 Specifying the directory for installing the Microsoft Transaction Server.

7. Next, Setup asks you to specify the directory for installing Microsoft Transaction Server (see Figure 3.3). Proceed by accepting the default option.

8. Setup then asks you to choose the type of administration: local (the default) or remote (see Figure 3.4). Proceed with the default option.

9. Setup starts copying the files. Upon successful completion, Setup reboots your machine. IIS 4.0 is now installed.

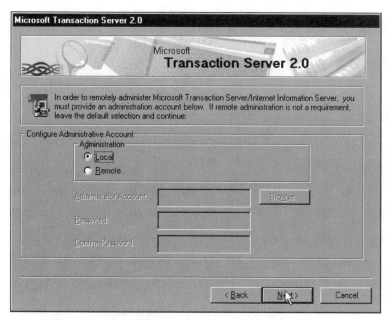

Figure 3.4 Choosing a local type of administration.

Exam Prep Questions

Question 1

> You format your machine and then install Windows NT under NTFS. There's no partition on the machine. Assume your Windows NT installation was not successful and NT crashes every time you load it. Which of the following approaches would you take to resolve this problem? [Check all correct answers]
>
> ❑ a. Use the emergency repair disk (ERD) to repair NT.
>
> ❑ b. Use Service Pack 3 to repair NT.
>
> ❑ c. Use the DOS **FORMAT** command to reformat the hard disk and then reinstall NT.
>
> ❑ d. Use FDISK to delete NTFS and create a primary DOS (FAT) partition.

The correct answers to this question are a and d. Using the ERD should be your first option. Chances are the ERD will fix the problem. If not, because there's no partition on the machine, you must use FDISK to delete NTFS and create a primary DOS (FAT) partition. Then, you can reinstall Windows NT. Typically, it's recommended you create a partition on your machine and then install NT. The Service Pack 3 cannot repair NT—that's not its purpose. Therefore, answer b is incorrect. The DOS **FORMAT** command does not work because there's no partition on the machine and the **FORMAT** command cannot recognize NTFS. Therefore, answer c is incorrect.

Question 2

> You have a 486/50MHz machine with 16MB of RAM and 200MB of available hard disk space. Can you install Windows NT and IIS on this machine?
>
> ○ a. Yes, absolutely.
>
> ○ b. No, you must first increase the RAM to 32MB.
>
> ○ c. No, you must first increase the available hard disk space to 400MB.
>
> ○ d. No, you must first increase both the available hard disk space to 400MB and RAM to 32MB.

The correct answer to this question is a. The minimum system requirements for installing Windows NT are a 486MHz machine, 16MB of RAM, and 124MB of free hard disk space. Therefore, answers b, c, and d are incorrect.

Question 3

Which of the following services are not directly supported by IIS 4.0? [Check all correct answers]

❑ a. WWW

❑ b. FTP

❑ c. Gopher

❑ d. RAS

The correct answers to this question are c and d. IIS 4.0 does not support Gopher. You can implement Gopher functionality by using the Index Server with IIS. IIS does not directly support RAS; that is a separate service of Windows NT. IIS 4.0 supports the other two services: WWW and FTP. Therefore, answers a and b are incorrect.

Question 4

How can you implement Gopher under IIS 4.0?

○ a. By using Microsoft Transaction Server

○ b. By using Microsoft Index Server

○ c. By using Microsoft Certificate Server

○ d. By using Microsoft FrontPage 97 Server Extensions

The correct answer to this question is b. Gopher is a large database that provides search capabilities. You can search by a keyword, a combination of keywords, or a phrase. Microsoft Index Server provides a search engine with similar capabilities. The other three—Microsoft Transaction Server, Microsoft Certificate Server, and Microsoft FrontPage 97 Server Extensions—don't provide any search engine capabilities. Therefore, answers a, c, and d are incorrect.

Question 5

> One of your users cannot connect to your IIS server. You have
> checked everything on the user's machine, including the TCP/IP
> configuration and IP address. Everything looks fine. How do you
> verify that the IIS server is installed and up and running on the
> server properly? [Check all correct answers]
>
> ❑ a. Open Internet Explorer 4.01 on the server and verify that
> the connection to the localhost is okay.
>
> ❑ b. Make sure both the network and IIS are running.
>
> ❑ c. Make sure the WWW service is configured properly.
>
> ❑ d. Make sure the TCP/IP protocol stack is installed.

All of these answers are correct (a, b, c, and d). First, you want to check if both
the network and IIS are running. Next, you want to check if the TCP/IP protocol stack is installed. Then, check if the WWW service is configured properly.
Finally, to test if everything is working right, open Internet Explorer on the
server and verify the connection to the localhost.

Question 6

> Which of the following features or improvements are found in IIS
> 4.0 that are not present in IIS 3.0? [Check all correct answers]
>
> ❑ a. Gopher
>
> ❑ b. Message Queue Server 1.0
>
> ❑ c. Internet Connection Services For Remote Access Service
> (RAS)
>
> ❑ d. Microsoft Transaction Server 2.0

The correct answers to this question are b, c, and d. IIS 4.0 does not support
Gopher, but it does install the other three components. Therefore, answer a is
incorrect.

Question 7

> Which NT Server 4.0 update installs the password-filtering secu-
> rity component?
>
> ○ a. Windows NT Service Pack 3
>
> ○ b. Windows NT 4.0 Option Pack
>
> ○ c. Internet Explorer 4.01
>
> ○ d. Windows NT Server 4.0

The correct answer to this question is a. Windows NT Service Pack 3 installs
a number of new security components and application programming interfaces, including the password-filtering security component. Windows NT
4.0 Option Pack installs IIS 4.0. Therefore, answer b is incorrect. Internet
Explorer 4.01 installs various system DLLs, providing functionality for the
Microsoft Management Console, the Microsoft Java VM, and so on. Therefore, answer c is incorrect. Windows NT Server 4.0 installs Windows NT.
Therefore, answer d is incorrect.

Question 8

> What version of Internet Explorer should you install before in-
> stalling IIS 4.0?
>
> ○ a. 3.0
>
> ○ b. 3.01
>
> ○ c. 4.0
>
> ○ d. 4.01

The correct answer to this question is d. Internet Explorer 4.01 installs various
system DLLs on the server, providing functionality for the Microsoft Management Console, the Microsoft Java VM, and so on. The other three versions
do not install the system DLLs necessary for IIS 4.0 to run properly. Therefore, answers a, b, and c are incorrect.

Question 9

> Why must you install Internet Explorer 4.01 before installing IIS 4.0?
>
> O a. To browse the Web.
>
> O b. Internet Explorer 4.01 installs various system DLLs on the server that provide functionality for the Microsoft Management Console, the Microsoft Java VM, and so on.
>
> O c. Internet Service Manager works only with Internet Explorer 4.01
>
> O d. None of the above.

The correct answer to this question is b. IIS 4.0 uses the system DLLs that Internet Explorer 4.01 installs. You don't need to use Internet Explorer to browse the Web—you can use any other browser. Therefore, answer a is incorrect. The ISM works with many other browsers, not just IE 4.01. Therefore, answer c is incorrect. Because both a and d are incorrect, then d is also incorrect.

Question 10

> When installing IIS 4.0, Setup reports an error "C:\winnt\ system32\odbc32.dll". How do you resolve this error?
>
> O a. Close all applications that use the ODBC drivers and stop the SQL Executive Service.
>
> O b. Reboot the server.
>
> O c. Restart the Internet Information Server Setup.
>
> O d. Install the Windows NT Service Pack 3.

The correct answer to this question is a. The error occurs because some other application or the SQL Executive Service is using the ODBC32.DLL. Therefore, when the Windows NT 4.0 Option Pack, which installs IIS 4.0, tries to upgrade ODBC32.DLL, the error occurs. None of the other options will resolve this error. Therefore, answers b, c, and d are incorrect.

Question 11

> When trying to install IIS, the installation fails due to insufficient privileges. How do you resolve this problem?
>
> ○ a. Reboot the machine.
>
> ○ b. Log on the machine as Administrator and reinstall IIS.
>
> ○ c. Reinstall IIS with all the components of Windows NT 4.0 Option Pack.
>
> ○ d. Share your root directory.

The correct answer to this question is b. While installing IIS, Setup needs to create some directories as well as give share access to others. Only an NT administrator can do this. None of the other options will resolve this problem. Therefore, answers a, c, and d are incorrect.

Question 12

> Which operating systems does the Internet Service Manager run on? [Check all correct answers]
>
> ❑ a. Windows NT Server 4.0
>
> ❑ b. Windows for Workgroups 3.11
>
> ❑ c. Windows 95
>
> ❑ d. Windows NT Workstation 4.0

The correct answers to this question are a, c, and d. The Windows 3.x platform does not support Internet Service Manager. Therefore, answer b is incorrect.

Question 13

Which of the following are needed to install Internet Information Server? [Check all correct answers]

- ❑ a. A local network connection
- ❑ b. An NTFS partition
- ❑ c. A computer with at least the minimum hardware required to support Windows NT Server 4.0
- ❑ d. TCP/IP protocol installed
- ❑ e. Access to the Option Pack distribution files

The correct answers to this question are c, d, and e. You need a machine that supports the minimum hardware requirements to install Windows NT Server 4.0. The TCP/IP protocol is also required for IIS. Access to the Option Pack distribution files can be via an Internet connection to the Microsoft Web site or on a CD-ROM. You don't need a local network connection (because IIS can be an isolated or standalone machine) or an NTFS partition for installing Windows NT or IIS. Therefore, answers a and b are incorrect.

Question 14

What is the Personal Web Server (PWS)?

- ○ a. A scaled-down version of IIS that works only on Intel-based Windows 95 or NT Workstation systems
- ○ b. A scaled-down version of Microsoft Transaction Server
- ○ c. A scaled-down version of Microsoft SQL Server
- ○ d. A scaled-down version of Microsoft Message Queue Server

The correct answer to this question is a. The PWS installs on Intel-based Windows 95 or NT Workstation systems. All others are not Web publishing servers. Therefore, answers b, c, and d are incorrect.

Need To Know More?

 Dyson, Peter. *Mastering Microsoft Internet Information Server 4.* Sybex, Alameda, CA, 1997. ISBN 0-78212-080-6. A nice introductory text on Microsoft's latest Web server technology. On the plus side, the book contains a lot of background information on Internet technologies and TCP/IP.

 Microsoft Corporation. *Microsoft Internet Information Server Resource Kit.* Microsoft Press, Redmond, WA, 1998. ISBN 1-57231-638-1. The kit goes much deeper into the internal workings of IIS and provides valuable clues for a successful implementation. The CD-ROM accompanying the book includes a copy of IIS version 4.0, additional utilities, a sampler of third-party tools, and detailed information on capacity planning and using IIS to set up an Internet Service Provider site.

 Sheldon, Tom and John Muller. *Microsoft Internet Information Server 4: The Complete Reference.* Osborne McGraw-Hill, Berkeley, CA, 1998. ISBN 0-07882-457-5. Provides a comprehensive coverage of IIS 4.0. You'll find a lot of information on installation, setup, monitoring, troubleshooting, and more.

 Microsoft TechNet. January, 1998. The technical notes for Microsoft Internet Information Server provide insight into its design and architecture. Perform a search on "IIS installation," "domain name," "boot and emergency repair diskettes," "DNS," "DHCP," "TCP/IP," "NetBIOS interface," "NetBEUI," and "RPC."

 Browse product documentation locally on your server at localhost/iishelp/misc/default.htm.

 The 15 Seconds Web site at http://www.15seconds.com/faq/ pg00058.htm includes an FAQ (frequently asked questions) on IIS as well as one on developing with IIS. The site also publishes an online newsletter for Internet developers and content providers about IIS, ISAPI, and Active Server.

Configuring
The WWW
And FTP Services

4

. . . .

Terms you'll need to understand:

√ Microsoft Management
  Console

√ TCP port

√ Connections

√ Connection timeout

√ Event logging

√ Performance tuning

√ Bandwidth throttling

√ ISAPI filter

√ Default document

√ Custom error

√ Automatic password
  synchronization

√ Maximum connections
  message

√ Unix- and MS-DOS-style
  directory listings

√ Directory security

√ Secure communication

√ HTTP headers

Techniques you'll need to master:

√ Configuring the WWW service

√ Configuring the FTP service

In these days of electronic media, providing access to electronic versions of information is increasingly important. Two of the most common forms of providing access to this type of information over the Internet are on the World Wide Web (WWW or Web) and via the File Transfer Protocol (FTP). This chapter explains how to configure the two basic publishing services in IIS: WWW and FTP. What these publishing services do and the options they have are also discussed.

Configuring The WWW Service

To configure the WWW Service, click Start|Programs|Windows NT Option Pack|Microsoft Internet Information Server|Internet Service Manager. Windows NT, in turn, starts the Microsoft Management Console 1.0, as shown in Figure 4.1.

 The Microsoft Management Console is the new interface used to administer all of IIS. Microsoft expects to add administration capabilities for the other servers, including Microsoft Transaction Server, Microsoft Proxy Server, and so on, within the realm of a single interface—the Microsoft Management Console.

Double-click IIS, then the computer name, then click the default WWW site and select Properties from the pop-up menu. Microsoft Management Console 1.0, in turn, displays the Default WWW Site Properties dialog, as shown in Figure 4.2.

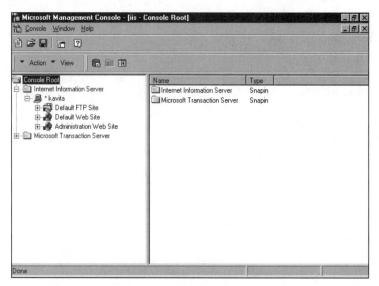

Figure 4.1 The Microsoft Management Console.

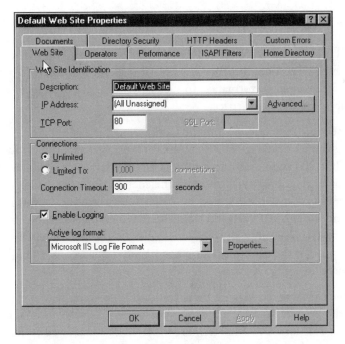

Figure 4.2   The Web Site tab of the Default Web Site Properties dialog.

The WWW service has nine items to configure. These are discussed in detail in the following sections.

General Properties

Configuring the WWW service's general properties includes specifying the following items:

➤ **Description** Within the Description text box, type the site's name. The default name is "Default Web Site". You can change the default to something that's more representative of the information contained on your site.

➤ **IP Address** Choose the IP address from the drop-down list box.

➤ **TCP Port** A TCP port represents a data stream. Multiple ports on the same machine represent multiple data streams within a single IP connection.

Within the TCP Port text box, you can specify the port number on which the WWW service runs. The default is port 80.

Note: It is recommended that you not change the default port number unless you have a compelling reason to do so.

➤ **Connection** To allow unlimited connections, click Unlimited. To limit
the number of connections, specify the number within the Limited To text
box. The default is 1,000. The fewer connections you allow, the better
your site's overall performance will be. More connections may hamper
your site's overall performance. In such cases, you may need to add more
memory and hard disk space.

➤ **Connection Timeout** Within the Connection Timeout text box, specify
the maximum time a client connection can exist without any activity. The
default is 900 seconds (or 15 minutes). Use the Connection Timeout
parameter to improve your server's efficiency. Change the default value,
if necessary, to a value that best suits your site's usage and performance.
You can use this parameter to eliminate the unused connections from
the server, thus improving your server's overall response time. On the
other hand, if the users are within a low bandwidth area, use a higher
Connection Timeout value.

➤ **Enable Logging** By logging the activities at your Web site, you can evaluate the WWW service's performance. Logging is also beneficial for
security reasons. You can determine which users are allowed to access
your site and what they may do once they are there. In addition, you can
track activities, such as maximum connections reached and connection
timeouts. You can configure the Web server to create logs at different
time periods, including daily, weekly, monthly, and so on.

To enable event logging, click Enable Logging and choose the format for
the log file from the Active Log Format drop-down list.

To specify additional properties for logging, click Properties. The Microsoft Management Console, in turn, displays the Microsoft Logging
Properties dialog, as shown in Figure 4.3.

Within the dialog, choose the time period option for creating the log file:
Daily, Weekly, Monthly, Unlimited File Size, or When File Size Reaches
(the server creates a new log file when file size reaches a number specified here).

In addition, within the Log File Directory text box, specify the directory
where the FTP server should place the log file.

Operators

Within the Operators tab, you can specify the Windows NT user accounts
for which you want to grant the operator privileges for the Web site (see
Figure 4.4).

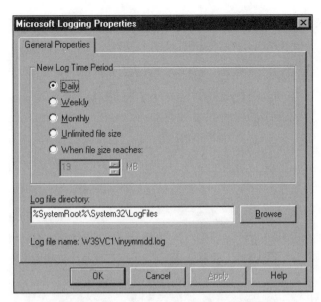

Figure 4.3   Specifying additional properties for logging.

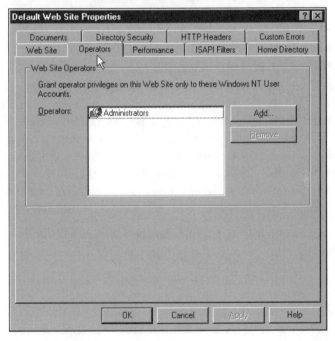

Figure 4.4   The Operators tab.

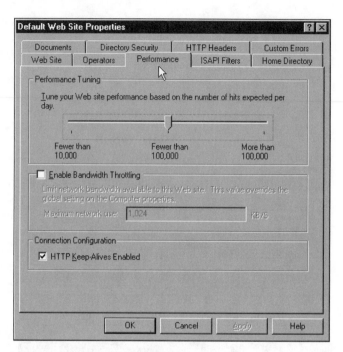

Figure 4.5 The Performance tab.

Performance Tuning

Within the Performance tab, you can specify the number of hits you expect per day on your IIS (see Figure 4.5). The range is from Fewer Than 10,000 to Fewer Than 100,000 (default) to More Than 100,000. The server allocates memory for the number of connections you specify. The more connections you specify, the more memory the server allocates. Therefore, if the actual number of connections is much lower than the allocated number, the server memory is wasted. Monitor the site regularly so you can adjust this number based on the actual site usage. This improves the server's overall performance.

To enable bandwidth throttling, check Enable Bandwidth Throttling. You can specify the maximum network size in kilobytes. The value you specify limits the bandwidth your Web site uses.

To direct the server to keep the HTTP connection alive, click HTTP Keep-Alives Enabled. This means the server does not create a new HTTP connection for every client request. This is an efficient use of the server resources, and it therefore improves the overall performance.

ISAPI Filters

An ISAPI filter is a program (typically an executable and always resident within the server's memory) that responds to the events during an HTTP request's processing.

The tab, as shown in Figure 4.6, indicates each filter's name, status (loaded, unloaded, or disabled), and priority (high, medium, or low).

To add a new filter, click Add. Microsoft Management Console, in turn, displays the Filter Properties dialog, as shown in Figure 4.7.

Specify the filter's name within the Filter Name text box. In addition, specify the executable within the Executable text box.

 IIS executes the filters in the order you specify.

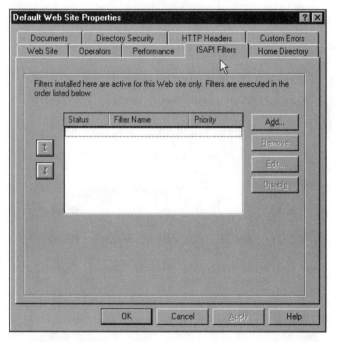

Figure 4.6   The ISAPI Filters tab.

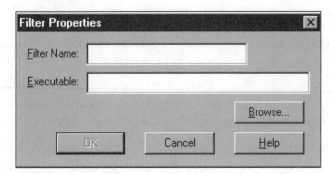

Figure 4.7   The Filter Properties dialog.

Home Directory

To change your site's home directory or the home directory's characteristics, use the Home Directory tab (see Figure 4.8). During IIS installation, the installation program creates a default home directory called "Wwwroot" (the default path is C:\InetPub\Wwwroot).

You can change the home directory's location to one of the following:

➤ A Directory Located On This (local) Computer (default)

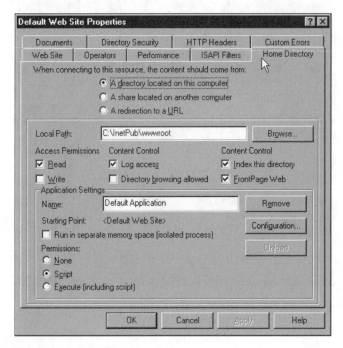

Figure 4.8   The Home Directory tab.

➤ A Share Located On Another Computer

➤ A Redirection To A URL

Depending on your choice, type the path of the directory on the same (or another) computer or the URL within the Local Path text box. For a local directory, specify the full path. For a network share, specify the Universal Naming Convention (UNC) and the name of the share (for example, \\Iis\Htmlfiles).

Within the Home Directory tab, you can modify access permissions, content control, and application settings:

➤ **Access Permissions** This section of the tab allows you to choose Read or Write access for a local directory or network share. Read access lets the Web clients download or read files within a home or virtual directory. Write access lets the Web clients upload files or change content within the write-enabled files.

 Grant Read access to the files you publish (for example, HTML files). Deny Read access to application files such as CGI programs (scripts or executables) and ISAPI filters.

➤ **Content Control** To record access to the directory within a log file, click Log Access. To let the user navigate through the directory structure on your IIS, click Directory Browsing Allowed. To direct Microsoft Index Server to include the directory within a full-text index of your site, click Index This Directory. To create a FrontPage Web for the site, click FrontPage Web.

➤ **Application Settings** Per the IIS documentation, an *application* is a collection of all the directories and files contained within a directory that is marked as an application starting point. Within the Home Directory tab, you can configure your home directory as the application starting point. You specify the application's name within the Name text box. To configure the application's properties, click Configuration.

To direct the server to run the application within a memory space isolated from the Web server, check Run In Separate Memory Space. The benefit is, if the application fails, the Web server and other applications still continue to run.

You can specify the following three types of permissions for executables or scripts within the home directory:

➤ **None** Do not allow any programs or scripts to run within this directory

➤ **Script** Allow only scripts to run within this directory, no executables

➤ **Execute (Including Script)** Allow both scripts and executables to run within this directory

Documents

You can configure the Web server to load a default document, typically your site's home page, when a user connects to your site. Using the home page as your site's default document provides the users with a method for navigating the site. The Documents tab is shown in Figure 4.9.

To specify the default document IIS loads when a user connects to the server, click Enable Default Document. To specify the document, click Add.

Note: The default document can be an HTML or ASP file.

To specify the default document footer, click Enable Document Footer. Specify the document footer file within the resulting dialog's text box.

Note: A document footer is an HTML-formatted file the server adds to the bottom of every Web document sent by the server.

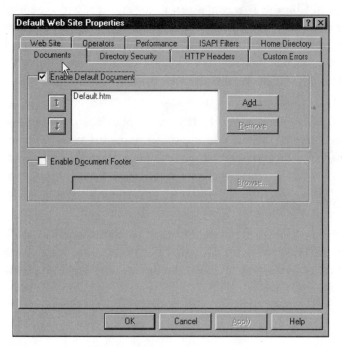

Figure 4.9 The Documents tab.

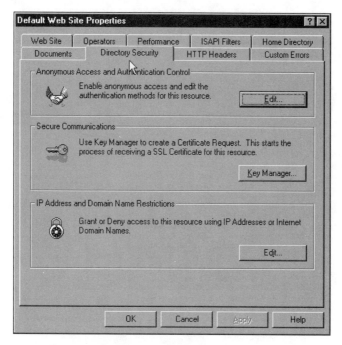

Figure 4.10   The Directory Security tab.

Directory Security

The Directory Security tab lets you configure your server's security (see Figure 4.10). It includes the following three options:

➤ **Anonymous Access And Authentication Control** Click Edit to configure anonymous access and confirm the identity of users before granting access to your server's restricted content.

➤ **Secure Communications** Click Key Manager to create an SSL key pair and server certificate request. By associating an SSL key pair with a server certificate request, you direct the client browser to establish an encrypted link to a directory or file on your IIS. This enables a secure communication link between the browser and the server.

➤ **IP Address And Domain Name Restrictions** To prevent specific users, Web sites, or domains from accessing your Web site, directory, or file, click Edit.

HTTP Headers

Figure 4.11 shows the HTTP Headers tab. You can add custom information to the HTTP headers; then the Web server sends it to the browser. The HTTP

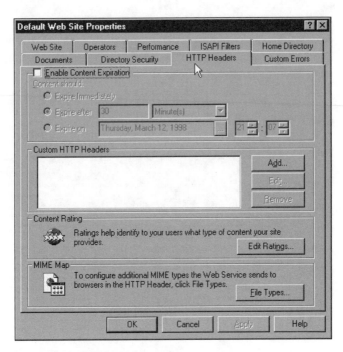

Figure 4.11   The HTTP Headers tab.

Headers tab lets you configure information such as content expiration, content rating, custom headers, and MIME maps, all of which are discussed here:

➤ **Enable Content Expiration**   Click Enable Content Expiration to include an expiration date in the HTTP header. The browser compares the expiration date to the current date and determines whether it should retrieve the page from the cache or request an updated page from the server.

➤ **Custom HTTP Headers**   You can configure the server to send a custom HTTP header to the client. For example, the server can send a custom header that prevents the proxy server from caching a page but lets the browser cache the page. To configure a custom HTTP header, click Add.

➤ **Content Rating**   The Web offers various types of content, some of which certain users may find potentially objectionable. The browser can use the content rating information to help users identify this type of information. You can include descriptive content labels within the HTTP headers. The browser detects these labels, thus helping users identify potentially objectionable content. You can set the content ratings for the Web site, a directory, or a file. To do so, click Edit Ratings.

➤ **MIME Map** To configure the Multipurpose Internet Mail Extensions (MIME) map, click File Types. The File Types dialog lists the file types registered on the server. To configure additional MIME mappings, click New Type.

Custom Errors

You can customize the errors IIS displays in the event of an error or exception. You can specify the message type and the corresponding HTML file or URL. Figure 4.12 shows the Custom Errors tab.

To edit the error message for an HTTP error, click the HTTP error and then click Edit Properties. Microsoft Management Console, in turn, displays the Error Mapping Properties dialog, as shown in Figure 4.13.

Within the dialog, you can change the message type. In addition, you can specify the HTML file or the URL (depending on the error type).

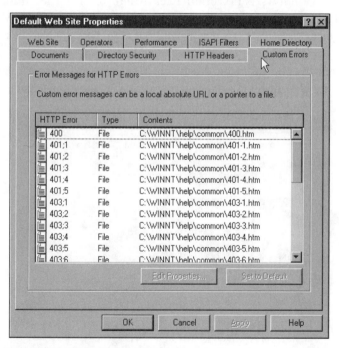

Figure 4.12 The Custom Errors tab.

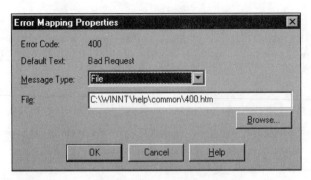

Figure 4.13 The Error Mapping Properties dialog.

Configuring The FTP Service

As mentioned previously, FTP is an application and a protocol used for re-
mote file manipulation. To configure the FTP service, click Start|
Programs|Windows NT Option Pack|Microsoft Internet Information
Server|Internet Service Manager. Windows NT, in turn, starts the Microsoft
Management Console 1.0. Once MMC has launched, double-click IIS and
then the computer name. Then, right-click Default FTP Site and select Properties from the pop-up menu. Microsoft Management Console 1.0, in turn,
displays the Default FTP Site Properties dialog, as shown in Figure 4.14.

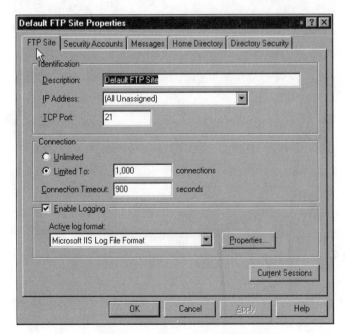

Figure 4.14 The Default FTP Site Properties dialog.

When configuring the FTP service, you have five tabs to configure. These tabs are discussed in detail in the following sections.

Configuring General Properties

Configuring the FTP service's general properties is very similar to the WWW service configuration, and includes specifying the following items:

➤ **Description** Within the Description text box, type the site's name. The default name is "Default FTP Site". You can change the default to something meaningful that's more representative of the information contained in your site.

➤ **IP Address** Choose the IP address from the drop-down list box.

➤ **TCP Port** Within the TCP Port text box, you can specify the port number on which the FTP service runs. The default is port 21.

 It is recommended that you not change the default port number unless you have a compelling reason to do so.

➤ **Connection** To allow unlimited connections, click Unlimited. To limit the number of connections, specify the number within the Limited To text box. The default is 1,000. The fewer connections you allow, the better your site's overall performance will be. More connections may hamper your site's overall performance. In such cases, you may need to add more memory and hard disk space.

Note: FTP connections consume more bandwidth than HTTP connections, because FTP connections handle larger file transfers than HTTP connections.

➤ **Connection Timeout** Within the Connection Timeout text box, you specify the maximum time a client connection can exist without any activity. The default is 900 seconds (or 15 minutes). Use the Connection Timeout parameter to improve your server's efficiency. Change the default value, if necessary, to a value that best suits your site's usage and performance. You can use this parameter to eliminate the unused connections from the server, thus improving your server's overall response time. On the other hand, if the users are within a low bandwidth area, use a higher Connection Timeout value.

➤ **Logging** By logging the activities at your FTP site, you can evaluate the FTP service's performance. Logging is also beneficial for security reasons. You can determine your site's users and their activities. In addition, you can track activities such as maximum connections reached and connection timeouts. You can configure the FTP server to create logs at different time periods, including daily, weekly, monthly, and so on.

To enable event logging, click Enable Logging and choose the format for the log file from the Active Log Format drop-down list box.

To specify additional properties for Logging, click Properties. The Microsoft Management Console, in turn, displays the Microsoft Logging Properties dialog, as shown in Figure 4.15.

Within the dialog, choose the time period for creating the log file: Daily, Weekly, Monthly, Unlimited File Size, or When File Size Reaches (the server creates a new log file when file size reaches a number specified here).

In addition, within the Log File Directory text box, specify the directory where the FTP server should place the log file.

➤ **Current Sessions** To display the active users at your FTP site at any given point, click Current Sessions.

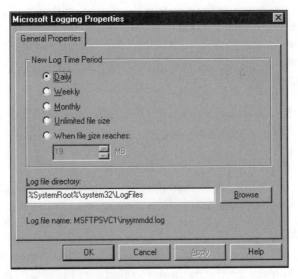

Figure 4.15   The Microsoft Logging Properties dialog.

Security Accounts

The Security Accounts tab lets you configure access for anonymous users to your FTP site. In addition, you can set up Windows NT user accounts as FTP site operators. Figure 4.16 shows the Security Accounts tab.

By default, anonymous users can connect to the FTP site. In the Username text box, specify the Windows NT user account the FTP service should use for anonymous access to this service. By default, the user account is "IUSR_*computername*" (where *computername* is the name of the system on which IIS is installed).

The Password text box specifies the password that goes with the user name within the Username text box. If you change the password here, you must also change the password for the server and domain controller. By default, the password synchronization is automatic. That is, the server automatically synchronizes the FTP site password with the Windows NT password for anonymous users. To disable this feature, deselect Enable Automatic Password Synchronization.

By default, the FTP server allows only anonymous connections.

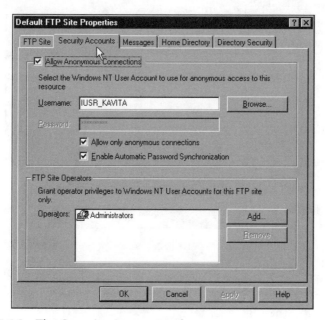

Figure 4.16   The Security Accounts tab.

To prevent the anonymous users from connecting and using the FTP site, deselect Allow Anonymous Connections.

Within the FTP Site Operators group, you can specify the Windows NT user accounts for which you want to grant the operator privileges for the FTP site.

Configuring The Messages

You can configure IIS to display the appropriate message when a user connects to the FTP service. IIS displays the following three types of message options in the Messages tab (see Figure 4.17):

➤ **Welcome** Within the Welcome text box, specify the greeting the users will see when they connect to the FTP site. You can also specify information about your company and the site, as well as display copyright and legal notices.

➤ **Exit** Within the Exit text box, specify the exit message the users will see when they disconnect from the FTP site.

➤ **Maximum Connections** Within the Maximum Connections text box, specify the warning message the users will see when they connect to the FTP site and it has already reached the maximum number of connections.

Figure 4.17   The Messages tab.

Home Directory

To change your site's home directory or the home directory's characteristics, use the Home Directory tab (see Figure 4.18). During IIS installation, the installation program creates a default home directory called "Ftproot" (the default path is C:\InetPub\Ftproot.

A user connecting to the home directory can see the context coming from a directory located on this computer or a share located on another computer.

Within the Local Path text box, specify the root directory for the FTP service (the default is C:\InetPub\Ftproot). The default access level is Read, which means the users have Read access to the directories on the FTP site. In addition, by default the server logs the access activities at the site. To provide Write access, click Write.

In addition, you can choose the directory listing style—Unix or MS-DOS. Most FTP hosts are Unix machines; therefore, the Unix directory listing style is a logical choice.

 If you change the directory listing style, you must stop and restart the FTP service for the change to take effect.

Default FTP Site Properties

| FTP Site | Security Accounts | Messages | Home Directory | Directory Security |

When connecting to this resource, the content should come from:
- ⦿ a directory located on this computer
- ○ a share located on another computer

FTP Site Directory

Local Path: `C:\InetPub\ftproot`   Browse...

- ☑ Read
- ☐ Write
- ☑ Log Access

Directory Listing Style
- ⦿ UNIX ®
- ○ MS-DOS ®

OK   Cancel   Apply   Help

Figure 4.18   The Home Directory tab.

Directory Security

Securing the directories on the server is one of the most important things you should consider when configuring your FTP server. In addition to protecting the site with a password authentication scheme, you can use the Directory Security tab to secure the directories on your FTP server (see Figure 4.19). You can choose to grant or deny access to all or specific directories on your FTP server. As a result, you can prevent unauthorized access to the server. By default, all computers are granted access.

To specify exceptions, click Add. Microsoft Management Console, in turn, displays the Deny Access On dialog, as shown in Figure 4.20.

Within the dialog, choose the type of computer (single computer, group of computers, or domain name) and specify the computer's IP address.

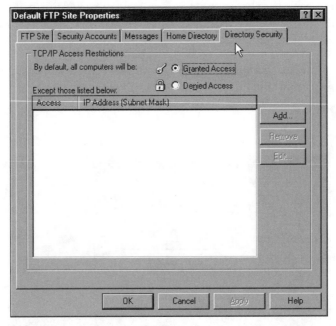

Figure 4.19 The Directory Security tab.

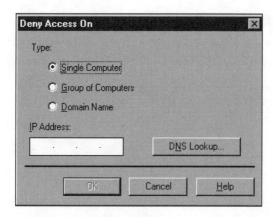

Figure 4.20   The Deny Access On dialog.

Exam Prep Questions

Question 1

> What is the default port for the WWW service?
>
> ○ a. 80
>
> ○ b. 81
>
> ○ c. 82
>
> ○ d. 83

The correct answer to this question is a. The default port for the WWW service is 80. Therefore, answers b, c, and d are incorrect.

Question 2

> What is the default port for the FTP service?
>
> ○ a. 20
>
> ○ b. 21
>
> ○ c. 22
>
> ○ d. 23

The correct answer to this question is b. The default port for the FTP service is 21. Therefore, answers a, c, and d are incorrect.

Question 3

> What is the maximum number of WWW connections allowed by IIS?
>
> ○ a. 1,000
>
> ○ b. 10,000
>
> ○ c. 100,000
>
> ○ d. Unlimited

The correct answer to this question is d. IIS can handle unlimited WWW connections. Therefore, answers a, b, and c are incorrect. However, practically speaking, the server is limited by its available resources (RAM and hard disk space).

Question 4

> What is the maximum number of FTP connections allowed by IIS?
>
> ○ a. 1,000
> ○ b. 10,000
> ○ c. 100,000
> ○ d. Unlimited

The correct answer to this question is d. IIS can handle unlimited FTP connections. Therefore, answers a, b, and c are incorrect. However, practically speaking, the server is limited by its available resources (RAM and hard disk space).

Question 5

> What is the maximum connection timeout (in seconds) you can set for the WWW and FTP services?
>
> ○ a. 900
> ○ b. 10,000
> ○ c. 100,000
> ○ d. Unlimited

The correct answer to this question is d. Although the default is 900 seconds, within the Connection Timeout text box you can actually specify any number—there is no limit. Therefore, answers a, b, and c are incorrect.

Question 6

> You designed and tested a Web site by using FrontPage 97 and the Personal Web Server. What should you do to port the site to IIS?
>
> ○ a. Port the site directly with little or no recoding (as long as you installed IIS with FrontPage Server Extensions).
> ○ b. Redesign the site completely under IIS.
> ○ c. Use Visual InterDev and Active Server Pages to port the site.
> ○ d. None of the above.

The correct answer to this question is a. Typically, you can port the site with little or no recoding. The PWS is, in fact, a scaled down version of IIS, so you don't need to redesign the site completely. Therefore, answer b is incorrect. Although Visual InterDev can read FrontPage 97 projects, FrontPage 97 does not support Active Server Pages, so you cannot use Visual InterDev and FrontPage 97 together to port the site. Therefore, answer c is incorrect. Because answer a is correct, answer d is incorrect.

Question 7

You can run multiple instances of FTP and WWW services on the same IIS.

○ a. True

○ b. False

The correct answer to this question is a. You can add virtual FTP and WWW services on the same IIS. Therefore, answer b is incorrect.

Question 8

The maximum number of FTP connections supported by your IIS is 1,000, and the server has reached its limit. When the next user connects to the server, what message does IIS display?

○ a. A warning message

○ b. An exit message

○ c. A welcome message

○ d. A welcome message, then a warning message

○ e. A warning message, then an exit message

○ f. A welcome message, then a warning message, then an exit message

The correct answer to this question is a. Because the maximum connections limit is reached, IIS displays a warning message (that is, the message you specify within the FTP Site Properties dialog's Messages tab). The server displays a welcome message only if the server lets the user access the site. Therefore, answers c, d, and f are incorrect. The server displays an exit message if a user has already connected to the site and then disconnects from the site. Therefore, answer b and e are incorrect.

Question 9

> Windows NT Challenge/Response is a built-in Windows NT security feature. What technology can you use to implement similar functionality independent of the operating system? [Check all correct answers]
>
> ❑ a. CGI scripts
>
> ❑ b. Active Server Pages with ActiveX controls
>
> ❑ c. Visual Basic
>
> ❑ d. Visual C++
>
> ❑ e. Perl

The correct answers to this question are a, c, d, and e. You can use any Visual Basic, Visual C++, and Perl to create CGI programs. A CGI program runs independent of the operating system, as long as the program does not use or call any functions specific to the operating system. Active Server Pages with ActiveX controls is Windows platform-specific. Therefore, answer b is incorrect.

Question 10

> How can you administer IIS? [Check all correct answers]
>
> ❑ a. Open the URL http://localhost:8782/iisadmin/iis.asp within Internet Explorer on your server.
>
> ❑ b. Open the URL http://localhost:80/iisadmin within Internet Explorer on your server.
>
> ❑ c. Use the Microsoft Management Console.
>
> ❑ d. Use the Internet Service Manager.

The correct answers to this question are a and c. You can take either approach: open the URL within the browser or use the Microsoft Management Console. You must specify the ASP file within the URL. Therefore, answer b is incorrect. There is no Internet Service Manager within IIS 4.0; Microsoft Management Console is now the primary interface for administering the entire IIS. Therefore, answer d is incorrect.

Question 11

> You are a consultant. The ISP (Internet Service Provider) asks
> you to improve the Web server's performance. How would you do
> this?
>
> ○ a. Enable SSL
>
> ○ b. Disable SSL
>
> ○ c. Disable Gopher
>
> ○ d. Disable FTP

The correct answer to this question is b. Disabling the SSL improves performance because the server does not need to go through the additional layer of
security check. Enabling SSL means you are adding an additional layer of
security check for IIS. Therefore, answer a is incorrect. IIS 4.0 does not support Gopher. Therefore, answer c is incorrect. Disabling FTP means the
users cannot use the FTP service to transfer the files. Therefore, answer d is
incorrect.

Question 12

> You recently joined a multinational organization that has
> Webmasters supporting heterogeneous platforms. The organiza-
> tion supports the growing demands of its employees for
> downloading popular software by using the FTP service running
> on IIS. Some of the users complain they have problems trying to
> access the directory listing on the FTP site. When investigating
> this problem, you find although this is true for some users, others
> have no problem getting the directory listing. How do you resolve
> this situation?
>
> ○ a. Reinstall IIS with the FTP option.
>
> ○ b. Enable directory browsing for FTP.
>
> ○ c. Disable the Windows NT Challenge/Response.
>
> ○ d. Set the directory listing to Unix.
>
> ○ e. Set the directory listing to MS-DOS.

The correct answer to this question is d. Because the organization supports
heterogeneous platforms, the Unix-style directory listing is appropriate. Reinstalling IIS with the FTP option is not necessary. Therefore, answer a is incorrect.
You do not need to enable directory browsing for FTP because some users can

already access the directory listing on the FTP site. Therefore, answer b is incorrect. The Windows NT Challenge/Response is a password authentication scheme. Therefore, answer c is incorrect. The MS-DOS-style directory listing works only with Windows systems. Therefore, answer e is incorrect.

Question 13

You're working for an accounting firm that has 26 Web administrators. The firm has one Windows NT Server to service all its needs. The firm has a mission critical application developed with SQL Server as the database back end running on the Windows NT Server. The client front end is in Visual Basic, and it resides on each user's machine. Recently, the firm also installed IIS and created an intranet. The intranet is yet within its nascent stage, where the firm posts all its notices, policies, procedures, and more. After deploying IIS, the network administrator began to complain that the network is becoming increasingly slower. This, in turn, affects the mission-critical application. How do you handle this request?

O a. Stop the FTP service on IIS.

O b. Disable the keep-alive HTTP connection

O c. Tune your Web site's performance for fewer than 10,000 hits per day.

O d. Enable bandwidth throttling.

The correct answer to this question is d. By enabling bandwidth throttling, you can limit the bandwidth your Web site uses. Stopping the FTP service on IIS is not a solution. You do not want to disable the FTP service. Therefore, answer a is incorrect. Disabling the keep-alive HTTP connection is no solution, either. In fact, keeping the HTTP connection alive helps improve the performance. Therefore, answer b is incorrect. Again, tuning your Web site's performance to fewer than 10,000 hits per day does not help. Although this may improve performance, your site will not be able to handle larger volume traffic. Therefore, answer c is incorrect.

Question 14

Your company has a single NT Server. The server's domain name is "Universe" and its computer name is "planet_intranet". You've installed IIS 4.0 and WINS on the server. Within the default WWW service directory (that is, Wwwroot), you create a subdirectory called "Arena". The directory Arena has an HTML page named "MYHOME.HTM". What URL should a client browser on your intranet use to load the MYHOME.HTM page?

○ a. http://localhost/arena/myhome.htm

○ b. http://Universe/planet_intranet/arena/myhome.htm

○ c. http://Universe/arena/myhome.htm

○ d. http://localhost/planet_intranet/arena/myhome.htm

The correct answer to this question is c. The computer name is not necessary, but the domain name is. Therefore, answers a, b, and d are incorrect.

Need To Know More?

Dyson, Peter. *Mastering Microsoft Internet Information Server 4.* Sybex, Alameda, CA, 1997. ISBN 0-78212-080-6. Nice introductory text on Microsoft's latest Web server technology. On the plus side, the book contains a lot of background information on Internet technologies and TCP/IP.

Microsoft Corporation. *Microsoft Internet Information Server Resource Kit.* Microsoft Press, Redmond, WA, 1998. ISBN 1-57231-638-1. The kit goes deep into IIS's internal workings and provides valuable clues for successful implementation. The CD-ROM accompanying the book includes a copy of IIS version 4.0, additional utilities, a sampler of third-party tools, and detailed information on capacity planning and using IIS to set up an Internet Service Provider site.

Oliver, Robert, Plazas Christian, John Desborough, and David Gulbransen. *Building a Windows NT 4 Internet Server.* New Riders Publishing, Indianapolis, IN, 1997. ISBN 1-56205-680-8. This is a good book that uses a tutorial-based approach to teach you how to implement and administer an Internet server. The book focuses on several security considerations and configurations for a Windows NT Internet server. The book's CD-ROM includes several software utilities from the *Microsoft Resource Kit* used to build an Internet server on the NT platform.

Sheldon, Tom and John Muller. *Microsoft Internet Information Server 4: The Complete Reference.* Osborne McGraw-Hill, Berkeley, CA, 1998. ISBN 0-07882-457-5. Provides a comprehensive coverage of IIS 4.0. You'll find a lot of information on installation, setup, monitoring, troubleshooting, and more.

Microsoft TechNet. January, 1998. The technical notes for Microsoft Internet Information Server provide insight into its design and architecture.

For discussions on Microsoft Management Console, subscribe to the newsgroup microsoft.public.management.mmc.

IIS Security

Terms you'll need to understand:

- √ NTFS (New Technology File System)
- √ User authentication and authorization
- √ Anonymous account
- √ NTLM authentication
- √ Home directory
- √ Secure Sockets Layer (SSL)
- √ Digital certificate
- √ Event auditing
- √ Directory browsing
- √ Secure communication
- √ Directory security
- √ Proxy server
- √ Access permission
- √ Firewall
- √ Packet filter

Techniques you'll need to master:

- √ Configuring Windows NTFS permissions
- √ Configuring IIS security
- √ Controlling access by IP address
- √ Using event auditing
- √ Securing a RAS connection

IIS is tightly integrated with Windows NT. As a result, IIS benefits and inherits Windows NT's security features. In this chapter, we'll explore the steps necessary to secure your IIS server. In addition to Windows NT, IIS is also tightly integrated with Microsoft Proxy Server, Certificate Server, Site Server, and BackOffice; therefore, we'll examine how security relates to those systems as well.

Basic Security Overview

Because security is such an important issue with IIS, you must fully understand what types of access you can allow on your system. The following security features are available for IIS:

➤ **User authentication and authorization** Because IIS is tightly integrated with Windows NT, any user accessing a Windows NT resource, such as IIS, must have a valid Windows NT user account. Therefore, if a user does not have a valid Windows NT account, he or she cannot use any of the Windows NT resources—including IIS. This also simplifies the logon process, because the user only provides the logon information once. In addition, Windows NT provides a number of features to further the process of user authentication and authorization, including password expiration, auditing the logon process, and forcing secure password policies.

➤ **Anonymous access** During the IIS installation, the installation program creates anonymous accounts for both Web and FTP services. Neither Windows NT nor IIS authenticates the anonymous access. The anonymous accounts can only access the files and applications for which the system administrator grants permission.

➤ **User name and password** You can configure IIS to authenticate the use of files and applications by specific users or groups of users only. That is, the user must provide a valid user name and password before he or she can use the files and applications. Windows NT compares the user name and password to the accounts in the Windows NT Server directory. Note that Windows NT does not encrypt the user name and password in such cases. Authentication that is not encrypted is called *basic authentication*.

➤ **NTLM authentication** NTLM (more commonly referred to as Windows NT challenge/response authentication) is an authentication technique the browser uses to encrypt and then send a password across the network. Microsoft Internet Explorer 3.0 and higher supports NTLM authentication. For other browsers, Microsoft provides the Software Developer's Kit (SDK), which other vendors can use to provide NTLM authentication techniques within their browsers and applications.

➤ **Access control by IP address** You can configure IIS to grant or deny access to specific IP addresses.

➤ **Access control by Windows NTFS permissions** You should install Windows NT on an NTFS partition because it includes built-in security that both Windows NT and IIS can use. Under an NTFS partition, you can configure the access permissions for individual files or an entire directory.

➤ **Digital certificates** For access control, IIS supports X.509 digital certificates. A *digital certificate* is like a driver's license: To validate your identity to the authorities, you must present a form of identification, such as the driver's license. Similarly, a client accessing the server's resources must present a valid ID, such as a digital (client) certificate. Just like the state authority that issues driver's licenses, there are trusted certificate authorities, such as VeriSign (www.verisign.com), that issue digital certificates. It is not enough to just have a valid digital certificate, a client must also know the password associated with the certificate. The combination of these two things is the key to successful access of a server's resources. Similar to a client certificate, a server can also have a certificate, called the *server certificate*. A client machine can use the server certificate to validate the server's authenticity. The support of both client and server certificates is an important part of the IIS security features.

Note: To issue digital certificates, you can use the Microsoft Certificate Server.

➤ **Secure Sockets Layer (SSL)** SSL encrypts the communication between the browser and server. You can, therefore, send sensitive data, such as credit card information, and so on, within an encrypted line of communication.

Note: Typically, encrypted communication is slower and requires more bandwidth than nonencrypted communication.

➤ **Auditing** Both Windows NT and IIS support event logging. You can log the activities on the server to a log file and then use the Crystal Reports engine (which comes with Windows NT) to generate reports of the log file. You can log the following types of activities:

  ➤ All logons

➤ Failed logon attempts

➤ Activities on the server, including file and directory accesses such as Read and Write operations

Auditing the activities on the server is an important part of configuring its security. If you sense unauthorized use of the server resources, you should enable auditing to track the activities.

You can complement Windows NT's security features by using one or more of the following techniques:

➤ **Packet filter** Think of a packet filter as a security guard. As an example, when you enter a Fortune 500 corporation's office complex, you'll probably notice a security guard in the lobby. The guard's responsibility is to let only authorized personnel into the building. A packet filter's function is similar: A packet filter analyzes the incoming TCP/IP packets. A packet filter resides between the two networks (the Internet and your corporation's LAN) and acts as a security guard. The Internet is the outside world and your corporation's LAN is the intellectual asset you want to protect from intruders and unauthorized users. Based on your specifications, the filter evaluates the validity of the incoming TCP/IP packets. If the incoming packet meets the set of rules, the filter lets the packet pass; otherwise, the filter blocks the packet. A packet filter is faster, but not as secure, as a firewall.

➤ **Firewall** A firewall is a computer that resides between the Internet and your corporation's LAN. Its function is similar to the packet filter. A firewall is typically more secure, but slower, than a packet filter. You can configure a firewall to block the communication between the two networks based on the following criteria:

➤ TCP/IP socket number

➤ Source computer's IP address (or IP network)

➤ Destination computer's IP address (or IP network)

A firewall could, for example, be used to block Internet users from using your server's file and printing services. The firewall blocks access to all services except HTTP and FTP.

➤ **Proxy server** A proxy server resides between the client machines and the Web server. A proxy server's primary responsibility is to cache Web pages. For example, a client machine sends a request to the Web server via the proxy server. The Web server responds with the page through the proxy server, and the proxy server caches this page. As a result, when another client machine sends the same request, the proxy server returns the page from its cache. As you can see, the proxy server expedites the response by eliminating the need for the request to make the trip from the proxy server to the Web server. In addition, the proxy server limits the possibilities of an intruder trying to reach the Web server, because the intruder must go through the proxy server before reaching the Web server.

Windows NT Security

In this section, we'll discuss Windows NT security and cover its features in detail, including setting up group and user accounts, directory sharing, file security, event auditing, and RAS. Because IIS is installed on Windows NT, these settings are used on both.

User And Group Accounts

When you install Windows NT, by default, the installation program creates two accounts automatically—Administrator and Guest, with the Guest account disabled. The Administrator account is very important because it is the only account you can use to log on to NT immediately after installation. As an administrator, you can add new Windows NT user accounts and create NT group accounts.

A user can belong to one or more groups.

For each user, you must create a valid user name and password. When assigning passwords, be careful yet creative. A simple and easy-to-guess password can be potentially harmful to your system. For example, assigning the user's first name as the user name and the user's last name as the password is easy for any intruder to guess. Typically, to create a password you should use a combination of numbers and uppercase and lowercase letters. For clients accessing sensitive data within certain directories on the server, enable SSL so that the password and other sensitive information the browser sends is encrypted. To learn more about SSL, refer to the section "Web Service: Directory Security" later in this chapter.

The IIS installation program automatically creates an anonymous account for both the Web and FTP services. The anonymous account's ID is IUSR_*computername,* where *computername* is the name of the machine on which you install Windows NT and IIS. IIS, by default, uses automatic password synchronization to validate the anonymous account.

By default, the Windows NT installation program assigns the Full Control permission for the Everyone group. This means that every user has complete access and control of all the files and directories. This is something you'll want to change!

Directory Sharing

For a directory residing on Windows NT Server, you can configure the directory's share permissions. To do so, right-click the directory and select Properties from the pop-up menu. Windows NT, in turn, displays a dialog, as shown in Figure 5.1.

To configure the sharing permissions, click the Sharing tab. To enable sharing, click Shared As. To specify the access permissions, click Properties. You can assign the following types of permissions to the NTFS directories:

➤ **No Access** The user can see the directory name but cannot do anything with the directory.

➤ **Full Control** The user has complete access and control over the directory.

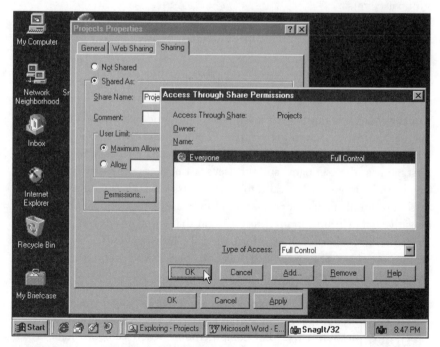

Figure 5.1 Only directories can be shared.

The user can read, write, execute, and delete files within the directory. In addition, the user can delete the directory itself. The user can also change the permissions for the directory and the files within the directory (assuming the files, themselves, do not have prior restrictions on them).

➤ **Read** The user can read and execute the files but cannot make any changes to the files in the directory.

➤ **Change** The user can read, write, execute, and delete files within the directory. However, the user cannot change the permissions for either the directory or the files within the directory.

 If needed, you can limit the number of users who can use this directory at the same time.

File Security

For a file residing on a Windows NT Server machine, you can configure the file's security permissions. To do so, right-click the file and select Properties from the pop-up menu. To configure the security permissions, click the Security tab within the resulting dialog. You can assign the following types of permissions to an NTFS file:

➤ **No Access** The user can see the file but has no control or access over the file.

➤ **Full Control** The user has complete access and control over the file. The user can read, write, execute, and delete the file. The user can also change the permissions for the file.

➤ **Read** The user can read and execute the file but cannot make any changes to the file.

➤ **Change** The user can read, write, execute, and delete the file but cannot change the permissions for the file.

Event Auditing

You can log the activities to access the files and directories on the server with event logging. Note that this is only possible if you have installed Windows NT on an NTFS partition. If you installed Windows NT on a FAT file system, this option is not available, because the FAT file system does not provide the built-in security features that NTFS does. By default, both Windows NT and IIS allow event logging. A log file includes the following data, typically in a comma-delimited format:

➤ **Client** The client machine accessing the server.

➤ **User Name** The user ID accessing the server. For anonymous users, the log file includes a hyphen (-).

➤ **Log Date** The log date.

➤ **Log Time** The log time.

➤ **Service** The IIS service that the client machine is accessing.

➤ **Machine** The server's computer name.

➤ **Server IP** The server's IP address.

➤ **Processing Time** The total time for IIS to process the request.

➤ **Bytes Received** The client request's size in bytes.

➤ **Bytes Sent** The server response's size in bytes.

➤ **Service Status** The service's status.

➤ **Win32 Status** The Win32 subsystem's status.

➤ **Operation** The specific client request.

➤ **Target** The client request's target (for example, Web page, FTP directory, and so on).

➤ **Parameters** The parameters for the request.

➤ **Other Info** Any other information.

You can use Windows NT's Event Viewer to view the log files. Alternatively, you can use the built-in Crystal Reports engine to view the log files. By default, the following Crystal Reports are available:

➤ Activity by day of the week

➤ Activity by hour of the day

➤ Most frequently requested pages

➤ Most frequently accessed directories

➤ Most frequently downloaded file types and sizes

➤ Server errors

Remote Access Service (RAS)

Windows NT supports RAS. By using a RAS connection, a remote computer can dial into your corporation's LAN. Obviously, to ensure the RAS connection is secure, you must undertake certain security measures. You can install RAS through the Network applet's Services tab.

RAS Encryption

Upon installation, you can configure the RAS connection's encryption settings to one of the following options:

➤ **Allow Any Authentication Including Clear Text (default)** This is basic authentication lacking any type of encryption. This method does not encrypt the password. You can use this method when connecting to a non-Microsoft server.

➤ **Require Encrypted Authentication** This method uses encryption to transmit the password. Use this method when connecting to a non-Microsoft server.

➤ **Require Microsoft Encrypted Authentication** Use this method when connecting to a Microsoft server. This method uses the Microsoft Challenge Authentication Handshake Protocol (MS-CHAP). If you check Require Data Encryption, the data sent over the RAS connection is also encrypted.

RAS Callback

RAS Callback disconnects the inbound call and reestablishes the RAS connection by calling back the client. You can configure RAS Callback to any one of the following options via the User|Properties|Dialin option within User Manager For Domains:

➤ **No Call Back (default)** The server does not call back the client.

➤ **Set By Caller** The server calls back the client at a number the caller specifies.

➤ **Preset To** The server always calls back the number you specify.

IIS Security

You can configure the security options for the Web and FTP services by using IIS's Microsoft Management Console. Click Start|Programs|Windows NT Option Pack|Microsoft Internet Information Server|Internet Service Manager. Windows NT, in turn, starts the Microsoft Management Console 1.0, as

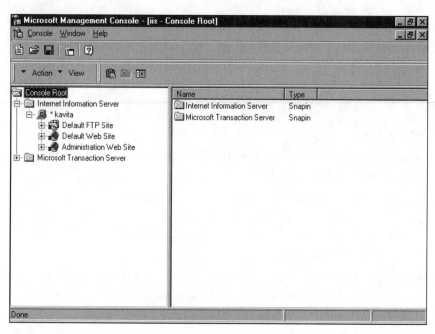

Figure 5.2 The Microsoft Management Console.

shown in Figure 5.2. The various security settings that can be configured for the Web and FTP services are detailed in the following sections.

Web Service: Home Directory

By right-clicking the site, and selecting Properties, then the Home Directory tab, you can change your site's home directory or the home directory's characteristics via the Default Web Site Properties dialog box (see Figure 5.3). During IIS installation, the installation program creates a default home directory, Wwwroot (the default path is C:\InetPub\Wwwroot).

You can change the home directory's location to one of the following:

➤ A directory located on the local computer (default)

➤ A directory (share) located on another computer

➤ A redirection to a URL

For a local directory, specify the full path within the Local Path text box. For a network share, specify the Universal Naming Convention (UNC) path, including the name of the share (for example, \\Iis\Htmlfiles).

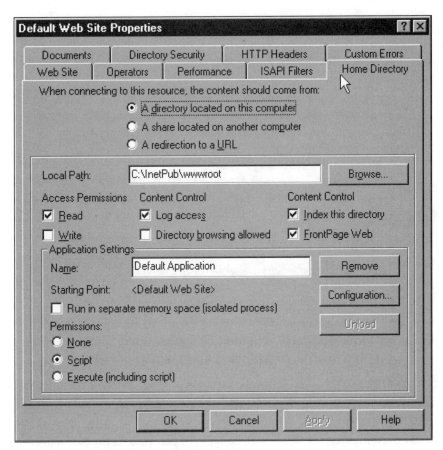

Figure 5.3   The Home Directory tab.

Access Permissions

You can configure the access permissions (Read and Write) for a local directory or network share through the Home Directory tab. Read access lets the Web clients download or read files within a home or virtual directory. Write access lets the Web clients upload files or change the content within the write-enabled files.

 Grant Read access to the files you publish (for example, HTML files). Deny Read access to application files, such as CGI programs (scripts or executables) and ISAPI filters.

Content Control

In addition to controlling access to IIS, you can also control access to its content. The server offers the following four options:

➤ **Log Access** Check this to record access to the directory within a log file.

➤ **Directory Browsing Allowed** Uncheck this to prevent users from navigating through the directory structure on the IIS server. By default, IIS lets users browse through the directory structure.

> You can disable directory browsing for the entire Web site but not for a single directory. You should not let users browse your server's directory structure unless absolutely necessary or your application requirements demand it.
>
> Providing a view of your server's directory structure indicates the type of information available on the server, thus increasing the potential for hacker and intruder attacks. Curiosity within the intruder's mind can spell trouble for you!

➤ **Index This Directory** Check this to direct Microsoft Index Server to include the home directory within a full-text index of your site.

➤ **FrontPage Web** Check this to create a FrontPage Web for the site.

Permissions

You can configure the following three types of permissions for executables or scripts within the Home Directory tab:

➤ **None** IIS does not allow any programs or scripts to run within this directory.

➤ **Script** IIS allows only scripts to run within this directory, no executables.

➤ **Execute (Including Script)** IIS allows both scripts and executables to run within this directory.

Be extremely careful when granting execute permission to users for the scripts and executables that reside on the server. Remember, the scripts and executables execute on the server, not on the client machine; therefore, you should not grant execute permission to just anyone; be sure there's a good reason.

Examples of scripts and executables include CGI scripts and ISAPI DLLs. You must grant execute permission for the directories containing ASP pages. The ASP pages execute and return HTML to the browser. However, you must disable Read access from such directories; otherwise, the users can modify the pages.

If there is a reason for users to execute a CGI script or ISAPI DLL, place all such scripts and DLLs within a single directory, grant execute permission on that directory alone, and disable the execute permission for all other directories.

Web Service: Directory Security

The sections that follow show you how you can use the Directory Security tab to configure your server's security. By using the Directory Security tab, you can perform the following tasks:

➤ Prevent specific users or domains from accessing your Web site

➤ Configure the anonymous access to the site

➤ Establish a secure communication link between the browser and the server

Figure 5.4 shows the Directory Security tab.

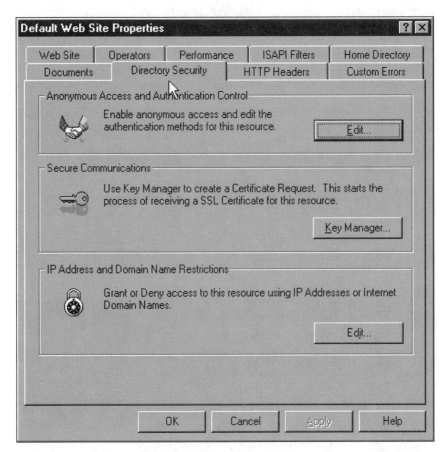

Figure 5.4   The Directory Security tab.

IP Address And Domain Name Restrictions

To prevent specific users, Web sites, or domains from accessing your Web site, directory, or file, click Edit in the IP Address And Domain Name Restrictions area.

Typically, you know the IP addresses of the machines within your company accessing the intranet. As a result, you can grant access to only those IP addresses and block the rest.

To grant access to the outside users of your company's intranet, first grant access to all and then selectively block the specific IP addresses as you detect potential intruder problems.

In addition to the IP address and domain name restrictions, you can introduce a firewall (or packet filter) between the Internet and your company's intranet as an added measure of security.

Anonymous Access And Authentication Control

To configure anonymous access and confirm the identity of users before granting access to your server's restricted content, click Edit in the Anonymous Access And Authentication Control. The Microsoft Management Console, in turn, displays the Authentication Methods dialog, as shown in Figure 5.5.

Within this dialog, choose one or more of the following authentication methods:

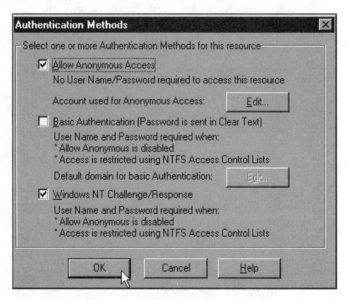

Figure 5.5 The Authentication Methods dialog.

➤ **Allow Anonymous Access** No user name and password are required for anonymous access.

➤ **Basic Authentication** A basic authentication scheme does not encrypt the password.

➤ **Windows NT Challenge/Response** Both user name and password are required.

Secure Communications

To create an SSL key pair and server certificate request, click Key Manager. By associating an SSL key pair with a server certificate request, you direct the client browser to establish an encrypted link to a directory or file on your IIS. This enables a secure communication link between the browser and the server. You should establish a secure communication link only if the directory or file contains sensitive information, because a secure communication link is typically slower and requires more bandwidth than a nonencrypted line of communication.

FTP Service: Security Accounts

By using the Security Accounts tab, you can configure the access for anonymous users to your FTP site. By default, anonymous users can connect to the FTP site. With this tab, you can also configure Windows NT user accounts as FTP site operators. Figure 5.6 shows the Security Accounts tab.

Within the Username text box, specify the Windows NT user account the FTP service should use for anonymous access to this service. By default, the user account is IUSR_*computername*, where *computername* is the name of the system on which IIS is installed.

The Password text box specifies the password that goes with the user name. If you change the password here, you must also change the password for the server and domain controller. By default, password synchronization is automatic. That is, the server automatically synchronizes the FTP site password with the Windows NT password for anonymous users. To disable this feature, uncheck Enable Automatic Password Synchronization.

To prevent anonymous users from connecting to and using the FTP site, uncheck Allow Only Anonymous Connections.

Within the FTP Site Operators section, you can specify the Windows NT user accounts to whom you want to grant the operator privileges for the FTP site.

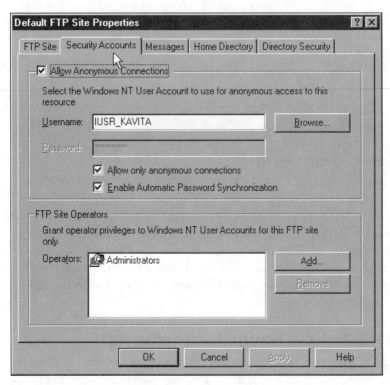

Figure 5.6 The Security Accounts tab.

FTP Service: Directory Security

Securing the directories on the server is one of the most important things you should consider when configuring your FTP server. In addition to protecting the site with a password authentication scheme, you can use the Directory Security tab to secure the directories on your FTP server (see Figure 5.7). You can choose to grant or deny access to all or specific directories on the server, thus preventing unauthorized access to the server.

By default, the FTP server grants access to all the computers.

To specify exceptions, click Add. Microsoft Management Console, in turn, displays the Deny Access On dialog, as shown in Figure 5.8.

Grant Read access to the FTP directories containing publicly accessible files for download and remove Write access from these directories. Create a separate directory for the users to upload files and grant both Read and Write access to this directory. By default, event logging is enabled for the FTP server. To detect potential unauthorized access or any other misuse, monitor the event log regularly.

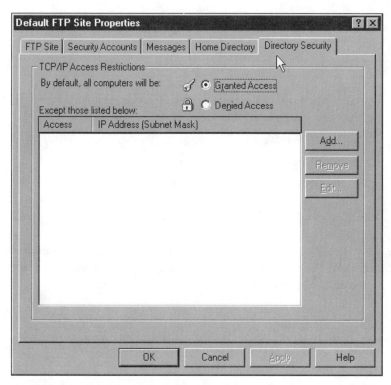

Figure 5.7   The Directory Security tab.

Within this dialog, choose the type of computer (Single Computer, Group Of Computers, or Domain Name) and specify the computer's IP address.

Figure 5.8   The Deny Access On dialog.

Exam Prep Questions

Question 1

> Windows NT's basic authentication scheme does not perform which of the following actions?
>
> ○ a. Encrypt the password
>
> ○ b. Encrypt the user name
>
> ○ c. Encrypt both the user name and password
>
> ○ d. None of the above

The correct answer to this question is d. The basic authentication scheme is just that, basic. The scheme does not encrypt anything involved in the authentication process. Therefore, answers a, b, and c are incorrect.

Question 2

> Which one of the following uses the NTLM authentication scheme?
>
> ○ a. The browser
>
> ○ b. Windows NT
>
> ○ c. IIS
>
> ○ d. All of the above

The correct answer to this question is a. The browser uses the NTLM authentication scheme to send the data to the server. Windows NT and IIS are on the server side. Therefore, answers b and c are incorrect. Because answer a is correct, answer d is incorrect.

Question 3

> You can configure IIS to block specific IP addresses from accessing and using which of the following services? [Check all correct answers]
>
> ❑ a. Web
>
> ❑ b. FTP
>
> ❑ c. Gopher
>
> ❑ d. Telnet

The correct answers to this question are a and b. You can configure both Web and FTP services to block specific IP addresses. IIS 4.0 does not support Gopher or Telnet. Therefore, answers c and d are incorrect.

Question 4

What can you specify using the Universal Naming Convention?

O a. Network share

O b. Redirection to a URL

O c. Local path

O d. None of the above

The correct answer to this question is a. A UNC (Universal Naming Convention) applies to a network drive that you configure as a share (for example, \\Iis\Htmlfiles). The UNC does not apply to URLs or local paths. Therefore, answers b and c are incorrect. Because answer a is correct, answer d is incorrect.

Question 5

Which one of the following file systems should you install IIS on so that IIS benefits from its tight integration with Windows NT?

O a. FAT

O b. NTFS

O c. Windows 95

O d. DOS

The correct answer to this question is b. NTFS is a secure file system. FAT does not have any built-in security. Therefore, answer a is incorrect. Both Windows 95 and DOS are operating systems, not file systems. Therefore, answers c and d are incorrect.

Question 6

> Which of the following can you use IIS's auditing services to audit?
>
> ○ a. Logons
>
> ○ b. Failed logon attempts
>
> ○ c. Access activities on the server
>
> ○ d. All of the above

The correct answer to this question is d. IIS's event logging capabilities let you record all types of information, including both successful and failed logon attempts. In addition, you can log the different types of access activities, including Web and FTP activities. Because answer d is correct, answers a, b, and c are incorrect.

Question 7

> For anonymous access, you can configure IIS so Windows NT automatically synchronizes the Windows NT password with the HTTP or FTP password.
>
> ○ a. True
>
> ○ b. False

The correct answer to this question is a, True. Synchronizing the Windows NT password with the HTTP or FTP password is IIS's default configuration.

Question 8

> Which is the default account created by the installation program during the IIS installation?
>
> ○ a. IUSR_*computername*, where *computername* is the name of the machine on which you installed IIS
>
> ○ b. USR_*computername*, where *computername* is the name of the machine on which you installed IIS
>
> ○ c. *Computername*, where *computername* is the name of the machine on which you installed IIS
>
> ○ d. IUSR_*servername*, where *servername* is IIS's name

The correct answer to this question is a. IUSR_*computername* is, in fact, the default user account. Therefore, answers b, c, and d are incorrect.

Question 9

> If you do not have Read access to a file on the FTP server, you cannot perform which of the following operations? [Check all correct answers]
>
> ❑ a. Download the file
>
> ❑ b. Read the file
>
> ❑ c. Write to the file

The correct answers to this question are a and b. Downloading a file is equivalent to a read operation. Because there's no Read access on the file, you can neither read nor download the file. To be able to write to the file, you must have Write access to the file, which is a separate permission from Read and does not rely upon Read access. Therefore, answer c is incorrect.

Question 10

> Netscape distributes the Navigator source code for free. Netscape Navigator does not inherently support the NTLM authentication scheme. How can you build this scheme into Navigator?
>
> ○ a. By using the Software Developer's Kit from Microsoft.
>
> ○ b. By using the Software Developer's Kit from Netscape.
>
> ○ c. By using the Microsoft Windows API.
>
> ○ d. NTLM authentication is Internet Explorer-specific only; you cannot add this functionality into Navigator.

The correct answer to this question is a. You can enhance Navigator by integrating the NTLM authentication scheme. To do so, you must use the Software Developer's Kit from Microsoft. The NTLM authentication scheme originates from Microsoft, so using the Software Developer's Kit from Netscape does no good. Microsoft Windows API does not include any such scheme, either. Although this scheme originates from Microsoft, the scheme is not Internet Explorer-specific. Microsoft provides a Software Developer's Kit you can use to integrate the scheme within other browsers, including Netscape Navigator. Therefore, answers b, c, and d are incorrect.

Question 11

> You have been the IIS administrator for your company for more than a year. The Internet content for your company's Web site has grown and you are asked to create a proprietary authentication program for the site. As the Web site administrator, you are asked to choose the design technique. What technique would you choose? [Check all correct answers]
>
> ❑　a. Create an ISAPI filter to authenticate all the users.
>
> ❑　b. Create a CGI script to authenticate all the users.
>
> ❑　c. Create a user account on Windows NT for all the users.

The correct answers to this question are a and b. Answer a is the most efficient technique because the approach uses an ISAPI filter. ISAPI implementation consumes fewer server resources compared to a CGI implementation. Answer b is less efficient (but still correct) because an ISAPI solution is faster than a CGI solution. Answer c is not an option because you do not want to create a Windows NT user account for each user. Therefore, answer c is incorrect.

Question 12

> Your company has developed a killer software product. The company would like potential customers to download the product's evaluation copy for free from its Web site. As the site's Webmaster, how do you propose to implement this in the best way possible?
>
> ○　a. Create a Web form where users register themselves and you mail them a disk with the free software.
>
> ○　b. Place the software on the FTP site and set the FTP directory to Read Only. Point the interested users to this site.
>
> ○　c. Use Microsoft Merchant Server to configure the download facility.
>
> ○　d. Install a proxy server and then use IIS's FTP service to facilitate the download.

The correct answer to this question is b. The FTP service's primary function is to allow users to download and upload files easily. Creating a Web form for users to register themselves and then mailing them a disk is not a state-of-the-art solution. Therefore, answer a is incorrect. You can use the Microsoft Merchant Server to design and build Web storefronts that may include a file download facility, but this is not really necessary because IIS's FTP service suffices. Therefore, answer c is incorrect. The proxy server has no role as far as implementing a download facility is concerned. Therefore, answer d is incorrect.

Question 13

The access permission on one of your server's directories, SalesData, is set to No Access. The Microsoft Index Server uses this directory within its full text search.

○ a. True

○ b. False

The correct answer to this question is b, False. An important point to understand about the Microsoft BackOffice products is that they are tightly integrated with each other. As such, if you set the access permission on a server directory to No Access, the Microsoft Index Server recognizes the access permission and does not use the directory within its full text search.

Question 14

Which one of the following characters represents anonymous access within an event log file?

○ a. -

○ b. !

○ c. @

○ d. None of the above

The correct answer to this question is a. The hyphen character (-) is the default. Therefore, answers b, c, and d are incorrect.

Need To Know More?

Buyens, Jim. *Building Net Sites with Windows NT: An Internet Service Handbook*. Addison-Wesley Publishing Company, Reading, MA, 1996. ISBN 0-20147-949-4. This book provides practical, accessible advice on selecting and installing hardware, operating systems, and application and administrative services. In addition, the book covers IIS. This book also supplies valuable guidance on site planning, security, and ongoing operation of an NT Internet site (information that can be difficult to find).

Edwards, Mark. *Internet Security With Windows NT*. Duke Communications, Loveland, CO, 1997. ISBN 1-88241-962-6. In this book, security guru Mark Edwards shares the wisdom he accumulated through his years within the security field to help you protect your network from attack, detect security breaches when they occur, and recover from problems as quickly as possible.

Rutstein, Charles B. *Windows NT Security: A Practical Guide to Securing Windows NT Servers and Workstations*. McGraw-Hill, Berkeley, CA, 1997. ISBN 0-07057-833-8. This authoritative guide provides essential information on how to tap the Windows NT operating system's sophisticated security capabilities. You can apply the book's pragmatic advice on designing secure NT networks to small, medium, and large organizations.

Sheldon, Tom. *Windows NT Security Handbook*. McGraw-Hill, Berkeley, CA, 1996. ISBN 0-07882-240-8. Sheldon's guide approaches security from the Windows NT perspective and addresses key issues, such as protective features available within NT, as well as potential security holes. You'll learn how to create defensive strategies and become familiar with the different security protocols.

Sheldon, Tom and John Muller. *Microsoft Internet Information Server 4: The Complete Reference*. McGraw-Hill, Berkeley, CA, 1998. ISBN 0-07882-457-5. This book provides a comprehensive coverage of IIS 4.0. You'll find a lot of information on installation, setup, monitoring, troubleshooting, and more.

Microsoft TechNet. January, 1998. The technical notes for Microsoft Internet Information Server provide insight into its design, architecture, and security. Also search the TechNet CD using the following keywords: "IIS security," "authentication and authorization," "NTLM authentication," "Secure Sockets Layer," "digital certificate," "event auditing," "directory security," "access permission," "firewall," and "packet filtering."

 Browse product documentation locally on your server at http://localhost/iishelp/misc/default.htm.

 For timely information about weaknesses within Internet software security, visit www.cert.org.

 The Microsoft Web Site at www.microsoft.com/iis provides a wealth of information regarding IIS, including datasheets, white papers, system requirements, a downloadable copy of IIS, case studies, tips, tricks, and lots more.

 The BHS Web site at www.bhs.com is a valuable resource center for information on Windows NT and tools that are dependent on Windows NT, such as the IIS.

Enhanced Security Through Authentication And Encryption

6

Terms you'll need to understand:

√ Encryption/decryption

√ Public key encryption

√ Digital signatures and secure envelopes

√ Certificate authorities (CAs)

√ Certificates

√ Secure Sockets Layer (SSL)

√ https://

√ Certificate Server

√ Public Key Cryptography Standards (PKCS)

√ CryptoAPI

Techniques you'll need to master:

√ Understanding the basics of encryption, keys, and certificates

√ Requesting and obtaining a certificate for IIS 4.0

√ Understanding how SSL works with IIS 4.0

√ Using client certificates

√ Using Certificate Server

√ Understanding the purpose of the CryptoAPI

Most Internet services are, by nature, distributed in a clear text format. There-fore, standard service communications can be intercepted anywhere between a server and client. Internet Information Server 4.0 (IIS 4.0) includes native support for secure communications through Secure Sockets Layer (SSL) cer-tificates. This chapter discusses IIS 4.0's support for SSL and other advanced security features.

Secure Internet Transmission

Secure transmissions over the Internet or an intranet using IIS 4.0 are possible through the use of *encryption*. Encryption is simply the process of scrambling data (whether it's a message, streaming multimedia, data files, or whatever) into a form that is unusable and unreadable by anyone except the intended recipient. *Decryption* is the necessary flip-side of encryption. Decryption is the process of unscrambling the encrypted data.

When data is encrypted, a tool known as an *encryption key* is used (see Fig-ure 6.1). An encryption key is an electronic mathematical formula used to scramble data. An encryption key can be thought of like any metal key—once it's used on a door, that door is inaccessible to anyone without the key because it's locked.

When data is decrypted, a tool known as a *decryption key* is used. A decryption key is the mathematical inverse of the encryption key. The decryption key unscrambles encrypted data to extract the original. Only the decryption key can unlock and restore encrypted data. It's very important to maintain control over the decryption key because anyone with access to it can unscramble any data encrypted by the related encryption key. Granting wide access to the decryption key will, in effect, circumvent the security of encryption.

IIS uses a form of cryptology known as *public key encryption*. In this system, both the server and the client use two keys—a private key and a public key. The client uses the server's public key and its own private key to encrypt a message; then, the server uses the client's public key and its own private key to decrypt the same message. The same pattern occurs when data is sent from the server to the client. In each case, once the data is locked, only the private key of the recipient combined with the public key of the sender will decrypt the data.

In the public key system, private keys are obviously kept secure and are not distributed. However, the public key is widely distributed. This gives both the sender and the recipient the ability to send and receive messages using the two-key encryption system.

A system related to public key encryption (shown in Figure 6.2) is known collectively as *digital signatures and secure envelopes*. In this system, the private

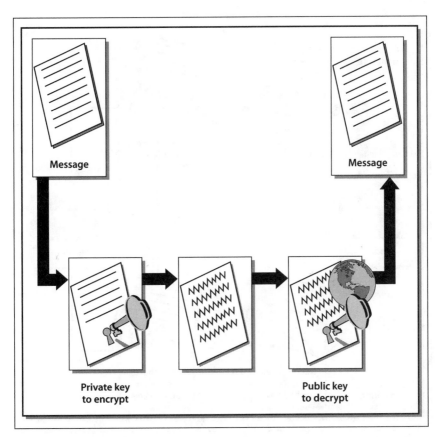

Figure 6.1   Basic key encryption.

key of the sender is the digital signature. Its presence verifies the origin and identity of the sender, rather than encrypting the message. The secure envelope is the public key encryption of the sender. This encrypts the message. Once the message is received by the recipient, the recipient's private key is used to decrypt the message from the secure envelope; then, the public key of the sender is used to verify the signature of the message.

The next logical step in the realm of digital signatures is identity verification. Because anyone can claim to be anyone via the anonymity of the Internet, identity verification is extremely important. For instance, you need to know that the Web site you're sending your credit card information to is, in fact, the flower store in San Francisco and not some hacker impersonating it. The scheme used in identity verification is called a *certificate*. A certificate is a digital signature issued by a third party (called a *certificate authority* or *CA*) that claims to have verified the identity of a server or an individual. The presence of a certificate from a CA indicates that some type of offline verification process was used to establish an identity.

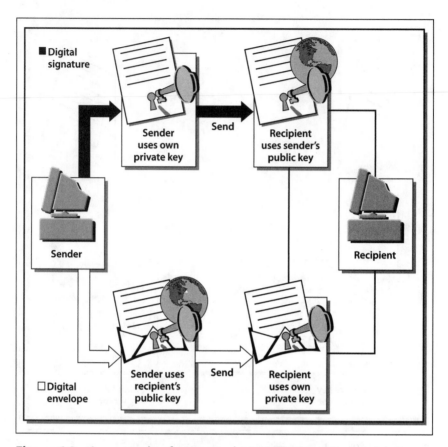

Figure 6.2 An example of encrypted message transmission using digital signatures and secure envelopes.

Certificates are used to create the private signature key for a sender and the public verification key for the recipient. The private signature key is given only to the entity whose identity is verified by the certificate. The public verification key is distributed either by the sender, the CA, or both. This enables a recipient to verify the identity of a communication partner by relying on the word and reputation of the CA.

In addition to issuing certificates, CAs are also responsible for renewing and revoking certificates. Once the life span of a certificate has expired, most organizations want to renew their certificates to continue to offer secure communications. A certificate can be revoked for several reasons, including expiration of life span, improper use of a certificate, and termination of a compromised certificate. A certificate revocation list (CRL) is maintained by the CA, which lists all invalid certificates. This grants servers and clients the ability to determine if an invalid certificate is being used.

SSL 3.0

SSL (*Secure Sockets Layer*) is an industry-standard protocol used to establish secure communications between a Web server (or other information service server) and a client. SSL is a dual-layered protocol. The lower layer—SSL Record Protocol—operates just above the Transport Control Protocol (TCP). It encapsulates higher-level protocols, thus making it a flexible and application protocol-independent security scheme. The higher layer—SSL Handshake Protocol—is used to coordinate an encryption algorithm for use between a client and server for secured communications. Figure 6.3 shows SSL in action.

Establishing an SSL session involves the following steps:

1. The client initiates communication by requesting a resource from a server. The request takes the form "https://...".

2. The server responds to indicate that it received the request for a secured resource.

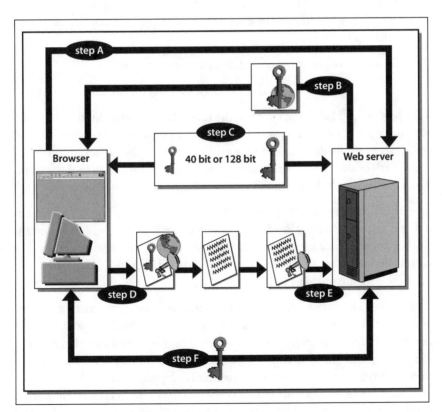

Figure 6.3 SSL in action.

3. The server sends its certificate to the client.

4. If required, the server requests the client's certificate.

5. The server indicates its transmission is complete.

6. The client responds by sending its own certificate to the server, if the server requested the client's certificate.

7. The client attempts to verify the server's certificate using the CA-distributed public key.

8. If verified, the client sends the encryption specification it needs to the server. This is typically called a *session key*. It's encrypted using the client's private key.

9. The client indicates its transmission is complete.

10. The server verifies the validity of the client's certificate, if requested.

11. The server receives the session key, decrypts it using the client's public key, and then modifies its (the server's) encryption to match that requested by the client.

12. The server indicates the end of normal transmissions.

13. Secure encrypted communication begins between the client and server.

This process will fail if the client or the server fails to respond to any request for information, or if a response indicates that no such information, data, or certificate is available. The communication link will also be severed if either the server's or the client's certificates are unable to be validated, or if the server is unable to comply with the encryption requirements of the client.

The certificates are used to establish the secure communication between a client and server, to verify the identity of one or both parties, and to secure the session key. It's the encryption technology defined by the session key, not the certificate, that governs the encryption of data between the client and server once the SSL channel has been established.

The session key is the key used by the client and server to encrypt all data communicated between them. The session key can have a range of strength based on its degree of encryption. Encryption degrees are measured in bits. The longer the session key, the stronger the encryption it provides. A 40-bit encryption key is typical and is the current maximum encryption that can be used when communications pass outside of U.S. borders. Within the U.S., 128-bit or more encryption can be used. The strength or bit length of an encryption key also affects the performance of communications: The stronger the encryption, the more complicated the encryption/decryption process becomes. For every additional bit added to a key, you double its effectiveness as well as the resources required to process it.

> *Note: Windows NT Server only supports 40-bit encryption schemes straight out of the box. To add support for 128-bit encryption, you must apply the 128-bit domestic version of Service Pack 3.*

Using SSL With IIS 4.0

To use SSL with IIS 4.0, you must obtain a server certificate from a CA (Microsoft recommends the VeriSign CA, but any will do). A server certificate is requested by creating a key request file using the Key Manager and sending it to a CA. Once the CA grants you a server certificate, it must be installed on the server.

The Key Manager is accessed by following these steps:

1. Launch the Microsoft Management Console (MMC) by choosing Start|Programs|Windows NT 4.0 Option Pack|Microsoft Internet Information Server|Internet Service Manager. Figure 6.4 shows the MMC.

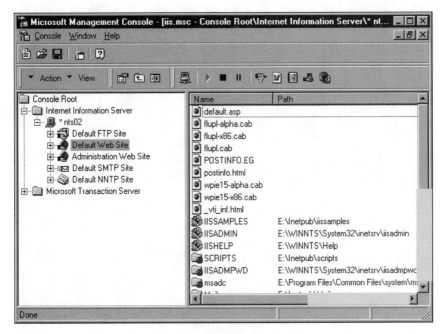

Figure 6.4   The Microsoft Management Console.

2. Select a local Web site from within the MMC.

3. Select Properties from the Action pull-down menu.

4. Select the Directory Security tab, as shown in Figure 6.5.

5. Click the Key Manager button. The Key Manager is shown in Figure 6.6.

To create a key request file, perform the following steps:

1. Select the WWW service listed for the local computer within the Key Manager.

2. Select Create New Key from the Key menu. The Create New Key Wizard then appears.

3. The first page of the wizard allows you to select whether to create a request file, which you must send to a CA, or for the wizard to send the

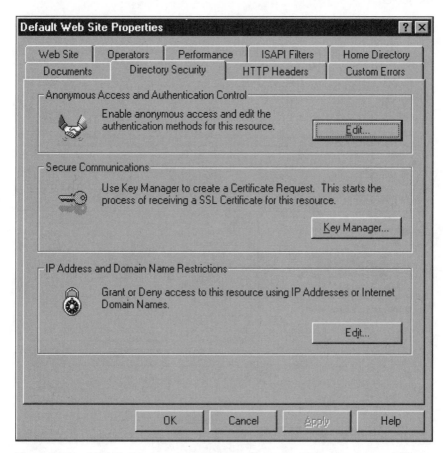

Figure 6.5   MMC's Directory Security tab on the Web Site Properties dialog (precertificate install).

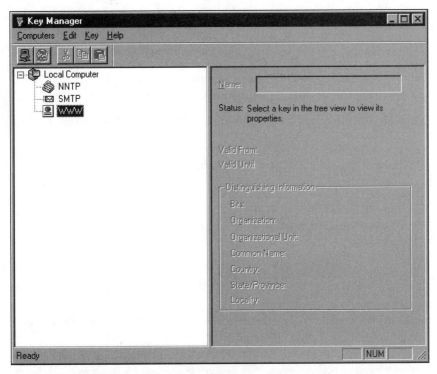

Figure 6.6 The Key Manager.

request file automatically to a known CA (typically only useful when the Certificate Server is installed). Choose to create a request file, specify the path, and then click Next.

4. Define a key name, a password, and a bit length. The key name is used to identify individual keys. The password is required for later installation of the issued certificate. The bit length determines the strength of the requested certificate. (Note that without the installation of 128-bit Service Pack 3, you do not have a choice of bit length. The only selection is 512. If you have applied the 128-bit Service Pack 3, you can select from 512, 768, or 1,024, with 1,024 being the default.) Click Next.

The bit length defined here is related only to the certificate and the key request. The bit lengths of 512, 768, or 1,024 are extremely secure and are used to protect identity certificates. Once a certificate is issued and installed, that certificate is used to establish the session key for data transmission, which can only be 40-bit or 128-bit encryption.

5. The next page of the wizard is where you define information about your organization, including name, unit, and common name (typically the domain name of the server). Fill in the information and then click Next.

6. You are asked to identify your geographic location by country, state/province, and city/local. Do this and click Next.

7. Next, identify yourself by name, email address, and phone number. Click Next.

8. The last page of the wizard informs you that your request file will be stored in the file name you specified in Step 3. Click Finish to complete the request generation.

9. You'll see animation while the request is generated. When completed, click OK.

The key request file is a plain text file that contains a section of encrypted information that only the CA will be able to decipher (see Figure 6.7). This file is sent to the CA via predefined means, such as email, FTP, or snail mail. Once your identity is verified and your certificate is granted, you'll receive your certificate via email, FTP, or snail mail.

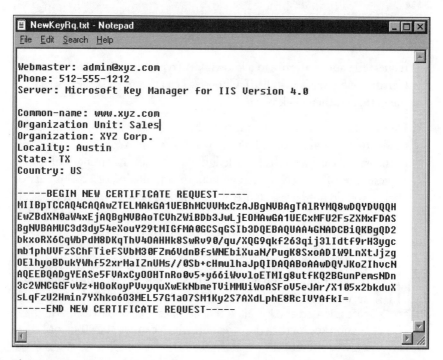

Figure 6.7 The contents of a sample key request file.

Once you receive the certificate, you must install it. This process is as follows:

1. Launch the Key Manager.

2. Select the named key item below the WWW service when you have received a certificate from a CA.

3. Select Install Key Certificate from the Key menu.

4. Use the Browse window to locate and select the certificate file; then click Open.

5. You'll be prompted for the password used to create the original key request file. Type in the password and then click OK.

6. If successful, the Server Bindings dialog appears. Through this dialog, you can define which IP addresses and port numbers on this server can use this certificate for SSL communications. After defining at least one IP address, click OK.

7. This returns you to the main Key Manager window. By selecting the newly installed key certificate, you can obtain information about the certificate, such as validity dates, bit length, and identification information (see Figure 6.8).

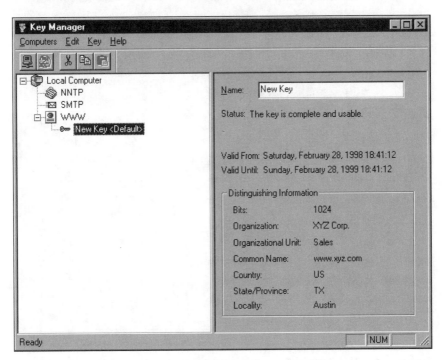

Figure 6.8   The Key Manager with a certificate installed.

Once a key certificate is installed, you can set the Web server to use SSL exclusively or only as needed. Several configuration settings are now available that can be made to manage how SSL is used by IIS. The first is made on the Web Site tab of the Properties dialog of the Web server, listed in the MMC. You can define the SSL port for secure communications. The default is 443. If you change this, users will need to add the port address to their URLs—for example, https://www.*domain*.com:812/.

The rest of the options are accessed on the Directory Security tab, but the button previously labeled Key Manager now reads Edit. Clicking the Edit button reveals a new dialog, enabled by the presence of a certificate, called Secure Communications (see Figure 6.9). In this dialog, you can force all communications for this site to use SSL by selecting Require Secure Channel When Accessing This Resource. By clicking the Encryption Settings button, you can choose to enable 128-bit encryption (only available if the 128-bit Service Pack 3 has been applied). By requiring 128-bit encryption, you limit your audience to domestic North American users with modern browsers. Remember that only Internet Explorer and Netscape Navigator versions 3.0 and newer support 128-bit encryption.

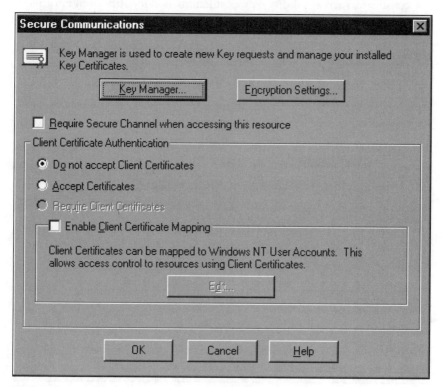

Figure 6.9 The Secure Communications dialog.

When a browser attempts to access resources from a secure server, but does not request a secure channel when required (https://) or does not support the required level of encryption (128-bit), the error message "HTTP/1.1 403 Access Forbidden (Secure Channel Required)" is sent to the browser.

IIS 4.0 supports SSL 3.0, SSL 2.0, and PCT 1.0. PCT, or Private Communication Technology, is an encryption technology similar to SSL. Through these secure communication protocols, IIS is able to offer the widest range of compatibility with client browsers.

Client SSL Features

Once your IIS 4.0-hosted Web site has a certificate installed, you can select to require client certificates before granting access to resources. Client certificates give you greater access control over your resources by forcing clients to properly identify themselves with a respected or trusted CA. Without a valid client certificate, all secure resources are restricted from use. SSL Client Authentication (SSLCA) is another, more secure authentication scheme (added to the existing set of three—anonymous, basic/clear text, and Microsoft Challenge/Response). However, with SSLCA, the identity of the client is verified.

SSL client certificates are enabled in the Secure Communications dialog. It's accessed by clicking the Edit button on the Directory Security tab of a Web site's Properties dialog. The default setting does not accept client certificates. The next option is to accept client certificates if available and when necessary. Forcing a client to have a certificate can only be enabled when Require Secure Channel When Accessing This Resource is selected for the entire site (that is, no insecure communications).

The purpose of client certificates is two-fold: to verify the identity of the client and to associate that client with a user account hosted by the system. When client certificate mapping is enabled, you can map client certificates to specific NT user accounts. Therefore, each time a client accesses an IIS 4.0-hosted resource, access is granted based on the access permissions of the user account associated with the validated certificate. Mapping can be a one-to-one relationship or multiple certificates to a single user account. One-to-many mapping can be performed using wildcards to match any field stored in a certificate.

SSL And Certificate Server

Included on the Option Pack for integration with IIS is the Microsoft Certificate Server. This application is used to organize, issue, renew, and revoke private certificates without relying on a third-party external CA. The role of Certificate Server is to receive Public Key Cryptography Standards (PKCS)

#10 certificate requests and to issue X.509 certificates in PKCS #7 format. Certificate Server gives you the ability to be your own CA, which gives you a wider range of control over certificates and what they can be used for.

Certificate Server is designed to support Web applications that rely on SSL-based secure communication and authentication. In addition to SSL, Certificate Server also supports other certificate-based applications, including Secure/Multipurpose Internet Email Extensions (S/MIME) and Secure Electronic Extensions (SET), plus Microsoft Authenticate digital signatures.

Certificate Server is installed through the Option Pack Setup program's custom setup. During the setup, you'll be prompted for several items, including the following:

➤ **Configuration Data Storage Location** A shared folder used by the Certificate Server to store certificates and configuration files.

➤ **Database Location** The location of the server's database. By default, this is Winnt\System32\CertLog.

➤ **Log Location** The location to store the server's log files. By default, this is Winnt\System32\CertLog.

➤ **Select CSP And Hashing (Advanced)** The Cryptographic Service Provider (CSP) and the hash algorithm used by the CSP. The default CSP is Microsoft Base Cryptographic Provider (MBCP) and the default hash algorithm is MD5.

➤ **Use Existing Keys (Advanced)** If existing keys are present, this selection retains those keys for use with Certificate Server.

➤ **Erase All Previous Configuration Information (Advanced)** Performs a fresh installation with new configurations. Deselect to retain existing settings.

➤ **Make This Installation The Default (Advanced)** On a network with multiple instances of Certificate Server, this option sets the current installation as the default.

➤ **Select Certificate Authority Hierarchy (Advanced)** Hierarchies are not supported in Certificate Server 1.0. However, you can select this server to be a root CA or a nonroot CA.

➤ **Identifying information** You must provide details about this installation, such as the name of the CA, the organization name, the department or unit, as well as the city, state, country, and a comment.

Once these items are defined, the server is installed. A public/private key pair is generated to be used as the self-signed root or site certificate for this installation. This key is written to the shared certificate folder, and the server is added to the list of CAs.

Certificate Server is installed as a Windows NT service that is launched automatically under the system account each time the system is booted. This is the preferred and default method of launching the application, but it can be set to manual and be set to launch under a different security level, if desired, through the Services applet.

Certificate Server is primarily managed through Web-based administration tools. Several command-line tools can be used in cases of restoring the system or performing operations more easily accomplished through the Web interface. The Web utilities are accessed by requesting the default URL: http://localhost/CertSvr/. The Web interface gives you quick access to the Log utility, the Queue utility, Enrollment Tools, and online documentation.

The Certificate Log Administration utility is used to manage active certificates and the CRL (see Figure 6.10). Each known certificate is displayed in the default List view. Individual certificates can be inspected more closely in the Form view by clicking a certificate's number or by using the Form View

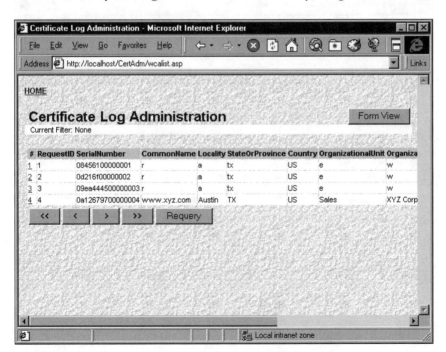

Figure 6.10   The Certificate Log Administration utility.

button and its arrows to select the certificate. In Form view, you can revoke a certificate by clicking the Revoke button followed by the Requery button.

The Certificate Server Queue Administration utility is used to manage requests. Each action requested or performed by the Certificate Server is listed here. Like in the Log utility, the Form view offers a more detailed look at individual items. In Form view, you can define a filter to reduce the number of displayed items in the List view (see Figure 6.11).

The Certificate Enrollment Tools perform three functions: install CA certificates, process certificate requests, and request client authentication certificates. Installing CA certificates adds a CA's certificate to the Web browser being used. This configures the browser to automatically support and accept secure communications from all Web sites using certificates issued by that CA. Processing a certificate request is where the contents of a key request file (as created by the Key Manager) can be sent via a Web form to obtain a certificate for your server. Requesting a client authentication certificate allows you to obtain a client certificate to prove your identity.

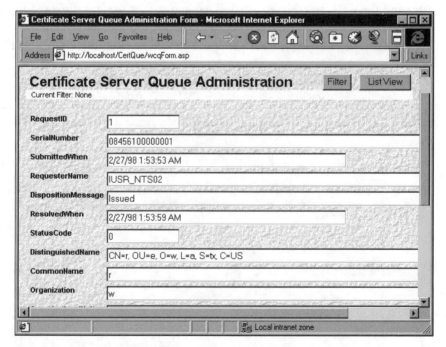

Figure 6.11   The Certificate Server Queue Administration utility.

The current version of Certificate Server is set to issue all certificate requests, by default. This is obviously a security problem. The evaluation of requests and the issuing of new certificates are governed through the use of *policies*. Policies are installed by an administrator; they instruct the Certificate Server to accept, deny, or delay a request based on the contents of the request. Policies are written in Java, Visual Basic, or C/C++. Brief details on writing custom policies for Certificate Server are included with the online documentation. We assume more information will soon be available via the Microsoft Web site or the *IIS Resource Kit*.

CryptoAPI

In an effort to move the underlying details of cryptography away from application developers, Microsoft has developed the CryptoAPI. This application programming interface (API) allows programmers to create applications that can use or even rely upon cryptography without requiring knowledge of the encryption system. The CryptoAPI separates applications from encryption, thus enabling an application without modification to use different types or new technologies of encryption. The ability to change the strength and type of encryption used by an application is provided by the Cryptographic Service Provider (CSP) interface. This component is supported by the Certificate Server and allows alternate CSPs to be used for certificate management. Certificate Server supports CryptoAPI 2.0.

Exam Prep Questions

Question 1

> Which technology is used most often to establish secure commu-
> nications over networks where data interception is possible?
>
> O a. CRC
>
> O b. Encryption
>
> O c. TCP/IP
>
> O d. DHCP

Encryption is the technology used to establish secure communications over
insecure networks. Therefore, answer b is correct. CRC is a technology used
to verify the integrity of transmitted data; it's not associated with security.
Therefore, answer a is incorrect. TCP/IP is a network protocol. Secure communications can occur over it, but TCP/IP does not directly provide for security.
Therefore, answer c is incorrect. DHCP is a technology used to dynamically
configure clients. Therefore, answer d is incorrect.

Question 2

> Which of the following are typical concepts or terms associated
> with encryption? [Check all correct answers]
>
> ❑ a. Public keys
>
> ❑ b. Identify verification
>
> ❑ c. Certificates
>
> ❑ d. Digital signatures

All of these items are associated with encryption. Therefore, answers a, b, c,
and d are all correct.

Question 3

> A digital signature performs two functions—it indicates the iden-
> tity of the sender as well as encrypts the signed message.
>
> O a. True
>
> O b. False

False, a digital signature is only used to indicate the identity of the sender; it's not used to encrypt data. Therefore, answer b is correct.

Question 4

What is a certificate's primary purpose?

○ a. Encrypting data

○ b. Advertising

○ c. Identifying a sender or a client

○ d. Proving the value of online products and services

A certificate is primarily used to identify a sender or a client. Therefore, answer c is correct. Certificates are not used to encrypt data. Therefore, answer a is incorrect. Certificates are not a form of advertisement. Therefore, answer b is incorrect. Certificates are not used to prove the value or worth of products and services found online; rather, they are only used to prove the identity of the owner of the site distributing such items. Therefore, answer d is incorrect.

Question 5

What is a certificate authority (CA)?

○ a. The single worldwide distribution point for client identities

○ b. An Internet standards organization, similar to IETF and IEEE, that sets the requirements for certificates

○ c. A division of the National Security Council (NSC) with the sole purpose of cracking down on computer fraud

○ d. A third-party organization that is trusted to verify the identity of servers and individuals

A certificate authority (CA) is a third-party organization that is trusted to verify the identity of servers and individuals. Therefore, answer d is correct. A CA is not a single world wide distribution point for client identities. This type of entity does not currently exist. Therefore, answer a is incorrect. A CA is not an Internet standards organization similar to IETF and IEEE that sets the requirements for certificates. Therefore, answer b is incorrect. A CA is not part of the NSC. Therefore, answer c is incorrect.

Question 6

SSL, or Secure Sockets Layer, is an industry-standard protocol used to establish secure communications between a Web server (or other information service server) and a client.

○ a. True

○ b. False

True, SSL (Secure Sockets Layer) is an industry-standard protocol used to establish secure communications between a Web server (or other information service server) and a client. Therefore, answer a is correct.

Question 7

Creating a key certificate request is an integral step of what process?

○ a. Installing IIS 4.0

○ b. Configuring a Web server to offer SSL-based secure communications

○ c. As a client, purchasing a product with a credit card over a secure link

○ d. Applying Service Pack 3 to Windows NT Server

Creating a key certificate request is an integral part of configuring a Web server to offer SSL-based secure communications. Therefore, answer b is correct. Installing IIS and applying Service Pack 3 do not require a key request. Therefore, answers a and d are incorrect. As a client, purchasing a product with a credit card over a secure link does not require a key request to be generated, but it does rely on the Web server to have already installed a certificate. Therefore, answer c is incorrect.

Question 8

> What is the maximum strength of data encryption that can be used by IIS 4.0 when communicating with clients outside of North America?
>
> ○ a. 40
>
> ○ b. 128
>
> ○ c. 512
>
> ○ d. 1,024

The strongest encryption that can be used across North America's borders is 40-bit encryption. Therefore, answer a is correct. One hundred twenty eight-bit encryption can only be used within North America. Therefore, answer b is incorrect. Five hundred twelve and 1,024 bits are encryption strengths for certificates that are used for identity verification, not data encryption. Therefore, answers c and d are incorrect.

Question 9

> In addition to IIS 4.0 and Windows NT Server, what is another component required to enable 128-bit data encryption?
>
> ○ a. An InterNIC-assigned domain name
>
> ○ b. Microsoft Transaction Server
>
> ○ c. Service Pack 3
>
> ○ d. Microsoft Certificate Server

Service Pack 3 is the component required for 128-bit data encryption. Therefore, answer c is correct. IIS does not need a true Internet domain name assigned by the InterNIC, Microsoft Transaction Server, or Microsoft Certificate Server to use 128-bit encryption. Therefore, answers a, b, and d are incorrect.

Question 10

> If you change the default SSL port from 443 to 1013, what is the syntax of the URL used to access the site?
>
> ○ a. http://www.*domain*.com/1013/
>
> ○ b. shttp:/www.*domain*.com:1013/
>
> ○ c. https://www.*domain*.com/
>
> ○ d. https://www.*domain*.com:1013/

The only correct URL for accessing an SSL-secured site with a nonstandard port is https://www.*domain*.com:1013/. Therefore, answer d is correct. All of the other selections are invalid. Therefore, answers a, b, and c are incorrect.

Need To Know More?

 Howell, Nelson, et al. *Using Microsoft Internet Information Server 4.* Que Publishing, Indianapolis, IN, 1997. ISBN 0-7897-1263-6. This book contains excellent information on using SSL with IIS (Chapter 21); however, it lacks coverage of Certificate Server.

 The best overview information for IIS 4.0 can be found in the Reviewer's Guide for IIS 4.0. This document can be found on the TechNet CD-ROM or online via the IIS Web area (http://www.microsoft.com/iis/).

A useful white paper from Microsoft is the "Internet Information Server Security Overview." This white paper is available from the IIS Web area (http://www.microsoft.com/iis/).

Virtual Directories, Virtual Servers, And Active Server Pages

7

Terms you'll need to understand:

- √ Virtual directory and site
- √ Access permissions
- √ Physical path
- √ Active Platform, Client, and Server
- √ ActiveX
- √ Server-side scripting
- √ Active Server Pages, Active Objects, and Active Components
- √ ASP scripts
- √ Microsoft Script Debugger
- √ ODBC
- √ Server extension
- √ IDC
- √ HTX

Techniques you'll need to master:

- √ Creating and configuring virtual directories
- √ Creating and configuring virtual servers
- √ Designing ASP applications

131

In this chapter, we take a look at a number of IIS features. We examine and show you how to configure virtual servers and virtual directories. In addition, we explore ActiveX and its controls, as well as a thorough examination of Active Server Pages, Active Objects, and Active Components. Finally, we show you how to design ASP applications. However, first, we'll begin with some IIS basics that are necessary to understand before making use of IIS's additional features.

Home Directory

An IIS directory is a location on IIS where you store files, including ASP scripts and other programs. To understand the concept of virtual directories within an IIS environment, you must understand the concept of an IIS home directory. When you install IIS, the installation program creates a default home directory for the WWW (C:\InetPub\Wwwroot) and FTP services (C:\InetPub\Ftproot). By default, IIS routes the user connecting to your Web site to the WWW service's home directory.

For an intranet, the Web site's home directory is mapped to the site's server name. For example, if the server name is your_edge, you can reach the Web site's home directory by typing "http://your_edge" within your browser's URL text box.

For the Internet, the Web site's home directory is mapped to the site's domain name. For example, if the domain name is www.yourcompany.com and the Web site's home directory is C:\WebSite\MyCompany, you can reach the Web site's home directory by typing "http://www. yourcompany.com" within your browser's URL text box.

WWW Service: Home Directory

To start the Microsoft Management Console, click Start|Programs|Windows NT Option Pack|Microsoft Internet Information Server|Internet Service Manager. Windows NT, in turn, starts the Microsoft Management Console 1.0, as shown in Figure 7.1.

After MMC is launched, right-click on the site to be configured and select Properties. By using the Properties|Home Directory tab, you can change your site's home directory or the home directory's characteristics (see Figure 7.2). At IIS installation time, the installation program creates a default home directory: Wwwroot (the default path is C:\InetPub\Wwwroot).

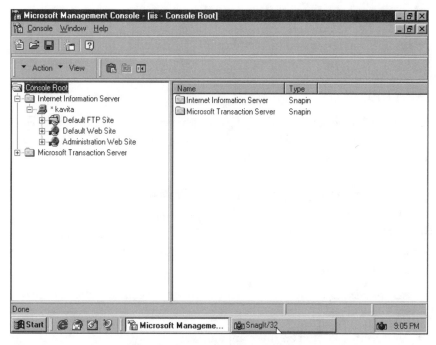

Figure 7.1   The Microsoft Management Console.

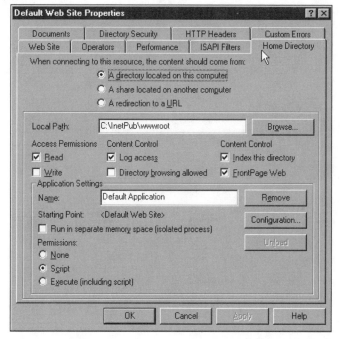

Figure 7.2   The Web Site Properties page's Home Directory tab.

You can change the home directory's location to one of the following:

➤ A directory located on the local computer (default)

➤ A directory (share) located on another computer

➤ A URL

For a local directory, specify the full path within the Local Path text box. For a network share, specify the Universal Naming Convention (UNC) and the name of the share (for example, \\Iis\Htmlfiles).

FTP Service: Home Directory

To change your site's home directory or the home directory's characteristics, use the Home Directory tab (see Figure 7.3). When you install IIS, the installation program creates a default home directory, Ftproot (the default path is C:\InetPub\Ftproot).

A user connecting to the home directory can see the context coming from one of the following:

➤ A directory located on this computer

➤ A share located on another computer

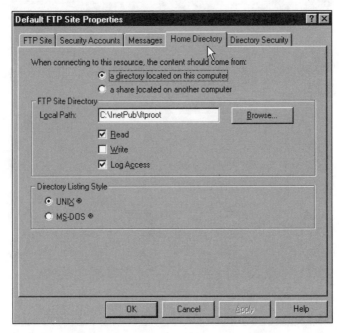

Figure 7.3   The FTP Site Properties page's Home Directory tab.

Within the Local Path text box, specify the root directory for the FTP service (the default is C:\InetPub\Ftproot).

In addition, you can choose the directory listing style—Unix or MS-DOS. Most FTP hosts are Unix machines; therefore, the Unix directory listing style is a logical choice.

 If you change the directory listing style, you must stop and restart the FTP service for the change to take effect.

Virtual Directory

Any directory that is not the home directory and not contained within IIS's home directory is a *virtual directory*. The following sections outline the steps to create and delete virtual directories on your WWW and FTP server.

Creating And Deleting A Virtual WWW Directory

To create a virtual WWW directory, follow these steps:

1. Click Start|Programs|Windows NT Option Pack|Microsoft Internet Information Server|Internet Service Manager. Windows NT, in turn, starts the Microsoft Management Console 1.0.

2. Click Default Web Site, click Action, and then select New|Virtual Directory. Microsoft Management Console, in turn, displays the New Virtual Directory Wizard (shown in Figure 7.4).

3. Within the dialog's text box, type an alias for the virtual directory you want IIS to create. An *alias* is a short name for the directory that is easy to use and remember. To proceed, click Next.

4. The wizard, in turn, prompts you to display the physical path of the directory containing the content you want to publish, as shown in Figure 7.5. To specify the path, click Browse. To proceed, click Next.

5. The wizard, in turn, prompts you to choose the access permissions you want to set for the virtual directory, as shown in Figure 7.6.

6. Now choose one or more of the following options:

   ➤ **Allow Read Access (default)** A user connecting to the Web site has only Read access to the files within this virtual directory. The user does not have Script, Execute, and Write access to these files.

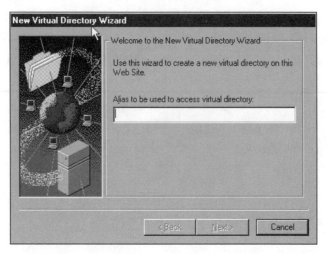

Figure 7.4 Creating a virtual Web directory with the New Virtual Directory Wizard.

➤ **Allow Script Access (default)** A user is limited to executing programs and scripts that are already stored within the home directory.

➤ **Allow Execute Access (Includes Script Access)** A user connecting to the Web site has both Script and Execute access to the files within this virtual directory. That is, the user can execute the files within this virtual directory.

➤ **Allow Write Access** A user connecting to the Web site has Write access to the files within this virtual directory. That is, the user can write to the files within this virtual directory.

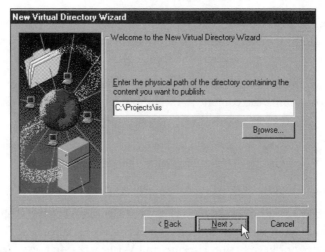

Figure 7.5 Specifying the virtual Web directory's physical path.

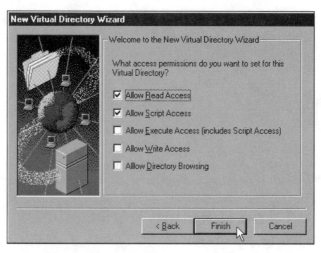

Figure 7.6   Specifying the access permissions for the virtual directory.

➤ **Allow Directory Browsing** A user connecting to the Web site can browse the files within this virtual directory.

Depending on your application requirements, click the appropriate options. To proceed, click Finish. The wizard, in turn, creates the virtual directory, as shown in Figure 7.7.

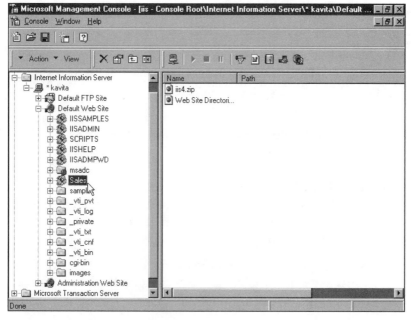

Figure 7.7   The virtual directory: Sales.

7. IIS denotes the virtual Web directory with a folder and a little globe at the bottom-right corner of the folder. Notice that IIS shows the directory's physical path mapped to the virtual directory.

 By default, IIS logs the activities on this directory.

To delete a virtual WWW directory, the process is pretty simple: right-click the WWW directory name and select Delete from the pop-up menu.

Creating And Deleting A Virtual FTP Directory

To create a virtual FTP directory, follow these steps:

1. Click Start|Programs|Windows NT Option Pack|Microsoft Internet Information Server|Internet Service Manager. Windows NT, in turn, starts the Microsoft Management Console 1.0.

2. Click Default FTP Site, click Action, and then select New|Virtual Directory. Microsoft Management Console, in turn, displays the New Virtual Directory Wizard.

3. Within the dialog's text box, type an alias for the virtual directory you want IIS to create. To proceed, click Next.

4. The wizard, in turn, prompts you to display the physical path of the directory containing the content you want to publish. To specify the path, click Browse. To proceed, click Next.

5. The wizard, in turn, prompts you to choose the access permissions you want to set for the virtual directory, as shown in Figure 7.8.

6. Now, choose one or both of the following options:

   ➤ **Allow Read Access (default)** A user connecting to the FTP site has only Read and Download access to the files within this virtual directory. The user can neither write to these files nor upload any files to this directory.

   ➤ **Allow Write Access** A user connecting to the FTP site has Write access to the files within this virtual directory. In addition, the user can upload files to this directory.

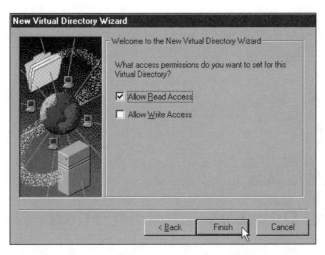

Figure 7.8   Specifying the access permissions for the virtual FTP directory.

Depending on your application requirements, click the appropriate options. To proceed, click Finish.

7. The wizard, in turn, creates the virtual directory, as shown in Figure 7.9.

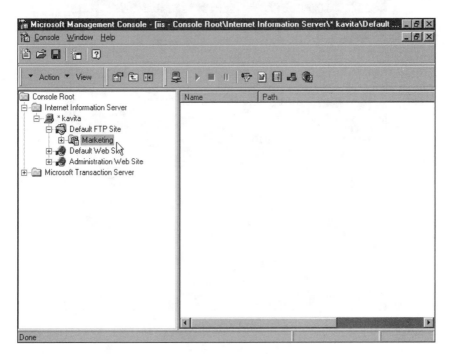

Figure 7.9   The virtual FTP directory: Marketing.

8. IIS denotes the virtual FTP directory with a folder and a little globe at the bottom-right corner of the folder. Notice that IIS shows the directory's physical path mapped to the virtual directory.

 By default, IIS logs the activities on this directory.

To delete a virtual FTP directory, right-click the virtual FTP directory name and select Delete from the pop-up menu.

Virtual Directory Administration

Right-click the virtual directory and then select Properties from the pop-up menu. The Microsoft Management Console, in turn, displays the Properties dialog, as shown in Figure 7.10.

At this point, you can configure two items: Virtual Directory and Directory Security. To learn more about configuring a directory's properties, refer to Chapter 4.

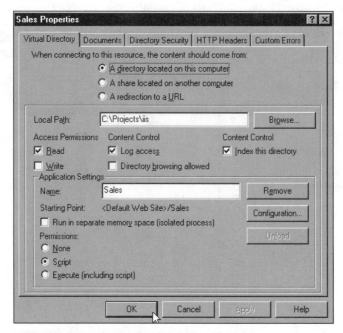

Figure 7.10 Configuring the virtual directory's properties.

Virtual Server

You can host several Web and FTP sites on the same IIS. At the time of installation, the IIS installation program creates a default Web and FTP site; you can create additional Web and FTP sites. Each such additional site is known as a *virtual server*.

Creating And Deleting A Virtual Web Server

To create a virtual Web server, follow these steps:

1. Click Start|Programs|Windows NT Option Pack|Microsoft Internet Information Server|Internet Service Manager. Windows NT, in turn, starts the Microsoft Management Console 1.0.

2. Click Default Web Site, click Action, and then select New|Virtual Site. Microsoft Management Console, in turn, displays the New Web Site Wizard, as shown in Figure 7.11.

3. Within the dialog's text box, type a name for the virtual Web site you want IIS to create. To proceed, click Next.

4. The wizard, in turn, prompts you to specify the IP address and TCP/IP port, as shown in Figure 7.12. If this is the second Web site you're creating in addition to the default Web site, you must specify a different TCP/IP port (the default is port 80). In addition, you must specify a different IP address. To host more than one Web site on IIS, each site must have its own IP address for the users connecting to that site. IIS

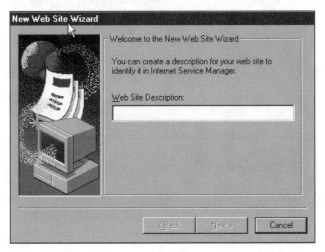

Figure 7.11   Creating a virtual Web site with the New Web Site Wizard.

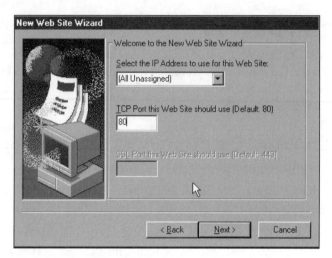

Figure 7.12 Specifying the IP address and TCP/IP port.

simulates the environment for the users to think each site corresponding to its IP address is hosted on a separate IIS. To proceed, click Next.

5. The wizard, in turn, prompts you to specify the path for the new Web site's home directory, as shown in Figure 7.13. Note that, by default, anonymous access is allowed to this Web site. To proceed, click Next.

6. The wizard, in turn, prompts you to choose the access permissions you want to set for the virtual Web site.

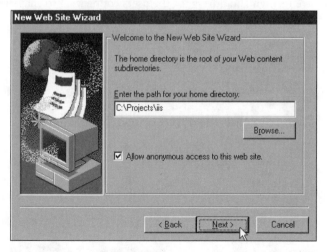

Figure 7.13 Specifying the path for the new site's home directory.

Now choose one or more of the following options:

➤ **Allow Read Access (default)** A user connecting to the Web site has only Read access to the directories and files within this virtual Web site.

➤ **Allow Script Access (default)** A user is limited to executing programs and scripts that are already stored within the home directory.

➤ **Allow Execute Access (Includes Script Access)** A user connecting to the Web site has Write access to the directories and files within this virtual Web site.

➤ **Allow Write Access** A user connecting to the Web site has Write access to the directories and files within this virtual Web site.

➤ **Allow Directory Browsing** A user connecting to the Web site can browse the directories within this virtual Web site.

7. Depending on your application requirements, click the appropriate options. To proceed, click Finish. The wizard, in turn, creates the virtual Web site, as shown in Figure 7.14. Notice that the virtual Web site's default state is Stopped. To start this server, right-click the Web server and then select Start from the pop-up menu.

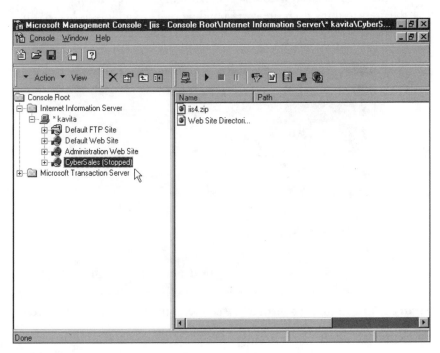

Figure 7.14   The new virtual site: CyberSales.

To delete a virtual Web server, right-click the server name and select Delete from the pop-up menu.

Creating And Deleting A Virtual FTP Server

To create a virtual FTP server:

1. Click Start|Programs|Windows NT Option Pack|Microsoft Internet Information Server|Internet Service Manager. Windows NT, in turn, starts the Microsoft Management Console 1.0.

2. Click Default FTP Site, click Action, and then select New|Virtual Site. Microsoft Management Console, in turn, displays the New Virtual Site wizard, as shown in Figure 7.15.

3. Within the dialog's text box, type a name for the virtual FTP site you want IIS to create. To proceed, click Next.

4. The wizard, in turn, prompts you to specify the IP address and TCP/IP port. If this is the second FTP site you're creating in addition to the default FTP site, you must specify a different TCP/IP port (the default port is 21). In addition, you must specify a different IP address. To host more than one FTP site on IIS, each site must have its own IP address for the users connecting to that site. IIS simulates the environment for the users to think each site corresponding to its IP address is hosted on a separate IIS. To proceed with the wizard, click Next.

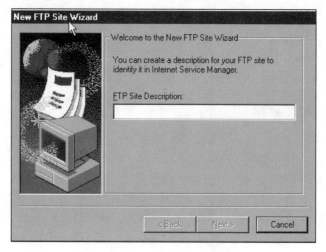

Figure 7.15 Creating a virtual FTP site with the New FTP Site Wizard.

5. The wizard, in turn, prompts you to specify the path for the new FTP site's home directory. To proceed, click Next.

6. The wizard prompts you to choose the access permissions you want to set for the virtual FTP site, as shown in Figure 7.16.

7. Now, choose one or both of the following options:

> **Allow Read Access (default)** A user connecting to the FTP site has only Read and Download access to the files within this virtual site. The user can neither write nor upload any files to this site.

> **Allow Write Access** A user connecting to the FTP site has Write access to the files within this virtual site. In addition, the user can upload files to this site.

8. Depending on your application requirements, click the appropriate options. To proceed, click Finish. The wizard, in turn, creates the virtual FTP server, as shown in Figure 7.17. Notice that the virtual FTP server's default state is Stopped. To start this server, right-click the FTP server and then select Start from the pop-up menu.

To delete a virtual FTP server, right-click the server name and select Delete from the pop-up menu.

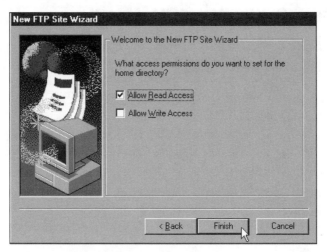

Figure 7.16 Specifying the access permissions for the virtual FTP site.

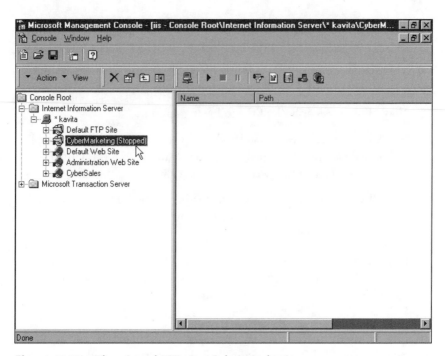

Figure 7.17 The virtual FTP site: CyberMarketing.

Virtual Server Administration

To administer a virtual server, right-click the virtual server and then select Properties from the pop-up menu. The Microsoft Management Console, in turn, displays the Properties dialog.

Within the WWW service, you can configure nine items:

➤ General Properties

➤ Operators

➤ Performance Tuning

➤ ISAPI Filters

➤ Home Directory

➤ Documents

➤ Directory Security

➤ HTTP Headers

➤ Custom Errors

To learn more about configuring the WWW service's properties, refer to Chapter 4.

The Active Platform

The Microsoft Active Platform is the foundation of designing and developing Internet and intranet business solutions by using Microsoft tools and technologies. A three-tier client/server model, the Active Platform is an extensible component-based architecture. The biggest advantage of using the Active Platform is the ease of use and reduced learning curve. To design both the client and server components of your application, you can use the same set of tools with which you are already familiar. As a developer, this reduces your learning curve, thus helping you deliver business solutions quickly and efficiently. The Active Platform includes the following three core components:

➤ Active Client (or Desktop)

➤ ActiveX

➤ Active Server

Active Client

Internet Explorer is a good example of Active Client. Internet Explorer includes built-in support for ActiveX technology and supports client-side scripting. That is, you can write Active scripts that execute on the client side by using scripting languages such as JScript, VBScript, and JavaScript. The scripts interact with HTML, Java applets, ActiveX controls, and so on, delivering information to the browser. The browser, in turn, displays the information to the end user.

ActiveX

ActiveX is not a programming language. In fact, ActiveX represents a suite of technologies you can use to deliver business solutions over the Internet and an intranet. ActiveX technology includes developing and integrating ActiveX controls, writing ActiveX scripts, and so on.

ActiveX Controls

ActiveX controls are stripped-down versions of OLE controls with their size and speed optimized for use over the Internet. Both ActiveX and OLE are based on Microsoft's COM technology. The basic premise of COM is that two objects can interact and communicate with each other over a network of heterogeneous systems, irrespective of the language and platform of their origin, as long as they are written to conform to the COM specification.

ActiveX Scripting

Microsoft develops and supports two scripting languages: JScript and VBScript. JScript is Microsoft's open implementation of JavaScript (Netscape's scripting language). Whereas JScript follows the C-style convention for writing scripts, VBScript is a subset of Microsoft's most popular programming language—Visual Basic.

Active Server

IIS is an Active Server. An Active Server supports server-side scripting, better known as Active Server Pages (ASPs). Check out Microsoft's Web site and you'll notice the Microsoft's server delivering client-side HTML by using Active Server Pages. Whereas an HTML file has the extension .HTML, an Active Server Page has the extension .ASP. To view ASP in action, visit the site at http://www.microsoft.com/search/default.asp.

An ASP script executes on the server, taking advantage of the server's processing power and delivering client-side HTML. Just as you can use scripting languages such as VBScript and JScript with reusable objects such as ActiveX controls and Java applets, you can use the same scripting languages with the same objects in conjunction with the five core server objects and Active Server Components to build ASPs. You'll learn more about the five core server objects and Active Server Components in the section titled "Prepackaged Active Server Components" later in this chapter.

ASP Vs. CGI

The advantage of using ASP over CGI is the ease of use in creating ASP scripts. To create ASP scripts, you can use the same set of tools and programming or scripting languages with which you're already familiar. For example, if you're familiar with creating client-side HTML by using HTML, JScript, ActiveX controls, Java applets, and so on, you can create ASP scripts by using the same set of tools and technologies. In addition, ASP embeds well within regular HTML. Another advantage of using ASP over CGI, is that you can use an Active Server Component to keep the HTTP connection alive with the database server. This helps improve your Web application's overall performance.

ASP Scripts

There are a few major differences between an ASP script and an HTML file. These include the following:

➤ An ASP script has the extension .ASP, whereas an HTML file has the extension .HTM (or .HTML).

➤ An ASP script executes on the server; an HTML file executes on the client.

➤ An HTML file can display a message box to the end user. On the other hand, including user interface objects and functions within an ASP script means nothing, because an ASP script's function is to return HTML to the client. Displaying message boxes on the server is meaningless from the end user's point of view. The end user cannot see anything that you display on the server.

ASP is actually an ISAPI DLL (ASP.DLL).

The following code is a sample ASP script. Notice the code between the pair of <% and %> tags. This is how you define ASP code. The first pair of <% and %> tags defines an ASP subroutine (**HelloASP**). Also, notice how the **HelloASP** subroutine uses the Response object's **write** method. The second pair of <% and %> tags calls the **HelloASP** subroutine. Notice also how these ASP routines are enclosed within the pair of HTML tags (**<HTML>...</HTML>**):

```
<HTML>
<HEAD>
<TITLE>
Welcome to the IIS Exam Cram
</TITLE>
</HEAD>
<BODY>
<%                '=== ASP begins
Sub HelloASP()
   Dim ASPGreeting

   ASPGreeting = "Hello ASP"
   Response.write ASPGreeting
End Sub
%>                '=== ASP ends
<% Call HelloASP %>        '=== Calling the ASP subroutine
</BODY>
</HTML>
```

Active Server Objects

The following are the five core server objects that constitute the core functionality of ASP. These server objects contain methods and properties that you can configure to meet your application's requirements:

➤ **Application** To manage your Web application's information, use the Application object.

➤ **Request** To retrieve information from the browser for processing at the server, use the Request object.

➤ **Response** To transmit information from the server to the browser, use the Response object.

➤ **Server** To administer and manage your Web server, use the Server object.

➤ **Session** To manage and track individual user sessions within your Web application, use the Session object.

Listing 7.1 is an example of an ASP script that uses three of the five server objects—Session, Response, and Request—to process the information. The script uses the Request object to retrieve and store information from the client form into the Session object's variables. The Session object's variables within this example are **User_ID** and **Officer**. The variable **User_ID** stores the ID of the user logging into the system. The variable **Officer** stores the user type (for example, Officer, Manager, Administrator, and so on).

Next, the script checks if the variable **User_ID** is empty. If this variable is empty, it redirects the user to the HTML file NOACCESS.HTM by using the Response object's **Redirect** method. If this variable is not empty, check the **Officer** variable's value. If the variable's value is Y, it displays the HTML file OFFICER.HTM by using the Response object's **Redirect** method. If the variable's value is N, it displays the HTML file MANAGER.HTM.

 The **RUNAT=SERVER** option indicates that the script executes on the server.

Listing 7.1 An example of an ASP script.

```
<% @LANGUAGE="VBSCRIPT" RUNAT=SERVER %>
<% Session("User_ID") = Request.Form("User_Id") %>
<% Session("Officer") = Request.Form("user_type") %>
<%
```

```
If IsEmpty(Session("User_Id")) Then
    Response.Redirect "noaccess.htm"
Else
    If Session("Officer") = "Y" Then
        Response.Redirect "officer.htm"
    Else
        Response.Redirect "manager.htm"
    End If
End If
%>
```

Prepackaged Active Server Components

IIS also comes with a number of predefined Active Server Components. You can use these components to build your ASP applications quickly and efficiently. Some of the components are described in the following subsections.

Active Data Object (ADO)

The ADO is probably the most important and popular ASP component. By using the ADO, you can build data-driven dynamic Web applications. You can use the ADO to connect your Web site to back-end relational database management systems such as Microsoft Access, Microsoft SQL Server, Sybase SQL Server, and Oracle. When you use the ADO within an ASP, the script communicates the SQL request that the browser sent to the ADO. The ADO, in turn, communicates the query to the database. The database processes the query and returns the result to the browser via the ADO and ASP.

Advertisement Rotator

The Web is not only today's medium of information but also the future's. The widespread dissemination of information and the amount of traffic on the Web only makes it logical for businesses to flock to the Web to advertise their products and services. IIS comes with an Active Server Component called the Advertisement Rotator. By using this component, you can display and dynamically change the advertisement banners within your Web site. This component—as well as its properties, methods, and events—makes it very easy for you to handle and display advertisement banners within your Web site.

Browser Capabilities

Even though Internet Explorer's market share has increased over the past few years, there are a number of clients using Netscape Navigator. Although both browsers confer to a basic set of technologies that they support, a number of differences exist between the two browsers. For example, Netscape Navigator does not include built-in support for ActiveX controls and Microsoft's ActiveX technology, in general. As a result, if a client using Netscape Navigator visits an ActiveX-enabled Web site, the client cannot really take advantage of the capabilities and features ActiveX technology offers. In some cases, this can even render a Web site useless. To resolve this type of problem, IIS comes with an Active Server Component called the Browser Capabilities component. By using this component, you can detect the type of browser the client is using. In addition, you can determine the browser's capabilities through an INI file and accordingly render HTML that the browser is capable of handling. For example, if the client browser does not support frames and tables, you can generate a simple HTML page that does not use the <FRAME>...</FRAME> and <TABLE>...</TABLE> tags.

Content Linking

Every site needs a navigation scheme. The Content Linking component makes it easy for you to design and develop a navigation scheme for your Web site so that users can access the information they need, with ease.

Page Counter

Probably every site you visit on the Web displays a page counter at the bottom of a site's home page. The page counter indicates the traffic the site generated since its inception. The Page Counter component helps you do exactly this. With this component, you can determine the amount of interest your site generates.

Permission Checker Component

To determine if a user has access permission to a given file on the server, use the Permission Checker component.

> *Note: In addition to using the prepackaged components, you can write your own Active Server Components. To write your own Active Server Component, you can use any of the programming tools you're familiar with, including Visual Basic, Visual C++, and so on.*

Microsoft Script Debugger

When you install IIS, you can choose to install the Microsoft Script Debugger. You use the Microsoft Script Debugger to debug your application scripts. Note, however, that the Microsoft Script Debugger works only with Internet Explorer; the debugger does not work with Netscape Navigator. In addition, you can invoke the debugger from within Internet Explorer only.

Features

The debugger is actually a nice little utility that offers the following useful features:

➤ **Breakpoints** You can set breakpoints within your scripts. At the breakpoint, you can evaluate expressions or examine a variable's value.

➤ **Code Coloring** The debugger uses color codes to display the script. Color codes make it easy for you to read, understand, and differentiate the code.

➤ **Immediate Expression Evaluation** In the Immediate window, you can evaluate new code or an expression within the call stack's context.

➤ **Integrated Call Stack** The debugger combines the VBScript and JScript call stacks into a single, seamless, integrated call stack. The Call Stack window displays the active procedure call.

➤ **Scripting Language Independent** You can use the debugger to debug scripts that may include both scripting languages (JScript and VBScript).

➤ **Stepping Through Code** You can use the debugger to step into, over, and out of the procedures within a script. In addition, you can step from a VBScript procedure to a JScript procedure, and vice versa.

Debugging Statements

You can use the following debugging actions within your script.

Here are the actions to stop the code execution:

➤ **VBScript statement: Stop** To stop the code execution and invoke the debugger from within your script, use the VBScript **Stop** statement.

➤ **JScript statement: debugger** To stop the code execution and invoke the debugger from within your script, use the JScript **debugger** statement.

Here are the actions to write a string to the Immediate window:

➤ **VBScript statement: Write** To write a string to the Immediate window, use the VBScript **Write** statement. The syntax for using the **Write** statement is

```
Debug.Write(string)
```

where the argument *string* is the string you want to write to the Immediate window.

➤ **JScript statement: write** To write a string to the Immediate window, use the JScript **write** statement. The syntax for using the **write** statement is

```
Debug.write(string)
```

where the argument *string* is the string you want to write to the Immediate window.

Here are the actions for writing a string and a new line to the Immediate window:

➤ **VBScript statement: WriteLine** To write a string and a new line to the Immediate window, use the VBScript **WriteLine** statement. The syntax for using the **WriteLine** statement is

```
Debug.WriteLine([string])
```

where the argument *string* is the string you want to write to the Immediate window. (Note that the argument string is optional.)

➤ **JScript statement: writeln** To write a string and a new line to the Immediate window, use the JScript **writeln** statement. The syntax for using the **writeln** statement is

```
Debug.writeln([string])
```

where the argument *string* is the string you want to write to the Immediate window. (Note that the argument string is optional.)

Open Database Connectivity

Open Database Connectivity (ODBC) is the industry standard for connecting your application to relational databases. The Internet Database Connector (IDC) that comes with IIS lets you connect IIS to 32-bit relational databases, including Microsoft SQL Server, Microsoft Access, Microsoft FoxPro, Sybase SQL Server, and dBASE. The IDC is a server extension—in fact, it's an ISAPI DLL (HTTPODBC.DLL). It's also a communication layer between IIS and the database. By using the IDC, you can build dynamic data-driven Web sites. Here's how the IDC mechanism works:

1. The browser issues a SQL request.

2. IIS routes the request to the IDC.

3. The IDC, in turn, routes the request to the database.

4. The database processes the request and returns the results to the browser via the IDC and IIS.

 The IDC file contains the SQL query the client browser wants the database server to execute.

Creating An IDC Application

To create an IDC application, perform the following steps:

1. Create the logical model of the database. To create the logical model, you can use tools such as LogicWorks' ERWin/SQL.

2. Generate the physical model from the logical model. You can do so with tools such as ERWin/SQL.

3. Create the ODBC datasource that works with the database.

4. Create the IDC file. In addition to the SQL query, the IDC file includes user name, password, and DSN (Data Source Name) to connect to the database by using ODBC. The following is an example of an IDC file that uses the **INSERT** statement:

```
Datasource: StatusReport
Template: statinsrt.htx
SQLStatement: INSERT INTO STATREPORT(ApplicationName,
ApplicationVersion, StatusNature, StatusDescription,
ReportedBy) + VALUES('%ApplicationName%',
'%ApplicationVersion%', '%StatusNature%',
'%StatusDescription%', '%ReportedBy%')
```

STATINSRT.HTX is the template page that the IDC uses to display the results of executing the SQL query. The values from the form replace the variables within the %...% signs. Place the IDC file within the \Scripts directory on the server.

5. Create the Web form that the user will use to input the data. To create the form, you can use any Web development tools, such as Microsoft FrontPage. Use the following form action line of code to specify the IDC file and the associated action (that is, **POST**):

```
<form action="/Scripts/statinsrt.idc" method="POST">
```

6. Build the template page (.HTX) that the IDC uses to display the results of executing the SQL query. The HTX file includes information for for-matting the data as HTML. The following is an example of an .HTX file:

```
<HTML>
<HEAD>
<TITLE>Status Report</TITLE>
</HEAD>

<BODY BGCOLOR="#FFFFFF" text="#008000">
<H1>Status Report</H1>

<HR>

<P>
Thank You, %ReportedBy%, for the status report.
</P>

</HR>

</BODY>
</HTML>
```

Exam Prep Questions

Question 1

You are the Webmaster within an organization. You have set the default document for your Web site to DEFAULT.ASP. However, whenever a user tries reaching your Web site, he gets the error message "Directory listing not allowed." What is the problem?

○ a. The .HTM extension should be used instead of the .ASP extension for the default page.

○ b. You cannot use an ASP page as your Web site's default page.

○ c. Execute rights need to be allowed on the directory where the DEFAULT.ASP page physically resides on your Web server.

○ d. The directory listing style needs to be set to Unix.

The correct answer to this question is c. You must enable Execute rights on the directory where the DEFAULT.ASP page physically resides on the server. It doesn't matter if you use an HTML or ASP page as your Web server's default page. You can, of course, use an ASP page as your site's default page. Setting the directory listing style to MS-DOS or Unix is not relevant. Therefore, answers a, b, and d are incorrect.

Question 2

> You have two virtual Web servers for two departments within
> your company. The first Web site, http://mainoffice.com, has a
> GLOBAL.ASP file that stores the session variables. The user must
> log in with this site before moving to the second Web site, http://
> dept-b.com. You've been using this Web application for more than
> six months on IIS 3.0 and it has been working fine. Now, you port
> your application to IIS 4.0 and you find that the application does
> not work. What is the reason?
>
> ○ a. IIS 4.0 did not install properly. You must reinstall it.
>
> ○ b. You must install Active Server Pages on IIS 4.0 before
> you can get any ASP applications to work with IIS 4.0.
>
> ○ c. IIS 4.0 provides an individual application scope for each
> application. You must have separate GLOBAL.ASP files
> for each Web site.
>
> ○ d. Active Server Pages must be ported for IIS 4.0.

The correct answer to this question is c. One of the main differences between
IIS 3.0 and IIS 4.0 is the application scope. Within IIS 3.0, the application's
scope covers the entire server. That is, if you had a couple of Web sites running
under IIS 3.0, both would share the same application scope. Within IIS 4.0,
you can have more than one application within each Web site and several application scopes on the entire server. There's no need to reinstall IIS 4.0. By
default, the IIS installation program installs ASP when you install IIS 4.0.
Porting ASP to IIS 4.0 is invalid because IIS 4.0 already supports ASP. Therefore, answers a, b, and d are incorrect.

Question 3

> Which of the following do you need before creating a virtual
> directory?
>
> ○ a. A physical path
>
> ○ b. Read and Write permissions
>
> ○ c. Gopher
>
> ○ d. An IP address

The correct answer to this question is a. When creating the virtual directory,
you need to provide the directory's physical path. If you do not grant the Read

and Write permissions for the directory, the client browser may not be able to browse the virtual directory; however, you can grant these permissions at a later stage. IIS 4.0 does not support Gopher. Also, you need an IP address for a virtual server, not for a virtual directory. Therefore, answers b, c, and d are incorrect.

Question 4

For each of the virtual servers you create on IIS, you must have a unique IP address.

○ a. True

○ b. False

The correct answer to this question is a, True. You can host more than one Web site on IIS; however, each site must have its own IP address for the users connecting to that site. IIS simulates the environment for the users to think each site corresponding to its IP address is hosted on a separate IIS. Therefore, answer b is incorrect.

Question 5

You would like to design an HTML form that accepts data from the user, processes the data on IIS, and returns results to the browser. Choose the IIS extensions for this type of implementation. [Check all correct answers]

❑ a. JScript

❑ b. VBScript

❑ c. CGI

❑ d. ASP

The correct answers to this question are a, b, c, and d. Both JScript and VBScript are scripting languages you can use with ASP. ASP is an alternative to CGI, which is the standard Web mechanism for transmitting data between the client and server.

Question 6

> JavaScript is Microsoft's open implementation of JScript.
>
> ○ a. True
>
> ○ b. False

The correct answer to this question is b, False. It's the other way around. JScript is Microsoft's open implementation of JavaScript. Therefore, answer a is incorrect.

Question 7

> You can use the Microsoft Script Debugger with Netscape Navigator.
>
> ○ a. True
>
> ○ b. False

The correct answer to this question is b, False. Microsoft Script Debugger works only with Internet Explorer. Therefore, answer a is incorrect.

Question 8

> Netscape Navigator can read and display an ASP page if the page uses which one of the following components to render HTML based on the client browser?
>
> ○ a. Browser Capabilities component
>
> ○ b. Active Data Object
>
> ○ c. Permission Checker component
>
> ○ d. Page Counter component

The correct answer to this question is a. By using the Browser Capabilities component, you can detect the type of client browser and accordingly render HTML. None of the other three components has anything to do with detecting the type of client browser. Therefore, answers b, c, and d are incorrect.

Question 9

> Which one of the following lines of code should you add to the
> first line within the following script so that the script runs on the
> server?
>
> ```
> <SCRIPT LANGUAGE=VBScript>
> <!--
> Option Explicit
>
> Dim validCreditCardNumber
> Sub Submit_OnClick
>      validCreditCardNumber = True
>      Call CheckCreditCardNumber(CreditCardNumber
>        Field.Value,
> "Please enter your credit card number.")
>      If validCreditCardNumber then
>           MsgBox "Thank you for your order"
>      End if
>      End Sub
> </SCRIPT>
> ```
>
> ○ a. **RUNAT=SERVER**
>
> ○ b. **EXECUTEAT=SERVER**
>
> ○ c. **PARSEAT=SERVER**
>
> ○ d. None of the above

The correct answer to this question is a. **RUNAT=SERVER** is the keyword.
The others are not. Therefore, answers b, c, and d are incorrect.

Question 10

> When creating a virtual FTP server, which of the following set of
> access permissions can you grant?
>
> ○ a. Read, Write, Script
>
> ○ b. Read, Write, Script, Execute
>
> ○ c. Read, Write
>
> ○ d. Read, Write, Script, Execute, Directory Browsing

The correct answer to this question is c. You can only read (download) and write (upload) files to an FTP server. The other options are not applicable to an FTP server. This is because an FTP server's primary function is to enable file download and upload. Therefore, answers a, b, and d are incorrect.

Question 11

You must manually start a virtual Web or FTP server.

○ a. True

○ b. False

The correct answer to this question is a, True. When you first create a virtual Web or FTP server, the server's default state is Stopped. Therefore, answer b is incorrect.

Question 12

Which one of the following objects handles session management for an ASP server?

○ a. Application

○ b. Server

○ c. Session

○ d. Request

○ e. Response

The correct answer to this question is c. To store and track session variables and their values, use the Session object. To manage the Web application, use the Application object. To manage the Web server, use the Server object. To request information from the browser, use the Request object. To return information to the browser, use the Response object. For these reasons, answers a, b, d, and e are incorrect.

Question 13

Netscape Navigator is an Active Client.

○ a. True

○ b. False

The correct answer to this question is b, False. Netscape Navigator does not include built-in support for Microsoft's ActiveX technology. Therefore, answer a is incorrect.

Question 14

A virtual directory cannot contain ASP files.

○ a. True

○ b. False

The correct answer to this question is b, False. Any directory that is not the home directory or not contained within the server's home directory is a virtual directory. A virtual directory, however, can host any files (including ASP files) that a home directory can. Therefore, answer a is incorrect.

Question 15

For an intranet, if the server name is "marketing", you can reach the Web site's home directory by typing which one of the following URLs within the browser's URL textbox?

○ a. http://localhost/marketing

○ b. http://marketing

○ c. http://www.iis.com/marketing

○ d. None of the above

The correct answer to this question is b. For an intranet, the Web site's home directory is mapped to the server name. http://marketing represents a direct mapping between the Web site's home directory and the server name. None of the other options represents this direct mapping. Therefore, answers a, c, and d are incorrect.

Need To Know More?

 Hiller, Scot and Daniel Mezick. *Programming Active Server Pages*. Microsoft Press, Redmond, WA, 1997. ISBN 1-57231-700-0. This book is a tutorial and guide for creating dynamic Web pages that uses all the relevant tools and necessary Microsoft technologies required to build state-of-the-art Web sites. Sections are included that introduce IIS, Personal Web Server as a development tool, and ODBC basics for connecting to databases.

 Johnson, Scot, et al. *Using Active Server Pages, Special Edition*. Que Publishing, Indianapolis, IN, 1997. ISBN 0-78971-389-6. This authoritative guide is your all-in-one guide to creating dynamic Web sites for both business and personal use. Jam-packed with timesaving advice and hands-on techniques, this tutorial and reference is your complete resource for using Active Server Pages to their fullest potential.

 Walther, Stephen. *Active Server Pages Unleashed*. Sams Publishing, Indianapolis, IN, 1997. ISBN 1-57521-351-6. This book is one of the few advanced-level books for Active Server developers. It gives you an in-depth examination of creating commercial-quality dynamic Web sites. This book assumes a knowledge of at least one language and Web site administration, and it builds on that knowledge to enhance your ability to provide dynamic pages for the World Wide Web. The CD-ROM contains the author's source code as well as third-party tools.

 Microsoft TechNet. January, 1998. The technical notes for Microsoft Active Server Pages provide insight into its design and implementation. Also, perform a search using the following key words: "virtual directory," "virtual site," "access permissions," "ActiveX," "server-side scripting," and "ASP scripts."

 The Microsoft Web sites at http://www.microsoft.com/iis/partners and http://www.microsoft.com/iis/guide provide a wealth of information regarding ASP, including white papers, FAQs, tips, tricks, and lots more. Performing a search using the same keywords as the TechNet will also yield a wealth of information at this site.

 The Web site at http://www.webnations.com/webnationsasp/ includes demos of ASP in action.

The Web site at http://www.ratio.org.uk/SoftLib/Soft/WinNT/ iis/asp/asp_tips.htm includes tips and techniques for trouble-shooting ASP.

Managing And Tuning IIS

8

. . . .

Terms you'll need to understand:

√ Microsoft Management Console (MMC)

√ Snap-in

√ MMC's scope pane

√ Results pane

√ Rebar

√ Internet Service Manager— MMC snap-in

√ Internet Service Manager HTML, HTMLA

√ http://localhost:port/ iisadmin/

√ Windows Scripting Host (WSH)

√ Metabase

√ Bandwidth throttling

√ HTTP keep-alives

Techniques you'll need to master:

√ Understanding the Microsoft Management Console (MMC)

√ Examining the available IIS administrative tools for local and remote management

√ Understanding Windows Scripting Host (WSH)

√ Understanding the Metabase

√ Identifying Performance Monitor objects for IIS activities

√ Tuning IIS performance, bandwidth, traffic, connections, HTTP keep-alives, pipeline size, and hardware

In this chapter, we'll discuss the administration tools used to manage IIS. Actual use of these tools is detailed in other chapters, where topic-, purpose-, and command-specific items are discussed. We'll also look briefly at the new Windows Scripting Host and the IIS Metabase. Finally, this chapter concludes with tips on performance monitoring and tuning IIS.

The Microsoft Management Console

The most obvious change or improvement to IIS 4.0 is the introduction of the Microsoft Management Console (MMC), which is shown in Figure 8.1. The MMC is a Windows-based tool that offers total management of all services and applications within a single utility. The MMC is also Active Desktop capable and will eventually be used to access management and control aspects of the entire Windows NT system. In fact, Windows NT 5.0's control mechanisms center around snap-ins for MMC.

MMC, itself, offers no management capabilities, but instead, offers a common environment where components called *snap-ins* reside. Snap-ins are product- or service-specific COM or DCOM object management utilities. When IIS 4.0 is installed, MMC is installed with the Internet Information Server snap-in.

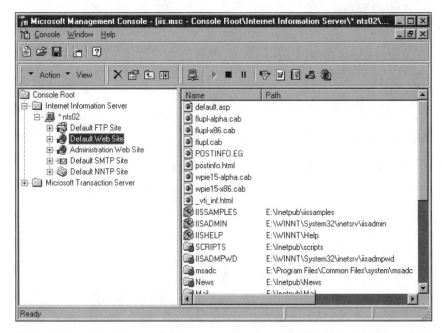

Figure 8.1 The Microsoft Management Console (MMC) with IIS and MTS snap-ins.

This snap-in gives you access to all the configuration and administration functions associated with IIS, which was accessed through the Internet Service Manager in previous versions of IIS.

If you only have IIS installed on your Windows NT Server system, you only have the IIS snap-in (and possibly the Transaction Server snap-in if it was selected for installation). Therefore, you don't have many configuration options for MMC. However, the MMC utility itself was designed to be a customizable interface. Most of the customization features center around adding and removing snap-ins to create a set of commonly used tools. Once MMC is configured, the state of the utility can be saved in a settings file with an .MSC extension. An MMC console configuration is stored using the Console|Save Console As command. An MSC file is loaded back into MMC with the Console|Open command.

Snap-ins are added to MMC using the Console|Add/Remove Snap-In command from the menu bar. This reveals the Snap-In Manager, where installed snap-ins can be removed or new snap-ins added. The extent of control of MMC is only to create new windows (where MSC layouts are displayed) and to add or remove snap-ins. All other functions are provided for through the snap-in itself, and those functions are dependent on the service, application, or protocol the snap-in is intended to administer. Thus, MMC offers a standardized administrative tool interface that is easy to use.

An MMC console is divided into two panes (refer to Figure 8.1). The left pane, known as the *scope pane*, displays the namespace tree where all items, called *nodes*, to be managed are listed. Each node is an object that can be managed through MMC by means of an installed snap-in. The right pane, known as the *results pane*, displays the contents of the selected node. Typically, you can right-click over a node or an item in the results pane to access object-specific commands in a pop-up menu. Most objects are managed by selecting Properties from such a pop-up menu. MMC also has three command bars: the top bar is a typical menu bar, the middle bar is a typical button bar, and the bottom bar is a new bar known as the *rebar*. The rebar lists node- and object-specific commands. Each time a new object is selected, the command selections in the rebar change.

IIS Administrative Tools

Earlier versions of IIS were managed through the Internet Service Manager (ISM). However, ISM has been replaced in IIS 4.0 by the MMC and the Web-based administration tool. Actually, what has occurred is that the previous standalone utility of the ISM has been transformed into an MMC snap-in and an HTML interface. These two methods are discussed in the following sections.

Internet Service Manager—MMC Snap-In

The Internet Service Manager MMC (ISM-MMC) snap-in is the primary means by which IIS is configured locally. ISM-MMC is accessed through the Start menu (Start|Programs|Windows NT 4.0 Option Pack|Microsoft Internet Information Server|Internet Service Manager). This brings up the MMC with the default MSC file (or the previously saved MSC file if it has already been accessed).

The ISM snap-in gives access to all computers hosting IIS services within the local network. As shown in Figure 8.1, the sample installation exists only on a single server named "nts02," where all the FTP, Web, SMTP, and NNTP sites are hosted.

The IIS snap-in also modifies the rebar to offer quick access to five standard Windows NT administration tools, which are commonly used in relation to IIS. These are the Key Manager, User Manager For Domains, Server Manager, Event Viewer, and Performance Monitor. These five tools are accessed using the five buttons located at the far right on the rebar.

Instead of reviewing and repeating all the management capabilities, commands, and actions that can be performed through the ISM snap-in, please refer to the other chapters in this book that focus on each of these issues.

Internet Service Manager—HTML

The HTML version of the ISM gives administrators remote access to the IIS server as a whole or to limited portions of IIS, such as a single hosted Web site (see Figure 8.2). The HTML ISM allows management to be performed from any Internet/intranet-accessible client. Through the remote Administration interface, you can perform most of the same functions you can through the locally accessed ISM snap-in. These include managing logging, adjusting performance, altering server properties (including stopping and restarting individual sites), creating new virtual directories, managing access properties, altering security, and customizing HTTP headers and error messages. Basically, the only function that can't be managed remotely is certificate mapping.

The HTMLA (HTML administration tool, also know as ISM) can be accessed through the URL http://localhost:port/iisadmin/. However, there are a few important items to take note of in regard to this URL. By default, HTMLA is only accessible on the same server that hosts IIS itself. In fact, you must use either "localhost" or "127.0.0.1" to access the Administration site. Using the correct IP address for the site won't grant access. This means that HTMLA cannot be accessed for remote administration until you enable this feature specifically. HTMLA is configured this way to provide the highest possible level

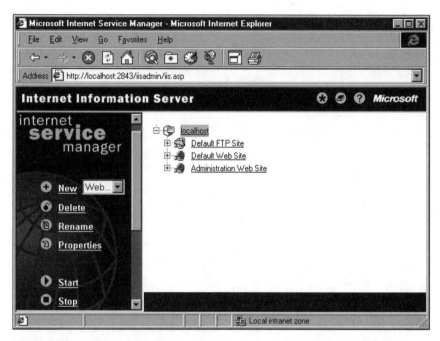

Figure 8.2   The Internet Service Manager HTML viewed through
Internet Explorer 4.0.

of security around administrative access. Remote access can be enabled by
HTMLA in the same way as granting or restricting access to any other Web
site—via the Directory Security tab of the Properties dialog of the Administrative Web site via the ISM snap-in of MMC. The following are the steps
required to grant access to HTMLA:

1. Launch MMC with the ISM snap-in (Start|Programs|Windows NT
   4.0 Option Pack|Microsoft Internet Information Server|Internet
   Service Manager).

2. Scroll down in the scope pane to reveal the Administration Web Site
   node and then select the Administration Web site.

3. Select Properties from the Action pull-down menu of the rebar.

4. Select the Directory Security tab.

5. Click the Edit button under the IP Address And Domain Name
   Restrictions area.

6. Notice that on the IP Address And Domain Name Restrictions dialog,
   all access is denied except for 127.0.0.1 (localhost). To enable access to
   HTMLA from other workstations or clients, either add an exception or
   change the default action to Grant Access.

If you change the default action to Grant Access, you should go to the \Winnt\System32\Inetsrv\Iisadmin folder and change its user/group NTFS access permissions. This is the default installation location of the Web-based administration tools. By default, this directory is set to grant Full Control to Administrators and Change To Everyone. Obviously, this is a security problem if it is not changed.

Another important item to note about the iisadmin URL is the use of a port address. When IIS is installed, a random port is selected to be used to gain access to the Web-based administration tools. To determine which port is selected or to change the port to your own preference, go to the Web Site tab on the Administration Web site's Properties dialog. The TCP Port field under Web Site Identification is where this value is set.

So, if you enable remote access, properly set access permissions on the folder, and determine the access port, the URL could be this: http://www.mydomain.com:2831/iisadmin.

Windows Scripting Host

The Windows Scripting Host (WSH) is a language-independent, shell-based host that adds a wide range of scripting capabilities to Windows NT. WSH is installed as part of the Option Pack when IIS 4.0 is installed.

Note: Windows NT 5.0 will include WSH as a standard component.

The version of WSH included in the Option Pack adds scripting support for VBScript and JScript as well as maintains compatibility with MS-DOS command scripts. WSH is based on the ActiveX scripting engine, which may encourage third-party vendors to develop add-in engines for other common Web/Internet scripting languages, such as Perl, TCL, REXX, and Python.

WSH can be used directly on the Windows desktop (WSCRIPT.EXE) or via a command console (CSCRIPT.EXE). Therefore, scripts can be executed without need of embedding them in an HTML document. This greatly expands the versatility of Windows NT-hosted Web activity by enabling both local and remote execution of scripts. The most significant benefit from WSH for IIS administrators is the ability to write administration scripts that can be launched locally or remotely.

For further information about WSH, please review the IIS documentation or consult the Technical Note document "Windows Scripting Host—A Universal Scripting Host for Scripting Languages" from TechNet.

IIS Metabase

Due to the nature of the services hosted by IIS, the Registry does not serve as an efficient storage device for most of the configuration parameters used by IIS. Instead, a high-speed, memory-resident, hierarchical system known as the *Metabase* is used. The Metabase is not a replacement for the Registry; in fact, it does not contain or duplicate Registry information. The Metabase holds only data that is key to IIS administration. Here are some examples:

➤ Computer and Web site properties

➤ Logging properties

➤ FTP and HTTP service-specific properties

➤ Virtual directory configurations

➤ Non-NTFS file properties

➤ Filter configurations

➤ SSL properties

The Metabase is stored in the \Winnt\System32\Inetsrv\METABASE.BIN directory. Each change is recorded in this file, but IIS uses the version stored in active memory. When the configuration information for a server is backed up through the MMC (using the Action|Backup/Restore Configuration command), the backup files are stored in \Winnt\System32\inetsrv\MetaBack as MD0 files. These files are encoded so that they can only be altered using the standard IIS administration tools (in other words, the Metabase cannot be edited directly). The IIS administration tools use Active Directory Service Interface (ADSI) to interact and interface with the Metabase.

Monitoring IIS Performance

The activity of IIS and its hosted services can be monitored through two tools native to Windows NT—namely Performance Monitor and the Event Viewer. IIS does include rich and versatile logging capabilities. These performance monitoring tools are discussed in Chapter 10.

 This book assumes you already have working knowledge of these tools. If not, please refer to *MCSE NT Server 4 Exam Cram* (1-57610-190-8) or *MCSE NT Workstation 4 Exam Cram* (1-57610-193-2), both published by Certification Insider Press.

IIS installs many objects and counters that can be monitored with the Performance Monitor. Here's a list of the objects added by IIS:

➤ **Internet Information Services Global** This object is used to measure performance for IIS as a whole, including request activity, bandwidth, cache activity, and object access.

➤ **Web Service** This object is used to measure Web service as a whole or Web site-specific performance, including request activity, bandwidth, throughput, CGI requests and activity, errors, connections, and users.

➤ **FTP Service** This object is used to measure FTP service as a whole or FTP site-specific performance, including request activity, throughput, connections, users, and logon activity.

➤ **Active Server Pages** This object is used to measure overall ASP performance, including errors, requests, sessions, transactions, and caching.

Other Option Pack services or IIS add-on applications add objects to Performance Monitor to broaden the scope of available monitoring points. These include the following:

➤ **Index Server** Content Index, Content Index Filter, HTTP Content Index objects

➤ **NNTP Service** NNTP Command and NTTP Server objects

➤ **SMTP Service** SMTP Server object

The Event Viewer is where many IIS events are logged with NT (a separate and distinct issue from IIS's own internal logging, see Chapter 10). You should check the system and application logs for IIS-related events. This includes service starts and stops, errors encountered on bootup, and the normal reporting of successful completion of administrative tasks.

Performance Tuning IIS

If your IIS-hosted site is not providing the performance you expect initially, you can tweak the performance of IIS through several built-in features. IIS is configured by default to adequately handle most standard sites, but fine-tuning Microsoft's defaults can often result in significant improvements. In the next few sections, we'll take a look at each of the IIS performance-tuning options available.

Restricting Bandwidth

By default, IIS attempts to use all the available bandwidth made available to the server for network or Internet connections. You may find that allowing IIS to allocate bandwidth use as it sees fit can cause non-IIS services to function poorly or to stifle one Web site in favor of another.

Bandwidth throttling can be enabled on a server (computer) level or on a service (site) level. Server- or computer-level throttling is configured on the Properties dialog of that computer (see Figure 8.3). This dialog is accessed through MMC by selecting the computer/server in the scope pane and then selecting the Action|Properties command. Marking the Enable Bandwidth Throttling limits the total bandwidth used by all IIS sites to the kilobytes per second defined in the associated field. The default value is 1,024.

Individual service or site throttling is enabled on the Performance tab of the Properties dialog of each site (see Figure 8.4). Once again, marking the Enable Bandwidth Throttling option limits the total bandwidth used by all IIS sites to the kilobytes per second defined in the associated field. However, defining a value for bandwidth throttling for a specific Web site overrides any setting made at the server/computer level for that site. The server/computer throttling setting will still apply to all other sites.

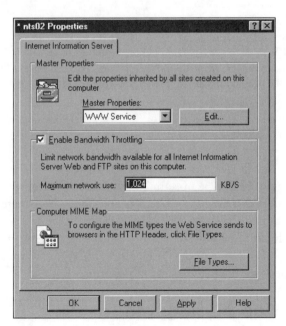

Figure 8.3   The Properties dialog of the server or computer.

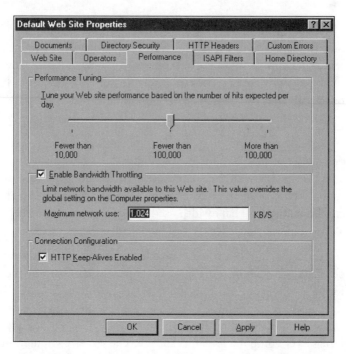

Figure 8.4 A Web site's Properties dialog with the Performance tab selected.

Traffic Estimation

By estimating the traffic you expect within a standard 24-hour period, you can set the memory management preferences to match. Here are your options:

➤ Fewer than 10,000

➤ Fewer than 100,000

➤ More than 100,000

This isn't a fine-tuning type of setting but more of a broad setting for low-, moderate-, and high-traffic sites. This is enabled on a site-by-site basis on the Performance tab of a Web site's Properties dialog (refer to Figure 8.4). This setting actually alters the way the server manages memory. By setting this slide bar to the selection that matches the closest to the reality of your traffic, your users will experience the highest level of performance.

Connection Management

By default, each Web site hosted by IIS can accept an unlimited number of simultaneous connections, whereas FTP sites are set to a limit of 100,000 connections. However, both these settings are unrealistic. Just compare that to the new record set by the RS/6000 IBM Unix mainframe machine that hosted the Nagano Games Official Web site. It had 103,429 hits in a single minute. If that's the record for the latest high-end mainframe, any Intel or Alpha machine you deploy IIS on won't be able to even get close!

If your site is flooded with resource requests, your server will be so tied up establishing communication pathways that it will never get around to actually sending the requested resource. It's often a good idea to limit connections to 1,000 users or fewer, especially if your site is comprised of an excessive number of items per document (such as 20+). As discussed in Chapter 2, one of the benefits of IIS is its ability to maintain a communication connection with clients and to send multiple resources over the same link, thus reducing system overhead and improving performance. However, even though fewer total connections are required per client, this does not imply that reducing the number of per-client connections can enable a corresponding increase in total clients without performance degradation. The connections limitation parameters are set on the Web/FTP Site tab of a Web or FTP site's Properties dialog (see Figure 8.5).

You can also define the connection timeout parameter on this tab. This determines how long a connection is kept alive by IIS before it is terminated. For both Web and FTP, this is 900 seconds (15 minutes). We think this is

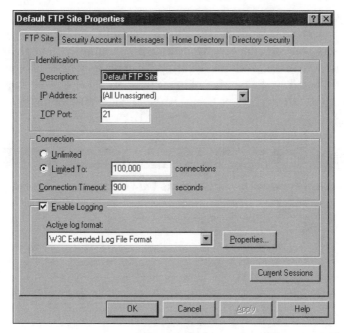

Figure 8.5   An FTP site's Properties dialog with the FTP Site tab selected.

extremely long, especially for popular sites. For FTP sites, a more reasonable value of 120 seconds (2 minutes) may improve performance by removing inactive users. For Web sites, a setting of 300 seconds (5 minutes) gives visitors time to read a lengthy document before making their next selection before their session is terminated. Remember, if fewer connections are being managed by IIS at any given moment, the performance of the server for all other sites and active connections is improved.

HTTP Keep-Alives

It has become a standard feature of modern browsers to request that the Web server keep a communication connection open across multiple requests. This request is known as an *HTTP keep-alive*. Keep-alives improve server performance by removing the overhead of tearing down and rebuilding connections between requests from the same browser. This means that a single document containing multiple items, such as graphics, can be sent over fewer connections instead of each over a separate connection. Keep-alives are enabled by default, which is the best performance setting for this item. If you need to disable keep-alives, you can do so on the Performance tab of a Web site's Properties dialog (refer to Figure 8.4).

Selecting A Pipeline

Your choice for the network connection to your intranet or the Internet can directly determine how much data you can transmit and how many simultaneous users you can support. By making an assumption that the average document or item on a Web site is 24K, you can see how large of a connection you'll need based on the number of items transferred per second, as shown in Table 8.1. (Note that Table 8.1 reflects the calculation assuming four bits of overhead are required for each eight bits of data.)

Table 8.1 Connection types and the objects transmitted per second.	
Connection Type	**Objects Transmitted Per Second**
28.8 to 56K modem	.3 to .6
56K Frame Relay	.9
ISDN	1.7
T1	24
T3	710
10MB Ethernet	163
100MB Ethernet	1,634

Table 8.2 Connection types and the number of simultaneous users.	
Connection Type	**Simultaneous Users**
28.8 to 56K modem	1 to 2
56K Frame Relay	2
ISDN	4 to 5
T1	52
T3	1,688
10MB Ethernet	353
100MB Ethernet	3,531

You can also make this decision depending on the number of simultaneous users you can support (as shown in Table 8.2). By selecting to deliver each document within 5 seconds, with an average document consisting of four 24K components plus overhead, you must deliver 144K in 5 seconds—about 29Kbps.

A final useful calculation for determining required bandwidth is the possible hits per day per connection type (as shown in Table 8.3). This value is determined by dividing the available bandwidth by 12 (8 bits data and 4 bits overhead), multiplying by seconds in a day (86,400), and then dividing by the average component size (24K).

Hardware Bottlenecks

In addition to tuning IIS itself, you may also need to improve Windows NT Server's performance. IIS can only operate at its best if NT gives it a reliable and responsive foundation. There are four main areas where NT's performance is crucial—storage devices, CPU, memory, and network.

Table 8.3 Connection types and the number of hits per day.	
Connection Type	**Hits Per Day**
28.8 to 56K modem	8,600 to 16,722
56K Frame Relay	16,7222
ISDN	38,222
T1	470,897
T3	13,760,000
10MB Ethernet	3,057,777
100MB Ethernet	30,577,777

Storage device or hard drive bottlenecks occur when the physical drive and/or the drive's controller are unable to process the number of requests or the volume of reads and writes demanded. Typically, a slow or below-par storage system will also be accompanied by low CPU and network activity. Through the Performance Monitor, check the PhysicalDisk object's % Disk Time counter. If this reads consistently over 60 percent, you should improve your storage subsystem. Another useful counter is the Current Disk Queue Length. If this reads consistently 2 or greater (per drive), your storage system is too slow. You should consider adding additional drives and using NT's software RAID for disk striping or purchase a hardware RAID solution. However, you should inspect the memory before making a storage system change because you may have a memory bottleneck instead.

CPU bottlenecks occur when requests devour all available processing cycles. Typically, a CPU bottleneck is accompanied by low network utilization and low disk usage. If the Processor object's % Processor Time is consistently over 85 percent, you should consider improving the system's CPU. Another related counter is the System object's Processor Queue Length. If this consistently reads one more than the total number of CPUs, the CPU is a bottleneck. This can be remedied by replacing the current CPU with a faster chip or by adding additional CPUs.

Memory bottlenecks occur when there's too little physical RAM, which forces the system to rely more upon the pagefile. Because the pagefile is stored on a hard drive, it operates at 10 to 1,000 times slower than physical RAM. By comparing the Memory objects' Page Faults/sec counter to the Page Inputs/sec counter, you can determine if your system needs more physical RAM. Page Faults/sec indicates the number of times per second a requested memory page is not immediately available and must be moved from another section of physical RAM or the pagefile. Page Inputs/sec indicates how many page faults must be read from disk. If Page Inputs is consistently more than 20 percent of Page Faults, you may be adding significant strain on your disk subsystem. This would indicate a need for more physical RAM.

Network bottlenecks occur when the network adapter card itself cannot handle the level of traffic or when the network media is saturated with other traffic. IIS can easily flood a 10MB Ethernet card and a network with traffic on a moderately active site. You can determine the network load by inspecting the Network Segment object's % Network Utilization counter. If this consistently reads 85 percent or more, you should consider improving the speed of your network from 10MB to 100MB or adding additional network interfaces to this server. If your network card's driver adds the Network Interface to Performance Monitor, you should inspect each interface's % Utilization and Queue

Length counters. If these counters read consistently more than 85 percent or one more than the total number of NICs, respectively, your network interface card is the bottleneck.

Exam Prep Questions

Question 1

IIS can be administered through which interfaces or utilities?
[Check all correct answers]

❑ a. Internet Service Manager MMC snap-in

❑ b. Internet Service Manager applet in the Control Panel

❑ c. Internet Service Manager Administrative wizard

❑ d. Internet Service Manager HTML via a Web browser

IIS is administered through an MMC snap-in and HTMLA. Therefore, answers a and d are correct. IIS does not have an applet or an Administrative wizard. Therefore, answers b and c are incorrect.

Question 2

The IIS MMC snap-in alters the rebar menu to grant you quick one-button access to which standard Windows NT Server utilities? [Check all correct answers]

❑ a. Performance Monitor

❑ b. Server Manager

❑ c. Registry Editor

❑ d. Event Viewer

❑ e. User Manager For Domains

❑ f. Network Monitor

The IIS snap-in modifies the MMC rebar to give single-button access to Performance Monitor, Server Manager, Event Viewer, and User Manager For Domains. Therefore, answers a, b, d, and e are correct. The Registry Editor and Network Monitor are not accessed via the MMC IIS snap-in rebar. Therefore, answers c and f are incorrect.

Question 3

With MMC, you have the ability to add or remove an individual snap-in; however, once it's added, you cannot save the configuration for future sessions.

○ a. True

○ b. False

False, MMC has the ability to save the configuration of each console as an MSC file for use in subsequent sessions. Therefore, answer b is correct.

Question 4

The Action and View pull-down command lists that are customized by each snap-in are found on or in which standard MMC component or area?

○ a. The scope pane

○ b. Nodes

○ c. The rebar

○ d. The results pane

The rebar hosts the Action and View command lists. Therefore, answer c is correct. The scope pane, nodes, and results pane do not host these lists. Therefore, answers a, b, and d are incorrect.

Question 5

If you need to make modifications to the certificate key mappings for a Web site, which administration utility can you use?

○ a. Internet Service Manager snap-in

○ b. Server Manager

○ c. Internet Service Manager HTML

○ d. Certificate Server

Only the locally accessible ISM snap-in can be used to manage certificate mappings. Therefore, answer a is correct. The Server Manager is not involved with certificate management. Therefore, answer b is incorrect. ISM HTML does not have the ability to manage certificate mappings. Therefore, answer c is incorrect. The Certificate Server is only used to issue certificates if you want to be a certificate authority—it is not used to map certificates to Web sites. Therefore, answer d is incorrect.

Question 6

> Immediately after installing IIS, you determine that the TCP port for the Administration Web site is 1234. You already know that the IP address of the site is 172.16.1.1. Which of the following URLs and access locations can be used to remotely administer IIS?
>
> ○ a. Remote Web browser: http://172.16.1.1:1234/iisadmin/
>
> ○ b. Local Web browser: http://172.16.1.1:1234/iisadmin/
>
> ○ c. Local Web browser: http://localhost/iisadmin/
>
> ○ d. Local Web browser: http://127.0.0.1:1234/iisadmin/

Only Local Web browser: http://127.0.0.1:1234/iisadmin/ will function without making other modifications to IIS's security. Therefore, answer d is correct. However, Local Web browser: http://localhost:1234/iisadmin/ is another method, which is not listed as a possible solution. Remote Web browser: http://172.16.1.1:1234/iisadmin/ will not function because access is limited to local access only, by default. Therefore, answer a is incorrect. Local Web browser: http://172.16.1.1:1234/iisadmin/ will not function because the default security settings will only work with localhost or 127.0.0.1, not the IP address of the server. Therefore, answer b is incorrect. Local Web browser: http://localhost/iisadmin/ will not function because the port is not included. Therefore, answer c is incorrect.

Question 7

> Where are the files that compose the Administrative HTML tools for remotely managing IIS stored by default?
>
> ○ a. \Inetpub\Iisadmin
>
> ○ b. \Winnt\System32\Inetsrv\Iisadmin
>
> ○ c. \Program Files\Inetput\Admin
>
> ○ d. \Inetpub\Adminroot

The IIS Administration HTML tool files are stored in \Winnt\System32\Inetsrv\Iisadmin, by default. Therefore, answer b is correct. The other listed folders are incorrect. Therefore, answers a, c, and d are incorrect.

Question 8

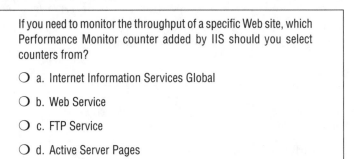

If you need to monitor the throughput of a specific Web site, which Performance Monitor counter added by IIS should you select counters from?

- ○ a. Internet Information Services Global
- ○ b. Web Service
- ○ c. FTP Service
- ○ d. Active Server Pages

You should use the Web Service object because it enables you to select the instance of a single site. Therefore, answer b is correct. The IIS Global object does not have granular focus on sites. Therefore, answer a is incorrect. The FTP Service object is not for Web sites. Therefore, answer c is incorrect. The ASP object is not related to a specific site's throughput but rather the overall performance of scripting. Therefore, answer d is incorrect.

Question 9

IIS is used to host four Web sites, named SITE1, SITE2, SITE3, and SITE4. You enable bandwidth throttling for the server/computer and set it to 4,096K. SITE3 and SITE4 are the most popular sites hosted by your installation of IIS. You want to grant each of them twice the bandwidth of the other sites. Which modification should you perform?

- ○ a. Set server/computer-level bandwidth throttling to 8,192K.
- ○ b. Set service/site-level bandwidth throttling to 2,046K for SITE1 and SITE2.
- ○ c. Set service/site-level bandwidth throttling to 8,192K for SITE3 and SITE4.
- ○ d. This cannot be done with IIS 4.0.

The correct modification is to set service/site-level bandwidth throttling to 8,192K for SITE3 and SITE4. This will grant twice the bandwidth granted to SITE1 and SITE2 for both SITE3 and SITE4. Therefore, answer c is correct.

Setting server/computer-level bandwidth throttling to 8,192K will not specifically grant twice the bandwidth to SITE3 and SITE4; instead, it will just double the total bandwidth shared by all four sites. Therefore, answer a is incorrect. Setting service/site-level bandwidth throttling to 2,046K for SITE1 and SITE2 will not double the available bandwidth to SITE3 and SITE4 but will only force SITE3 and SITE4 to compete for the 4,096K server/computer throttle limit. Therefore, answer b is incorrect. Throttling by site and by computer is possible with IIS. Therefore, answer d is incorrect.

Question 10

Which of the following setting changes will improve the performance of a high-volume Web site?

O a. Disable HTTP keep-alives

O b. Set Web timeouts to 1,800 seconds

O c. Set Performance Tuning to fewer than 10,000

O d. Connect a T3 to IIS

Using a T3 line will improve the site's performance by allowing more hits per day, more simultaneous users, and more objects transmitted per second. Therefore, answer d is correct. Disabling keep-alives, increasing Web timeouts, and setting Performance Tuning to fewer than 10,000 will only degrade the performance of IIS. Therefore, answers a, b, and c are incorrect.

Need To Know More?

 Howell, Nelson, et al. *Using Microsoft Internet Information Server 4.* Que Publishing, Indianapolis, IN, 1997. ISBN 0-7897-1263-6. This book discusses at length MMC (Chapter 13), performance tuning (Chapters 15 and 16), and using Performance Monitor (Chapters 15 and 16).

 The best overview information for Internet Information Server 4.0 can be found in the Reviewer's Guide for IIS 4.0. This document can be found on the TechNet CD-ROM or online via the IIS Web area (www.microsoft.com/iis/).

 IIS's own online documentation, accessed through Start|Programs|Windows NT 4.0 Option Pack|Product Documentation, contains extensive detail on the subjects of IIS management, performance monitoring, and IIS tuning.

Indexing Web Sites With Index Server

. . . .

Terms you'll need to understand:

√ Index Server

√ Unicode

√ CATALOG.WCI

√ Corpus

√ Query

√ Content filters

√ Word breaker

√ Normalizer

√ Noise word and noise word list (NOISE.ENU)

√ Index

√ Word list

√ Shadow index, persistent index

√ Master index

√ Catalog

√ .HTM (HTML form document)

√ .IDQ (Internet Data Query file)

√ .HTX (HTML extension file)

√ Merge

Techniques you'll need to master:

√ Learning the basic installation and configuration requirements

√ Understanding the indexing process

√ Understanding of the parts and process of queries

√ Administering and maintaining Index Server

√ Maintaining security with Index Server

In this chapter, we'll discuss Index Server's content indexing and searching application. Index Server is designed to operate pretty much automatically without requiring administration after its initial configuration. This chapter will familiarize you with Index Server. To really use this application in a live environment, you'll need to spend the time reading the online documentation.

Index Server: Explored And Explained

As the sheer size and volume of information on the Internet, an intranet, or even on a single Web site grows, it becomes increasingly difficult to locate items of relevance. In response to this problem, Microsoft has developed Index Server, a solid indexing and content-searching application. Index Server, currently in its 2.0 release, is an add-on product for Internet Information Server and Peer Web services.

Using Index Server 2.0, you can index and search the full text and properties of documents hosted by your Web and FTP sites. In fact, Index Server 2.0 can index and search any document or file on any accessible drive in the UNC namespace of a Windows NT system hosting IIS or PWS. Out of the box, Index Server 2.0 supports full content indexing of the following file types:

➤ Text files (.TXT)

➤ HTML 3.0 and later documents (.HTM, .HTML)

➤ Microsoft Word 95 and Word 97 documents (.DOC)

➤ Microsoft Excel 95 and Excel 97 documents (.XLS)

➤ Microsoft PowerPoint 95 and PowerPoint 97 documents (.PPT)

All other file and document types are indexed by their NTFS properties. You can add support for other Microsoft or third-party documents and file types, such as Adobe PDF or WordPerfect documents, by installing content filters, and all OLE linked documents and elements within a document are indexed as well. For example, an Excel chart contained in a Word document is indexed and searchable.

Index Server 2.0 includes native support for indexing and querying in several languages, including Dutch, French, German, Italian, Japanese, Spanish, Swedish, UK English, and U.S. English. Index Server's multilingual support also applies to documents that contain several languages; Index Server maintains indexes in Unicode, and all queries are converted to Unicode before they are processed.

Index Server was designed with zero maintenance in mind; once it's installed and its query pages are configured, no further administration is required. Index Server automatically maintains its indexes, and all changes and additions to Web sites, FTP sites, and network/local directories monitored by Index Server are automatically incorporated into the master index.

Users interact with Index Server through the use of Web-based forms that help construct a query to be processed against the index of all monitored documents. Index Server comes with sample query forms to help you get up and running quickly. These forms can be used as templates in constructing your own query forms.

Understanding The Terminology

To understand how Index Server works, you need to become familiar with the Index Server concepts and terms described in the following list:

➤ **Corpus** The collection of all documents that Index Server is configured to monitor and index.

➤ **Content filters** The file format-specific add-ons that enable Index Server to index contents of non-Microsoft documents.

➤ **Word breaker** A software tool that takes the stream of characters emitted by a content filter and breaks it into words based on known language-dependent syntax and structure rules.

➤ **Normalizer** A software tool that standardizes words produced by a word breaker. Standardization includes removing capitalization, plurality, and punctuation. In addition, the normalizer identifies and removes noise words from the index.

➤ **Noise word list** A *noise word* is a language-specific word with no useful content that is not stored in the index. "The," "a," "of," and "you" are common English noise words. Index Server maintains a customizable list of noise words that can be used to fine-tune data stored in the index. The list of noise words is stored in \Winnt\System32\NOISE.ENU.

➤ **Index** The database of all remaining words extracted from the corpus after it has been handled by the content filters, word breakers, normalizers, and noise word filters. Index Server uses two types of indexes. The first is a *word list*, which is the list of non-noise words and relevant properties extracted from a document. This list exists only in memory, so all word lists are lost if the server loses power; however, the next time Index Server is active, the word lists will be rebuilt. The second is a *persistent index* or *shadow index*, which is the combination of one or more word lists located on a file stored on the hard drive. The process of moving word lists into shadow indexes is known as a *shadow merge*. Because they are stored on the hard disk, shadow indexes can survive a power loss or a system reboot.

➤ **Master index or catalog** Created when all current shadow indexes and the current master index are integrated into a new master index; there's never more than one master index. Index Server attempts to move all word lists into shadow indexes, and all shadow indexes into the master index. When Index Server "catches up" on all new items, there will be only the master index. The user is unaware of any multiple word lists and shadow indexes that may exist in addition to the master index because all queries are processed against all indexes—from word list, to shadow index, to master index.

Running Index Server

Index Server is installed through the Option Pack installation wizard; you select the languages for which to install support as a subcomponent of Index Server. During the installation process, you'll be prompted for the location in which to store the catalog directory. The catalog is the highest level of content organization within Index Server. Because the CATALOG.WCI file created by Index Server in the catalog directory can be as large as 40 percent of the corpus (all indexed documents), you need to point the installation wizard to a location with significant free space.

During installation, the following items are added:

➤ Sample query documents and script files are copied to \InetPub\Iissamples (http://localhost/iissamples/)

➤ Administration files are copied to \Winnt\System32\Inetsrv\Iisadmin\Isadmin (http://localhost/iisadmin/isadmin/)

➤ Documentation is copied to \Winnt\Help\Ix (http://localhost/iishelp/ix)

Once the installation is complete, Index Server starts indexing all the local and virtual default IIS directories. Index Server remains active in memory until the Content Index service is stopped or the machine is powered down. Index Server is launched when the first query is initiated, not when IIS is launched; Index Server can continue to update indexes even when all IIS-hosted sites are stopped. To stop or pause Index Server, use the Services applet in the Control Panel. Select the Content Index service to start, stop, or pause the service.

Each Web site hosted by Index Server can be configured so that it has its own unique master index; however, queries cannot span multiple indexes. If you divide your hosted Web sites into multiple Index Server master indexes, you limit the user's ability to search multiple Web sites with a single query.

The Index Server's indexing process allows the application to operate without an administrator. The indexing process begins when a new file is added to the corpus or an existing file is changed and these systems are recognized by the Content Index service scanning process. The Content Index service, or CISVC.EXE, scans the known corpus at a regular interval that's defined by the HKEY_LOCAL_MACHINE\SYSTEM\CurrentControlSet\Control\ ContentIndex\ForceNetPathScanInterval Registry entry. This default value for this interval is 120 seconds.

Index Server performs a full scan the first time it scans a directory. After that, a full scan is necessary only if a catastrophic failure damages the master index; only an incremental scan is necessary to index new or changed items. An administrator can force a full scan through the Index Server MMC snap-in or the HTML Administration tool.

Index Server Queries

A query or search is performed by means of a Web form. A form submits a query to Index Server using Standardized Query Language (SQL). Index Server can use simple standard HTML forms or complex ASP or SQL forms. Here are some important points concerning the Index Server query language:

➤ It supports Boolean operators: **AND, OR**, and **NOT**.

➤ It supports the proximity operator: **NEAR**.

➤ It is case-insensitive.

➤ It supports wildcards: *frag**.

➤ It supports stem roots: *stem***.

➤ It ignores punctuation.

➤ It ignores noise words except those in phrases enclosed with double quotes.

➤ It supports free-text queries (phrases proceeded by $).

➤ It supports properties searches (property operator value; for example, size < 1024).

Query controls can be entered manually or included as part of the Web form to simplify user interaction. The actual resolution of a query involves three files—form, IDQ, and HTX. The form can be a standard HTML file (.HTM, .HTML) or an ASP file (.ASP). The IDQ (Internet Data Query) file specifies how the query is to be processed. The HTX (or .HTML extension) file is used to format query results for presentation back to the user.

HTML Form

As mentioned earlier, the HTML form functions as the interface for initiating queries, and it can be simple or complex. Several examples of HTML forms are included with Index Server. These forms are stored in \InetPub\ Iissamples\Issamples\. You can also design your own forms. Here are the key elements in a form:

```
<FORM ACTION="query.idq" METHOD="GET">
<INPUT TYPE="TEXT" NAME="CiRestriction" SIZE="60" MAXLENGTH="100"
 VALUE=" ">
<INPUT TYPE="SUBMIT" VALUE="Excecute Query">
<INPUT TYPE="RESET" VALUE="Clear">
</FORM>
```

This form simply offers a field in which a query string can be typed. It also offers a Submit button that executes the query. Further details about constructing HTML, ASP forms, and SQL queries can be found in Index Server's online documentation.

The IDQ File

The IDQ file defines a query's parameters, including the scope of the search (which portions of the corpus are to be searched), the restrictions of the search (format type, file properties, and so on), and how hits are displayed back to the user (number of records per page, highlighting hits, and so on). A basic IDQ file may contain the following data:

```
[Query]
CiCatalog=d:\
CiColumns=filename,size,rank,characterization,vpath,DocTitle,write
CiRestriction=%CiRestriction%
CiMaxRecordsInResultSet=150
CiMaxRecordsPerPage=10
CiScope=/
CiFlags=DEEP
CiTemplate=/iisamples/issamples/query.htx
CiSort=rank[d]
CiForceUseCi=true
```

The following items contained in an IDQ file each have a specific function, as described in the list:

➤ **[Query]** Identifies the following items as query restrictions.

➤ **CiCatalog=d:** Defines which master index to use.

➤ **CiColumns=filename,size,rank,characterization,vpath, DocTitle, write** Determines what types of information are returned for each document hit.

➤ **CiRestriction=%CiRestriction**% A variable placeholder for the query string from the HTML form.

➤ **CiMaxRecordsInResultSet=150** Sets the maximum number of returned results.

➤ **CiMaxRecordsPerPage=10** Sets the maximum number of returned results per page.

➤ **CiScope=/** Sets the level or virtual directory within the corpus to restrict the query.

➤ **CiFlags=DEEP** Sets the query to search all subfolders of the scope.

➤ **CiTemplate=/iisamples/issamples/query.htx** Defines the template file to use to format the results.

➤ **CiSort=rank[d]** Sets the results sort method (descending in this case).

Note: Further details about customizing IDQ files can be found in Index Server's online documentation.

The HTX File

The HTX file is used to format query results into HTML to be displayed in the user's Web browser. An HTX file defines the layout of each result record, the navigation among multiple returned pages, and the footer of the result's documents. The following code is a header definition from an HTX file:

```
<%if CiMatchedRecordCount eq 0%>
<H4>No documents matched the query "<%CiRestrictionHTML%>".</H4>
<%else%>
<H4>Documents <%CiFirstRecordNumber%> to <%CiLastRecordNumber%> of
<%if CiMatchedRecordCount eq CiMaxRecordsInResultSet%> the first
<%endif%>
<%CiMatchedRecordCount%> matching the query
<%CiRestrictionHTML%>".</H4>
<%endif%>
```

If the search phrase "network segment" is used, this code will return:

```
Documents 1 to 10 of the first 150 matching the query "network segment".
```

For more information about HTX files, consult Index Server's online documentation.

Administering An Index

Index Server administration takes place through either the Index Server MMC snap-in or the HTML Administration interface.

The MMC snap-in (see Figure 9.1) offers you basic status information about each defined corpus. The status items include the size of the master index, the number of documents in the corpus, the number of memory-resident word lists, and the number of persistent indexes. Selecting the Directories item under a catalog allows you to view the virtual roots that comprise a particular corpus. Selecting the Properties item under a catalog allows you to view the indexed properties and which of these properties is stored in cache.

You can add new catalogs by selecting Index Server On Local Machine in the left pane and then issuing the command Action|New|Catalog. You'll be prompted for a name and a location in which to store the catalog.

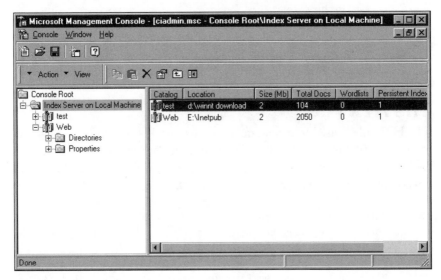

Figure 9.1 MMC with Index Server snap-in.

You can add directories to control the scope of a corpus, with an option to include or exclude the added directory from the indexing process. New directories are added by selecting the Directories item below a catalog and then issuing the command Action|New|Directory. You'll be prompted for the path, an alias, a user account and password (if required) for access, and you'll be asked whether to include or exclude the directory from the corpus.

You can modify the global generation properties for all catalogs by selecting Index Server On Local Machine and issuing the command Action|Properties. The global generation options allow you to decide whether to filter files with unknown extensions, whether to generate characterizations (abstracts and summaries), and to establish the maximum size of the summaries in characters. These settings are also available on a catalog level; any changes made on the Generation tab of a catalog's Properties dialog override the global settings.

A catalog's Properties dialog is accessed by selecting a catalog and then issuing the Action|Properties command, and it also offers a Web tab that enables you to turn off automatic indexing of virtual roots based on a virtual server and to determine whether to track NNTP messages.

If you make a change to Index Server—such as changing the characterization or adding or removing a filter—you can force a rescan of the corpus on a per-directory basis. First, select Directories below a catalog and then select one of the listed directories from the right pane. Issue the Action|Rescan command and then choose Yes for a full rescan (choosing No results in an incremental rescan).

 You can force a merge of all word lists to shadow indexes to the master index on a per-catalog basis. First, select the catalog and then issue the Action|Merge command.

The HTML Administration interface is mainly to be used as a remote status monitor and to force merges, and it offers a slightly different set of administration features. As shown in Figure 9.2, this interface offers four main controls or selections:

➤ Index Statistics

➤ Unfiltered Documents

➤ Virtual Root Data

➤ Merge Index

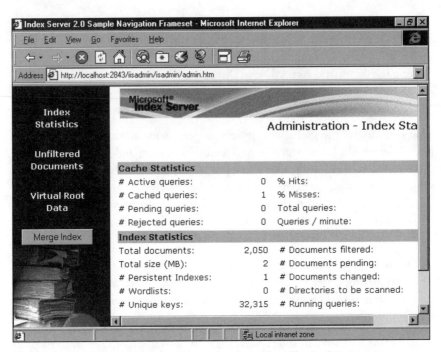

Figure 9.2 The HTML Administration interface for Index Server.

Index Statistics displays cache and index statistics, as well as the status of the indexing process. Unfiltered Documents lists information about unfiltered documents. Virtual Root Data allows you to set the type of scan to perform on a per-directory basis. Once changes to the scan type are submitted, the Merge Index button will instruct Index Server to rescan based on the settings made on the Virtual Root Data page.

Index Server Security

When Index Server is first installed, the location of the initial catalog is securely set up; Index Server defines the Access Control List (ACL) on the catalog directory and defines its contents so that access is restricted to the system and administrators. This prevents users from accessing the catalog directly or attempting to decipher a catalog's contents. If additional catalogs are created elsewhere on the system, be sure that the correct ACLs are defined for the catalogs. Because Index Server runs as a service, additional catalog directories should be set so the system and administrators have Full Control access.

Index Server's filtering process retains the ACLs in the index. When a user performs a query, his or her access credentials are checked against the ACLs stored for each document. If a user does not have proper permissions, Index

Server will not return that document as an item in the query results. Users with valid accounts, other than anonymous, should properly authenticate with their user name and password before issuing queries.

There are three possible situations under which a particular document will not be returned as an item in the results of a query:

➤ The user failed to authenticate before issuing a query

➤ The user does not have at least Read access to the document

➤ The document is outside the corpus of the catalog used in the query.

If authentication is required to gain access to most documents on your particular system, incorporate authentication into your query form by adding a name and password field. These data items can be used during the query process to authenticate a user when the query is submitted. However, it's recommended that this be used only in circumstances where SSL communications are taking place to ensure the integrity of the password transmission.

Index Server Performance Monitoring

You can monitor the performance of Index Server via one of two methods. You can use the Windows NT Performance Monitor utility to watch counters from the Content Index objects, or you can use an IDA script and an HTX template. The Index Statistics selection of the HTML Administration tool uses the IDA and HTX method. The Performance Monitor method gives you real-time information and a graphical display. The IDA method updates only when refreshed and allows remote monitoring.

For details on the contents and syntax of performance monitoring IDA and HTX files, consult Index Server's online documentation.

Exam Prep Questions

Question 1

> You want to create a new Index Server catalog for a Web site. The
> corpus of the Web site is 500MB. How much space will be re-
> quired by the catalog?
>
> ○ a. 100MB
>
> ○ b. 200MB
>
> ○ c. 500MB
>
> ○ d. 800MB

The index catalog is typically 40 percent of the corpus, so 200MB is required
in this scenario. Therefore, answer b is correct.

Question 2

> How many Index Server catalogs can be selected for searching
> from a single query?
>
> ○ a. 1
>
> ○ b. 2
>
> ○ c. 10
>
> ○ d. Unlimited

Only a single catalog can be searched per query. Therefore, answer a is correct.

Question 3

> Which do you use to monitor the performance of Index Server?
> [Check all correct answers]
>
> ❑ a. Index Server MMC snap-in
>
> ❑ b. Performance Monitor
>
> ❑ c. Server Manager
>
> ❑ d. Use an IDA script

You can monitor Index Server's performance via the Performance Monitor or
an IDA script. Therefore, answers b and d are correct. The Index Server MMC

snap-in is not used to monitor Index Server's performance, but instead it is used to manage indexed directories and indexes. Therefore, answer a is incorrect. Server Manager is not used in any way with Index Server. Therefore, answer c is incorrect.

Question 4

What Index Server file type is used to format the results from a query?

○ a. HTM

○ b. IDQ

○ c. HTX

○ d. ENU

An HTX is an HTML template extension file that is used to format a query's results. Therefore, answer c is correct. An HTM is an HTML document that usually contains the query form. Therefore, answer a is incorrect. An IDQ is a parameters file used to define the scope and restrictions of a query. Therefore, answer b is incorrect. An ENU is the extension of the noise word list file. Therefore, answer d is incorrect.

Question 5

Which of the following Index Server indexes are stored only in memory?

○ a. Word lists

○ b. Persistent index

○ c. Shadow index

○ d. Master index

Only word lists are stored only in memory. Therefore, answer a is correct. Persistent, shadow, and master indexes are stored on a hard drive. Therefore, answers b, c, and d are incorrect.

Question 6

> The Index Server service is started only when a query is issued by a user.
>
> ○ a. True
>
> ○ b. False

True, Index Server is not launched until a query is initiated. Therefore, answer a is correct.

Question 7

> A user performs a query using an Index Server query form on the office's intranet. The results from his query fail to list the SALES1997.DOC file, which he knows contains the words "April" and "1997." What could be the reason for this? [Check all correct answers]
>
> ❑ a. The user was not authenticated.
>
> ❑ b. The user does not have Read access to the file.
>
> ❑ c. Another user was accessing the document at the time the query was performed.
>
> ❑ d. The file is not included in the corpus.

The nonappearance of a known file in a results list can be the result of a user not being authenticated, a user not having at least Read access, or the file not being part of the corpus. Therefore, answers a, b, and d are correct. Because a query is performed against an index and not the original file, it is not affected by the use status of the document. Therefore, answer c is incorrect.

Question 8

> Which of the following words are most likely to appear in the
> NOISE.ENU file? [Check all correct answers]
>
> ❑ a. and
>
> ❑ b. 7
>
> ❑ c. expensive
>
> ❑ d. which
>
> ❑ e. very
>
> ❑ f. Williams

The words "and," "7," "which," and "very" are most likely to appear in the
NOISE.ENU file. Therefore, answers a, b, d, and e are correct. The words
"expensive" and "Williams" are not likely to appear in the NOISE.ENU file.
Therefore, answers c and f are incorrect.

Question 9

> Your public Web server also hosts a private data area. You have
> configured Index Server to index every document stored on the
> server in both the Web root and the data directory. All the files in
> the data directory are set so that only internal users have Read
> access. If an external user performs a search using a word that
> exists in one or more files from both the Web root and the data
> directory, how will items from the data directory appear in the
> results lists?
>
> ○ a. They will appear without hyperlinks
>
> ○ b. They will appear with authentication fields to gain access
>
> ○ c. They will appear just as any item from the Web root
>
> ○ d. They will not appear, and the external user will be
> unaware of their presence

Items from an ACL restricted directory will not appear in the results list for a
user without proper access privileges. That user will be unaware of the existence of those documents because Index Server will not even show the filename
of restricted items to nonauthorized users. Therefore, answer d is correct. Because Index Server will not display restricted items to unauthorized users in

any way, answers a, b, and c are incorrect. The fact that even when items are included in the index files used by a search to which the current user does not have valid access, these items are not displayed in the results, thus this is a trick question.

Question 10

> How many shadow indexes and master indexes can exist within a single Index Server catalog?
>
> ○ a. One shadow index; sixteen master indexes
>
> ○ b. Sixteen shadow indexes; four master indexes
>
> ○ c. Unlimited shadow indexes; one master index
>
> ○ d. Four shadow indexes; unlimited master indexes

Only one master index can exist within a single catalog, whereas an unlimited number of shadow indexes can exist. Therefore, answer c is correct.

Need To Know More?

 Howell, Nelson, et al: *Using Microsoft Internet Information Server 4.* Que Publishing, Indianapolis, IN, 1997. ISBN 0-7897-1263-6. Chapter 12 discusses Index Server.

 The best overview information for Index Server 2.0 can be found in the "Reviewer's Guide for IIS 4.0." This document can be found on the TechNet CD-ROM or online via the IIS Web area at http://www.microsoft.com/iis/.

 IIS's online documentation, accessed through Start|Programs|Windows NT 4.0 Option Pack|Product Documentation, contains extensive detail on Index Server.

Web Site Management And Analysis

Terms you'll need to understand:

- √ Content Analyzer
- √ Cookie
- √ Hits/requests/visits/users/ organizations
- √ Inference algorithm
- √ Report Writer
- √ Robot, spider, Robot protocol
- √ Site Server Express
- √ Usage Import
- √ W3C extended log file format
- √ Web maps (tree and cyberbolic views)

Techniques you'll need to master:

- √ Automating log imports, database filters, and reports with Usage Import
- √ Creating Web site reports with Report Writer
- √ Filtering and importing log files
- √ Organizing data on site structure with quick searches and site summary reports
- √ Setting log parameters on IIS
- √ Using Content Analyzer to examine the structure of a Web site
- √ Using spiders to test links

Web sites are becoming increasingly complex. To examine Web site performance, a hit count is not enough. With the right tools, it's possible to maintain a Web site as well as to collect profiles of Web site users. Microsoft developed the Site Server utilities (Site Server Express, Site Server, Site Server Enterprise) to address this need.

Microsoft makes it relatively easy to install Site Server Express with IIS 4.0, both of which are included in the Windows NT 4 Option Pack 3. Although Site Server Express is the least functional member of the Site Server series, it's still a marvelous tool for identifying everything on a Web site, from bottlenecks to user habits.

Site Server Express includes three major tools: Content Analyzer, Usage Import, and Report Writer. Content Analyzer maps and tests the integrity of the Web site. Usage Import brings Web site logs into a database, which can then be refined by Report Writer into any number of formats. The calculation, filtering, and report generation functions of Usage Import and Report Writer can be set up and run on a preset schedule.

Content Analyzer: Explored And Explained

Site Server Express Content Analyzer is a fantastic tool used to visualize what is and is not working on a Web site. It eases the burden of managing a large number of pages, resources, and links. Its tree structure and cyberbolic views are customized ways to visualize site structure. Its preformatted reports highlight various problems, from broken Web links to pages big enough to annoy typical modem users.

Web Maps

A Web site is more than just a series of linked pages. The other objects in a Web page, such as images and Java applets, require more memory and download time than a text-only Web page. Content Analyzer organizes these components in two ways—the tree and cyberbolic views. The level of detail can be customized through the View|Display Options menu.

Content Analyzer begins with a visual representation of a Web site. At a minimum, each view shows Web pages and their links. Other significant objects can be added through the View|Display Options menu. General properties of each object are then available through the Object Properties option of the View menu.

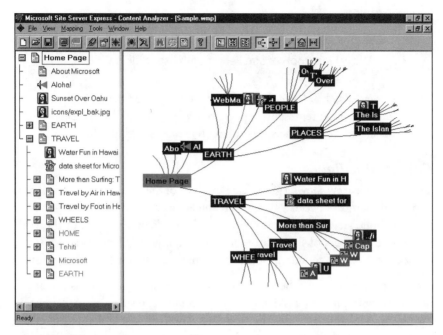

Figure 10.1   A sample Web map: tree and cyberbolic views.

Tree View

As shown in Figure 10.1, the tree view was designed to look like the directory pane of NT Explorer. Starting at the home page, every object that is a part of the home page is directly linked one level below it. Each page with links is like a directory that contains subdirectories and files in NT Explorer.

There are four different control icons associated with each page—the plus, minus, question, and robot icons. The plus and minus icons work the same way as they do in Explorer: If a plus sign is next to a Web page, you can click it and view more detail about that page. Conversely, the minus icon condenses the view. The question icon indicates a page for which the Content Analyzer has not yet explored the links.

The robot icon is shown next to pages in which the Robot protocol is active. Generally, the Robot protocol stops the Content Analyzer Explore Site and Verify Links tools from checking links on or beyond that page. Details of these two commands are included in the subsection on tools.

The difference between robots and the Robot protocol can be confusing. It's important to remember that the Robot protocol stops robots. A robot, also called a *spider*, is an automated tool used to explore links. In the General tab of the Mapping Options dialog, the Content Analyzer default is set to Honor Robot Protocol, which prevents robots from checking the page. The Explore Site and Verify Links tools of Site Server both use spiders.

The tree view also has object icons. They are rather self-explanatory. For example, the page icon represents a page in a Web site, the Mona Lisa picture represents an image, and the speaker icon represents an audio file.

Cyberbolic View

The cyberbolic view shows a graphical flowchart of the Web site. At first glance, it looks like a mix between a spider web and an overgrown bush. The power of the cyberbolic view is in how it shows the demands on each part of the Web site. Large numbers of links can represent potential bottlenecks and a small number of links can represent objects that may be difficult for a user to find.

Maneuvering around a cyberbolic view of a Web site is as easy as moving a mouse. As with program taskbars, a cursor over an icon shows the full name of the object. A left-click focuses the view on the links closest to that object in the Web site. A left-click and drag on the object changes perspectives relative to other objects linked to that page.

Functions

Content Analyzer may be customized through the Program Options menu (see Figure 10.2). The default browser is set in the General tab. Proxies that contain the structure of the Web site are specified or bypassed in the Proxy tab.

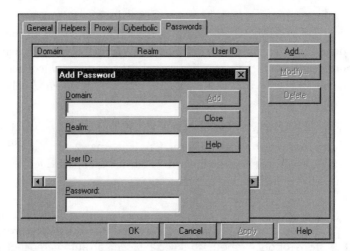

Figure 10.2 Content Analyzer program options: setup for password-protected areas.

The Cyberbolic tab adjusts how this view moves in response to mouse commands. In the Passwords tab area, domain and user IDs are set to allow Content Analyzer to search through restricted areas of a site. (The Helpers tab is not active in Site Server Express.)

Tools

Content Analyzer includes several important tools to help you search through a Web site to verify objects, Uniform Resource Locators (URLs), and links as far as you can go within or outside a site:

➤ **Mapping Options** Sets the defaults for searches by the Content Analyzer spider through the site and through links to other sites. Search engines use spiders to glean content from new areas of the Internet.

➤ **Site Statistics** Creates a quick visual count of what the spider has found, inside and outside of a Web site. Site Statistics counts include relevant objects such as pages, links, images, Web maps, gateways, Internet services, Java applets, application calls, and audio, video, and text files.

➤ **Mapping|Explore Site Command** Sends the spider to get URLs through as many pages and/or levels as set for that particular search. A spider does not connect to a link any faster than you do; therefore, calling too many Web pages via the Internet may create performance problems. When this command is complete, unverifiable links are highlighted in red in both the tree and cyberbolic views.

➤ **Mapping|Verify Links Command** Checks the status of all links (or just the broken links) internal and/or external to the site. When complete, all unverifiable links turn red in both the tree and cyberbolic views.

Site Summary Reports

The Site Summary report is a big picture snapshot of the Web site that takes data from wherever the Content Analyzer spider has searched. Components include statistics on the major Web site objects, collected into an easy-to-read HTML-formatted file. A sample Site Summary report is shown in Figure 10.3.

Quick Search

Content Analyzer includes a number of quick search tools. These searches go one step further than the summary report. They specify everything needed to get to the Web page with the problem. The different searches (listed in Table 10.1) include some of the key criteria needed to determine if a Web site is working properly.

Object Statistics			Status Summary			Map Statistics	
Type	**Count**	**Size**		**Objects**	**Links**	**Map Date**	Mar 21 11:16 1998
Pages	62	47325	Onsite	62	177	Levels	7
Images	26	711579	OK	2	25	Avg Links/Page	3
Gateways	0	N/A	Not Found (404)	0	0		
Internet	0	N/A	Other Errors	61	153	**Server Summary**	
Java	0	0	Unverified	0	0	Domain:	site-analyst.backoffice.microsoft.com
Applications	3	55299				Server Version:	Microsoft-IIS/4.0
Audio	3	595320	Offsite	34	34	HTTP Version:	1.1
Video	0	0	OK	0	0		
Text	0	0	Not Found (404)	0	0		
WebMaps	5	529712	Other Errors	34	34		
Other Media	0	0	Unverified	0	0		
Totals	99	1939235	Totals	99	214		

Figure 10.3 The Site Server Express Site Summary report.

A more comprehensive analysis of the Web site requires the tools and filters included with Usage Import and Report Writer.

Table 10.1 Content Analyzer quick search tools.

Quick Search	Searches For
Home Site Object	Objects in the same domain as the home page.
Images Without ALT	Images without the HTML **<ALT>** label. Not usable by text browsers.
Load Size Over 32K	Web pages (including inline images, and so on) with more than 32K of data.
Non-Home Site Objects	Pages and resources on a different domain than the site's home page.
Not Found Objects (404)	Pages and resources that could not be found (also know as an "HTTP 404 file not found" error).
Unavailable Objects	Pages and resources that could not be reached, including all searches that return "HTTP 404 file not found," "server down (502)," and "object is password protected (401)" errors.
Unverified Objects	Pages and resources for which links have been found, but where the Content Analyzer has not searched.

Usage Import And Report Writer: Explored And Explained

When boiled down to their essence, Usage Import and Report Writer are a series of filters and algorithms. Usage Import reads in log files from Internet servers, such as IIS 4.0, into a relational database. Report Writer uses a series of filters to provide statistics on everything from browser profiles to a geographical distribution of users. All these tasks can be set to extrapolate and filter logs and databases, as well as create reports on a regular basis.

Log Files

The Microsoft Management Console (MMC) is the tool for setting up and administering Web servers and Web sites under IIS 4.0. In MMC, log files are set up in the properties page of each IIS Web site. Among the available choices for logging, the emerging standard is the World Wide Web Consortium (W3C) extended logging format.

Also required in the properties page is the HYPEREXT_LOG.DLL ISAPI filter. This filter adds logging capabilities for Referrer and User Agent to IIS (see Table 10.2 for a description of these categories). Although HYPEREXT_LOG.DLL is not included in the Option Pack, it can be downloaded from the Microsoft Web site.

Table 10.2 Usage import database categories.		
Database	**Description**	**W3C Extended Category Logging Property**
Internet address	To and from Internet address (IP address or host name)	Client IP Address
Time stamp	Date and time of server response	Date, Time
File name	File name or URL sent to the client IP address	URI Query, URI Stem
User name	User name used to log in to a site requiring registration	User Name
Size	Size of response in bytes	Bytes Sent
User agent	Browser name, version, security level	User Agent

(continued)

Table 10.2   Usage import database categories _(continued)_.

Database	Description	W3C Extended Category Logging Property
Referrer	The page (URL) from where the user linked to your site	Referrer
Cookie	User ID code allows tracking through multiple visits	Cookie
HTTP code	The HTTP code (200, 304, or 302) for a request	Http Status
Site type	The type of Internet site (Web, Gopher, FTP)	Protocol Version
Server IP	The IP address of the individual server doing the logging	Server IP

For a log file to be compatible with Site Server Express, Open Database Connectivity (ODBC) 2.5 or higher must be installed on the NT Server.

The W3C extended logging format can collect considerable detail on every hit to a Web site. Several of these options (shown in Figure 10.4) work well with Site Server Express. With this much potential data, the performance penalty from collecting every detail in an IIS log file could be serious. It's important to keep the data requirements for each hit to a minimum.

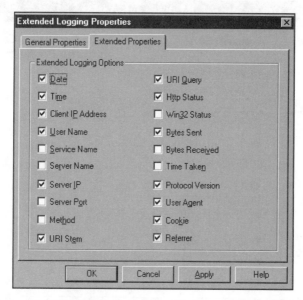

Figure 10.4   IIS 4.0 W3C extended log file format: Extended Properties.

In the following section, we examine how Usage Import brings log data into a database. As shown in Table 10.2, there are a number of important categories. Each of these categories can be associated with W3C Extended Properties logging fields. Most of these associations are fairly straightforward.

Importing Log Files

Log files can be imported from different Web sites. Each IIS Web site is associated with a server. The Usage Import Server Manager tool allows proper identification of all log files. In Server Manager, each log file source is associated with a server and site. If logs are being imported from more than one server, their IP addresses are also used. Sites are uniquely identified through their URL. All logs require the applicable server default pages (usually DEFAULT.HTM and DEFAULT.ASP).

> *Note: The Usage Import Server Manager tool is not the NT 4.0 Administrative Server Manager.*

Some of the larger Web sites have mirror sites in different time zones. When importing logs from different physical locations of the same site, it's important to synchronize these logs to one time zone. This is done by establishing a server's time zone through the hosting facility settings of the server's properties.

The Usage Import Log File Manager coordinates the different log files that make up the Usage Import database. Normally, IIS log files are created on a regular (daily or weekly) basis. With the Scheduling tool, these log files can be imported and processed automatically on a regular schedule.

Inference Algorithms

Usage Import uses *inference algorithms* to extrapolate some basic properties. Essentially, an inference algorithm is a statistical correction factor for situations, such as hits, that are not recorded due to proxy server caching. Usage Import applies inference algorithms to five categories of data:

➤ **Hits** Any line in a log file is a *hit*. Every request for content creates a hit. For example, a request to a page with five pictures creates six total hits. Even search errors such as the "HTTP 404 file not found" error are recorded as hits. The inference algorithms adjust hit counts. For example, the inference algorithm makes sure that one page does not look more popular just because it has twice the number of pictures.

➤ **Requests** Any hit that successfully retrieves content is a *request*. However, some requests never get logged. Browsers, gateways, and proxy servers have caches that send the data to the user without the Web site ever getting the request. The inference algorithms provide correction factors that more accurately reflect the popularity of the page.

➤ **Visits** Because TCP/IP uses discrete packets, it's not possible to calibrate the start and stop of a visit with the start and stop of data transfer. To determine the duration of a visit, the inference algorithm sorts requests based on IP address, user name, user agent (browser type), cookie data, and a preset "timeout" period (default is 30 minutes).

➤ **User** Within a TCP/IP packet, the one way to uniquely identify the user is through the source IP address. However, the way TCP/IP is set up, there are not enough IP addresses to uniquely identify all users. *Cookies* were developed to address this problem. A cookie is a marker downloaded to a PC that identifies a specific user to a Web site. However, with the use of proxy servers, gateways (firewalls) and anti-cookie software, not all cookies make it to user PCs.

➤ **Organization** Loosely, an *organization* is any group that connects its users to the Internet (for example, microsoft.com). By definition, IP addresses have four octets of binary digits. If the IP address cannot be resolved to an organization name, the first three octets of the IP address are designated as the organization.

Filters

It may be useful to apply a few more filters in the log file import process. In the Usage Import process, filtering is a balancing act between quality of the information and server performance. The following is a brief description of the Import Options tabs (see Figure 10.5):

➤ **Import** Although database indexes can slow the import, they take time to reconstruct for larger log files. Excluding spiders eliminates hits from the spiders shown under the Spider List tab.

➤ **Default Directories** Logs are imported from this directory.

➤ **Spider List** The list of spiders that won't have their hits counted.

➤ **IP Resolution** Includes caching and timeout options to optimize IP-to-host name resolution. Caches generally include the most common host name addresses.

➤ **IP Servers** Specifies domain and proxy servers best able to manage host name (DNS) and Whois query resolution.

Figure 10.5   Usage Import Options menu: sample list of spiders.

➤ **Log File Overlaps and Log File Rotation** Log files are generally made for a set time period (for example, noon to 11:59 A.M.). These settings address what to do with data from visits that overlap multiple logs.

There are three special filters: HTML Title, IP Address Resolution, and Whois Organization lookups. Because these are resource-intensive operations, use these filters only if and when necessary. Briefly, their functions are as follows:

➤ **HTML title lookup** Pulls the words associated with the HTML <TITLE> tag on each page.

➤ **IP address resolution** Looks for host names associated with IP addresses.

 Be careful! For Site Server, IP address resolution is essentially the same as a reverse DNS lookup. In some TCP/IP books, IP address resolution is the Address Resolution Protocol (ARP). IP address resolution in Usage Import has nothing to do with ARP!

➤ **Whois organization lookups** Identifies organizations associated with host names after IP address resolution.

Usage Import collects log data from a number of servers and time periods into a single database. In general, the size of a daily log file from a business Web site is anywhere from 150K to 1GB (for the most heavily used commercial sites).

Databases are usually a collection of logs from a number of days. It generally pays to compact the database on a regular basis.

Reports

Site Server Express Report Writer is a versatile way to mine information from the Usage Import database. With the right types of logs from IIS 4.0, reports can be generated on anything from how users navigate through your site to identifying the sites from where they came.

Report Writer is essentially another series of filters, but this time on the database assembled in the Usage Import utility. When Report Writer is opened, the user is given a series of prompts and options, similar to a program setup wizard. Before we get into an actual report, here are the main steps:

1. When Report Writer is opened, the first step is to select the desired report, either from a preset list (see Table 10.3) or from previously customized report filters. If there's more than one database (for example, if there are multiple Web sites), Report Writer adds this step to allow a choice on the database(s) to be used.

Table 10.3 Preformatted reports.	
Report Type	**Description**
Executive Summary	Top-level activity report. Requires Usage Import IP filters.
Bandwidth Report	Byte transfer loading averages and peaks. Key for network planning.
Browser/OS	Shows browser/operating system market share. Can be used to customize Web sites.
Geography	Correlates users by city, U.S. state/Canadian province, and country. Useful not only for market customization but also may show the need for a mirror site. Requires IP filters.
Hits	Shows server hits on an hourly, daily, and weekly basis.
Organization	This report identifies the domain origins of your Web site visitors. Requires Usage Import IP resolution and Whois queries.
Path	Summarizes how users navigate through the Web site. Helps highlight changes that can optimize Web site structure. Requires HTML **<TITLE>** lookups.
Referrer	Statistics on sites where users are coming from. Helps evaluate effectiveness of ads. Requires referrer data and IP resolution in server log files.

(continued)

Table 10.3   Preformatted reports *(continued)*.

Report Type	Description
Request	Popularity of different Web site documents. Requires HTML **<TITLE>** lookups.
User	Trends for user visits and frequency. Requires user registration or cookie data.
Visits Detail	Visits on an hourly, daily, and weekly basis.

2. The next step is to filter the database(s) for the desired time period (see Figure 10.6). Include/exclude filters can be added for the database. Some care is required; for example, it would not be a good idea to filter a database to use only information from March 23, 1998 and then to exclude all information from the week of March 22, 1998.

Note: For more information on Boolean filters, see Chapter 10 of MCSE NT Server 4 in the Enterprise Exam Cram *(ISBN 1-57610-191-6), also published by Certification Insider Press.*

3. Output properties (usually in the Row Dimensions) can be changed in the Report Request Detail. For example, one default property in the Geography report is to show the top 15 user origin cities in the U.S. Double-clicking the "cities" block allows you to adjust the number of

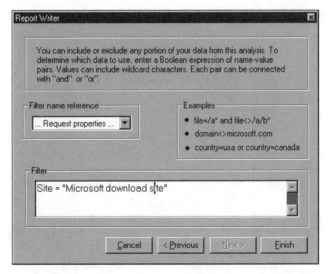

Figure 10.6   Example of Boolean expression database filtering.

cities listed. In a similar fashion, the appearance properties of the report can also be changed; fonts can be added, cell sizes can be changed, and colors can be revised.

4. When adjustments are complete, the Create Report Document command of the File menu allows you to choose output file formats. The default format is HTML. If MS Word and Excel are installed, reports can also be formatted for these programs.

5. Once everything is ready, you are not prompted. The command to finally generate the report is File|Create Report Document. To save what was customized, the command is File|Save Report Definition.

Scheduler

The Scheduler is a common linked component of both Usage Import and Report Writer. Seven basic tasks are associated with the Scheduler. These tasks can carry out the functions of both Usage Import and Report Writer. The Scheduler can be set to schedule jobs to automate task execution. Figure 10.7 shows the sequence of the tasks available through the Scheduler. Although not significant, here is the sequence of tasks:

➤ **Analysis** Because this task creates the output from the Report Writer, it should come after any other task that processes data for a report.

➤ **Compact database** This is a good task to do on a regular basis. Because Compact Database is resource-intensive, it's a good idea to set this function up to run after the analysis.

Figure 10.7 Task sequence in the Scheduler.

➤ **Delete** All filtering from Usage Import and Report Writer can be made part of this function with the help of Boolean expressions.

➤ **Import** For log files. Normally, this will be at the top of the task list.

➤ **IP resolution** As explained before, this is similar to a reverse DNS lookup. Do not confuse this with the TCP/IP ARP.

➤ **Title lookups** As described earlier, draws data from the HTML <TITLE> tags in each Web page.

➤ **Whois organizations** Lookup for organizational names.

Exam Prep Questions

Question 1

Which views are available in the Site Server Express Content Analyzer? [Check all correct answers]

❏ a. Orthogonal

❏ b. Tree

❏ c. Cyberbolic

❏ d. Visual

❏ e. Web

The correct answers to this question are b and c. The tree and cyberbolic views are the two views available in Site Server Express Content Analyzer. The other answers are not options in Content Analyzer. Therefore, answers a, d, and e are incorrect.

Question 2

As one of several Webmasters for the growing company Web site, you have been asked to publish a Web map. For security reasons, the sales manager has asked you to exclude information from the internal sales servers. The password-protected entry page to the sales server is several levels below the Web site home page. The Honor Robot Protocol box in the General tab of the Mapping Options dialog is not checked. In your Content Analyzer Web map, you see a robot icon at the firewall to the sales server. What do you do to protect the sales server from searches?

○ a. The Robot protocol is bad news in a secure area. If you see the Robot protocol icon where the Web site links to the secured part of the sales server, you need to do whatever is necessary to get rid of this robot; otherwise, the rest of the world will have easy access to your company's confidential sales information.

○ b. When you explore the site, limit the levels explored so that the Content Analyzer spider can't get to the secured area of the sales server.

○ c. Create a separate secure Web site for the sales server. Delete all links from your Web site to the secure area.

○ d. The Robot protocol icon is okay, but you need to make sure that the Honor Robot Protocol checkbox in the General tab of the Mapping Options dialog is checked.

○ e. If you see the Robot protocol icon, it's too late. The secure part of your site has already been penetrated by someone else's spider.

The best answer to this question is d. The Robot protocol, when honored, actually acts as a firewall to the automated Content Analyzer and search engine spiders. This can be confusing, because spiders are actually sometimes known as robots, and the Robot protocol actually stops robots. Therefore, answers a and e are incorrect. Although limiting the levels searched may prevent getting to the secured area entry page, it would also prevent searching through other areas of the site that could also be important. Therefore, answer b is incorrect. Even though it's technically possible to create a separate Web site for the secure sales area, anyone creating a Web page on the main site can create links to the secure area. Without the Robot protocol, the sales area is not as secure as it could be. Therefore, answer c is incorrect.

Question 3

As a busy Webmaster, you would like to automate the process of creating regular reports on the popularity of your Web site. However, you're concerned about the performance of your severely under-powered server. You've already set up the W3C extended log to take the data you need. Which of the following actions can you add to the Scheduler that won't compromise performance on your server?

○ a. Look up HTML titles.

○ b. Resolve IP addresses.

○ c. Perform Whois organization queries.

○ d. All of the above. This is all good information for reports to management.

○ e. None of the above. Each of these actions is performance-intensive on the server.

The best answer to this question is e. HTML title lookup, IP address resolution, and Whois organization queries are all resource-intensive operations and should be avoided whenever possible when performance is an issue. However, if you can find a time of day when demand on this server is low, it's certainly possible to schedule these operations for specific times. It would be helpful to find out when these times are through the appropriate report. However, you don't know what these times are right now. Therefore, answers a, b, c, and d are incorrect.

Question 4

Your manager has asked you for a quick "big picture" review of the Web site. He has heard complaints that there are a number of links at various places in the Web site that "just lead out into space." You are confident that this is not so, but need data to back you up. Which type of report do you need?

○ a. Report Writer Context Detail report

○ b. Report Writer Comprehensive Analysis

○ c. Quick search for broken links and unavailable objects

○ d. Content Analyzer Site Summary report

○ e. Report Writer Cookie report

The best answer is d. The Content Analyzer Site Summary report will give you and your manager a quick big picture view on the status of your Web site, including the required data. A quick search for broken links and unavailable objects will give you quick, detailed information on links that are no longer working and pages and other objects that are no longer available. Because these searches provide heavy detail on each problem link and object, they are not appropriate for an overview of the site. Therefore, answer c is incorrect. Because we're looking for data on specific pages and links on the Web site, Report Writer is not necessary. Besides, the Report Writer options given in answers a, b, and e do not exist, making those answers incorrect.

Question 5

As the Webmaster of the growing company Web site, you're getting a number of complaints from users: pages are too slow to load, text browsers just can't search through your site, and a number of links just end up in space.

You've already used the Verify Links tool. Which type of data can you get on these issues without having to go through the time and trouble of a Usage Import of a log file? [Check all correct answers]

❑   a. Perform a quick search for all images without HTML **<ALT>** tags.

❑   b. Do a quick search for all pages above 32K.

❑   c. Create a Site Summary report.

❑   d. Check the links and HTML tags on each page one by one. There's no other way to be sure what is and isn't working.

The correct answers to this question are a, b, and c. Not everyone has a browser that shows images. When a text-based browser gets to an image without an HTML <ALT> tag, it stops the browser. For test purposes, all pages with more than 32K are too slow to load for all modem users. A Site Summary report is a useful overview of the status of key quick search items on the Web site. Because you've already used the Verify Links tool, broken links will be reported. It isn't necessary to go into a Web page to check all the links. Therefore, answer d is incorrect.

Question 6

Log files in IIS 4.0 are set up by Web site. To use the IIS 4.0 log files, a number of parameters have to be set in Usage Import to match what has been set in the properties of each Web site. Which of the following do these settings include? [Check all correct answers]

❑ a. Default home page

❑ b. Time zone

❑ c. Spider list

❑ d. HTML **<ALT>** tags

❑ e. Domain

The correct answers to this question are a and e. Without the default home page and server domain, Usage Import cannot identify the right database for the site. The time zone is set in Usage Import to make sure that log data from different servers of a Web site, such as a mirror "site" in a different part of the world, is synchronized. By definition, you want times in a site to match their local time zones. Therefore, answer b is incorrect. Spider lists and images without HTML <ALT> tags are not part of the setup for IIS logging. Therefore, answers c and d are not correct.

Question 7

Your supervisor has just read an article that mentioned the power of inference algorithms. She asks you to explain to her what an inference algorithm is and what it has to do with measuring the performance of the Web server. Which of the following would be an accurate description?

○ a. An inference algorithm is a program that uses fuzzy logic to perform tasks such as HTML title lookups and IP address resolution. Because it simplifies the lookup of things such as DNS files, it improves performance of these otherwise high-intensity tasks.

○ b. An inference algorithm is a set of calculations that improves logging speed in IIS. Without it, ODBC logging would be a process that would overcome all but the fastest processors with at least 64MB of memory.

○ c. An inference algorithm works like a statistical correction factor for things such as request data in an ODBC-compliant log file. Without it, Web pages with 100 thumbnail images would appear to be many times more popular than they really are.

○ d. An inference algorithm works like a set of statistical correction factors for things such as IP address resolution and database caching. Without it, database references to cached data would not be possible.

○ e. An inference algorithm is a set of calculations that improves the speed of Site Server Express Report Writer.

The correct answer to this question is c. Without inference algorithms, a Web page with 100 thumbnail images would get 101 hits each time a user links to it, which would make the page seem much more popular than a text-only page that gets only one hit for each time a user links to it. Inference algorithms correct for this discrepancy. However, they only address the data related to hits, requests, visits, users, and organizations. Although IP address resolution is loosely related to organizations, database caching is not an inference algorithm function. Therefore, answer d is incorrect. None of the other answers are related to the function of inference algorithms. Therefore, answers a, b, and e are incorrect.

Question 8

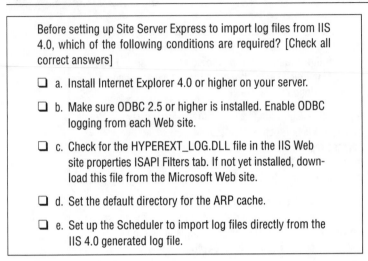

Before setting up Site Server Express to import log files from IIS 4.0, which of the following conditions are required? [Check all correct answers]

❑ a. Install Internet Explorer 4.0 or higher on your server.

❑ b. Make sure ODBC 2.5 or higher is installed. Enable ODBC logging from each Web site.

❑ c. Check for the HYPEREXT_LOG.DLL file in the IIS Web site properties ISAPI Filters tab. If not yet installed, download this file from the Microsoft Web site.

❑ d. Set the default directory for the ARP cache.

❑ e. Set up the Scheduler to import log files directly from the IIS 4.0 generated log file.

The correct answers to this question are b and c. ODBC 2.5 or higher and HYPEREXT_LOG.DLL are prerequisites before IIS will work with Site Server Express. Although Internet Explorer 4.0 is a requirement for installing Site Server Express, you can set a different default browser in the Content Analyzer Program Options dialog's General tab. Therefore, answer a is incorrect. Although IP address resolution in TCP/IP refers to the ARP, it does not apply here. Besides, IP address resolution as a Usage Import filter is completely different from ARP. Therefore, answer d is incorrect. Although the Scheduler can import log files from IIS 4.0, it cannot check for ODBC installation or the HYPEREXT_LOG.DLL filter. Therefore, answer e is incorrect.

Question 9

> You are running a Web site for a winery in the state of Washington. There's a steady stream of users from all over the country who go to your Web site to purchase wines and to get advice on winemaking. You're looking to customize the site to provide the best possible experience for your users. You're even considering the use of a mirror site in Delaware if you can show sufficient demand from the East Coast. Which of the following preformatted Report Writer reports could help you meet this need? [Check all correct answers]
>
> ❑ a. IP Server
>
> ❑ b. Geography
>
> ❑ c. Browser and Operating System
>
> ❑ d. Referrer
>
> ❑ e. Path

The correct answers to this question are b, c, and e. A Geography report will help you determine the distribution of where your users are coming from. Knowing the browser of most of your users will help determine the type of add-ons that are more important for your site (for example, ActiveX for MSIE or Java for Netscape). The Path report shows how your users are navigating through the site, and therefore helps determine whether you need to change the locations and sizes of some pages, images, and other objects to make navigation easier. There is no IP Server report. Therefore, answer a is incorrect. The Referrer report provides data on where users are coming from, meaning what ISP they log in to to gain Internet access. Although this can provide useful data on where your advertising is working best on the Web, this does not address the user experience once he or she has reached your site. Therefore, answer d is incorrect.

Need To Know More?

It's unfortunate that the *Microsoft IIS 4.0 Resource Kit* barely addresses Site Server Express. The best sources of information for Site Server Express are the user guides included with each SSE program. However, be cautious: several areas in the Site Server Express user guides seem to apply to the more functional Site Server versions.

 Amirfaiz, Farhad. *Official Microsoft Site Server 2.0 Enterprise Edition Toolkit,* Microsoft Press, Redmond, WA, 1998. ISBN 1-57231-622-5. Source for full capabilities of the most scalable version of Site Server.

 Muller, John Paul and Tom Sheldon. *The Complete Reference, Microsoft Internet Information Server 4,* Osborne/McGraw-Hill, Berkeley, CA, 1998. ISBN 0-07882-457-5. See Chapter 16 for a brief overview of IIS 4.0 logging as well as Site Server Express Usage Import and Report Writer.

The Other Servers: Transaction, SMTP, And NNTP

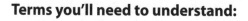

Terms you'll need to understand:

✓ Transactions

✓ SMTP (Simple Mail Transfer Protocol)

✓ Email messages

✓ NNTP (Network News Transfer Protocol)

✓ Discussion groups

✓ UA (user agent)

Techniques you'll need to master:

✓ Examining the capabilities of Transaction Server

✓ Installing and configuring the SMTP service

✓ Installing and configuring the NNTP service

✓ Using SMTP and NNTP services

In this chapter, we discuss the value of adding the servers and services included on the Option Pack with IIS 4.0. Specifically, we briefly investigate Microsoft Transaction Server 2.0, the SMTP service, and the NNTP service. This chapter does not contain details about Certificate Server, Index Server, and Site Server Express Server, because they are covered in other chapters throughout this book.

IIS Components

As discussed in Chapter 2, IIS 4.0 is distributed as part of the Windows NT Option Pack. The Option Pack contains seven distinct software components or applications that can be installed as an integrated whole to provide a wide range of Internet publishing and management capabilities. As Microsoft continues to integrate its products, the division line between one product or service and another becomes fuzzy. In addition to the individually named components on the Option Pack (IIS 4.0, Service Pack 3, Internet Explorer 4.01, Transaction Server 2.0, Message Queue Server Standard Edition, Site Server Express, and Connection Services for Microsoft RAS), there are several other components that are installed with IIS's Web and FTP services. These include Index Server 2.0, Certificate Server 1.0, several data access (database) and development (SDK) components, the SMTP service, the NNTP service, the Microsoft Management Console (MMC), and the Microsoft DNA (Distributed interNet Applications) architecture. It can be argued that these are not strictly IIS components; however, IIS does not function correctly or as flexibly if they are not present.

Each of these components is actually a product in its own right. In your endeavor for IIS certification, there's only a minimal amount of information you need to know about these additional products. However, to deploy and operate these products in the real world, you need to learn considerably more. If you plan on using these products in a production environment, we stress the need for you to read the online documentation and everything else you can find on TechNet regarding these products.

In the following sections, we'll take a look at three of the additional IIS components that ship as part of the Option Pack—Microsoft Transaction Server 2.0, the SMTP service, and the NNTP service.

Transaction Server: Explored And Explained

Microsoft Transaction Server (MTS) 2.0 is a transaction-processing system designed to offer additional robustness, fault tolerance, and programmable extensibility to IIS and Web applications. This Component Object Model (COM) application defines a programming environment in which high performance, scalable enterprise, Internet, and intranet applications can be developed quickly and easily. MTS is less like an application that is used to perform functions but more like a programming model that is used to take advantage of specific features.

The primary benefit of MTS is derived from its support of a three-tiered programming architecture. A three-tiered programming architecture is a system in which the components of an application are positioned in three distinct locations. First, presentation logic and interactive components are placed on the client. Second, the application logic and supporting execution code are placed on the server. Third, data is stored on a dedicated file server or database server. An application developed with this three-tiered approach is often considered to be "server centric," which implies that most of the actual execution or work of the application occurs on the server instead of on the client.

MTS is a great tool and specification for building COM-based applications. MTS offers several benefits, including:

➤ Support of several widely used development tools, including Visual Basic, Visual C++, and Visual J++.

➤ Automatic transaction support.

➤ Role-based security features.

➤ The ability to interface with popular database systems, such as SQL, Sybase, Oracle, and ODBC-compliant databases.

➤ The ability to interact with several message queuing products, such as Microsoft Message Queue Server.

➤ The ability to communicate with mainframe-based applications.

➤ Improved performance with database connection pooling.

➤ Improved fault tolerance with individual virtual machines for process isolation.

➤ The establishment of a runtime environment for server-side execution of applications.

MTS installs several sample applications. These applications can be used as examples or models for building custom MTS applications. The online documentation contains extensive details about the programming specifications, interface properties, and development environments. If you're a programmer planning on developing distributed transactional applications, you'll greatly benefit from reading the online documentation. If you are just pursuing IIS certification, you'll only need a little more information about MTS beyond what's covered in this chapter.

MTS is administered and managed through the MTS Explorer MMC snap-in. You can access this tool through Start|Programs|Windows NT 4.0 Option Pack|Microsoft Transaction Server|Transaction Server Explorer. Through this interface, you can perform several administrative tasks, including the following:

➤ Adding and removing MTS host computers, packages, and applications

➤ Altering package security, shutting down after idle timeout; its operational account and activation type are noted in the alert

➤ Issuing and viewing trace messages to inspect the status of the MS Distributed Transactional Coordinator (MS DTC)

➤ Viewing the current active transactions

➤ Viewing the current and cumulative statistics of transactions

These are only a few of the high-level functions of MTS Explorer. MTS Explorer is a fairly complex and in-depth tool for developing, managing, and operating transactional applications. Most of the functions of MTS Explorer are unintelligible to anyone unfamiliar with this type of programming. Fortunately, knowledge at this level is not required to obtain your IIS certification.

SMTP Service: Explored And Explained

IIS 4.0 includes an SMTP service that enables IIS to route SMTP email messages. The SMTP service does not include a POP3 server; therefore, it cannot deliver messages to POP3 user agents (UAs; also known as *standard email client utilities*). However, it can accept messages from UAs that use SMTP.

The SMTP service allows Web applications to send and receive email messages. In addition, Web server events can trigger email notification to administrators. The SMTP service gives the Web server an email message box in which error messages, user feedback, or undelivered messages can be deposited for manual administrator processing.

The IIS SMTP service is a relay agent for email messages. Messages originating from IIS, sent to IIS by a UA, or routed from another SMTP server can be deposited in a local drop box or forwarded onto other SMTP servers.

The SMTP service is installed as an optional component through the Option Pack setup routine. The only configuration option defined during installation is the location of the Mailroot directory. This directory is where all the messages handled by the SMTP service are stored. This directory cannot be changed without reinstalling the SMTP service. The default location for this directory is in the InetPub directory (C:\InetPub\Mailroot).

Within the Mailroot directory are several other directories, each key to the operation of the SMTP service:

➤ **Badmail** All undeliverable messages that cannot be returned to the sender are saved in this directory with a .BAD extension.

➤ **Drop** All the messages for the domains hosted by IIS are placed in this directory.

➤ **Pickup** Any outgoing messages copied into this directory as a text file are automatically processed.

➤ **Queue** All active messages in the process of being delivered are held in this directory.

➤ **SortTemp** Temporary files are stored in this directory.

When an email message is manually placed into the Pickup directory or when a UA or an SMTP server sends an email message via SMTP to IIS, the message is placed into the Queue directory. The SMTP service then inspects the header of the message. If the header is invalid, the SMTP service attempts to return the message to the sender. If this fails, the message is moved into the Badmail directory. If the header is valid, the SMTP service determines if the destination is local (a domain hosted by IIS) or remote. If it's local, the message is placed in the Drop directory. If it's remote, the SMTP service attempts to forward the message on to the remote destination.

The SMTP service is managed primarily through the same MMC snap-in as IIS (Start|Programs|Windows NT 4.0 Option Pack|Microsoft Internet Information Server|Internet Service Manager). Notice that the node below the IIS computer is named Default SMTP Site. Below this node are Domains and Current Sessions. Domains lists the default domain and all aliased domains for which the SMTP service can receive email. Through a listed domain's Properties menu, you can alter its remote routing, relaying, and security settings. Current Sessions lists the current active connections to the SMTP service.

You can also manage the SMTP service through its HTML interface. It's accessed via the URL http://localhost:port/mail/Smtp/Admin/Default.htm. This interface offers you the same controls and information as the MMC snap-in.

Configuration of the SMTP service is handled through the Properties dialog. This is accessed by selecting the Default SMTP Site node and then issuing the Action|Properties command. Here are the options on the SMTP Site tab of this dialog (see Figure 11.1):

➤ **Description** Enter a name for the site.

➤ **IP Address Of The SMTP Site** Enter the IP address of the site.

➤ **Incoming and Outgoing Connection Parameters** TCP port (the default is 25), limitation of simultaneous connections (the default is No Limit), and connection timeout (the default is 600 seconds).

➤ **Enable Logging** Records SMTP activity in NCSA, ODBC, or W3C extended format.

The Operators tab (shown in Figure 11.2) is where the administrators of the SMTP site are defined. It is a simple, standard, add-user-to-list interface.

The Messages tab (shown in Figure 11.3) is where message parameters are defined:

➤ Size limitations for a single message (default 2048K) and a single session (default 10240K)

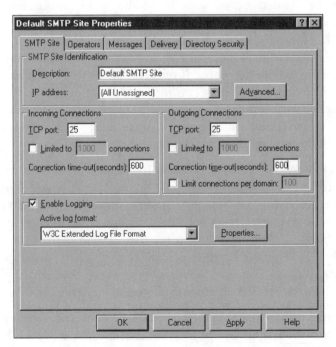

Figure 11.1 The SMTP Site tab of the SMTP Site Properties dialog.

Figure 11.2   The Operators tab of the SMTP Site Properties dialog.

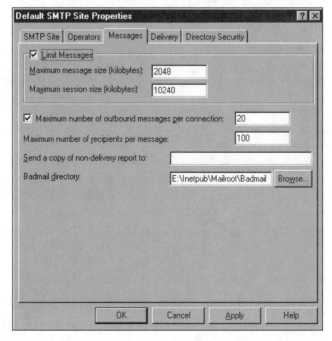

Figure 11.3   The Messages tab of the SMTP Site Properties dialog.

➤ Maximum number of outbound messages per connection (default 20)

➤ Maximum number of recipients per message (default 100)

➤ Email a copy of the nondelivery report to a user

➤ The directory in which to store badmail

The Delivery tab (shown in Figure 11.4) is where the delivery parameters are defined:

➤ **Maximum Retries and Retry Interval (Minutes)** The number of retries (default 48) and retry intervals (default 60 minutes) for both local and remote queues.

➤ **Maximum Hop Count** Maximum number of hops a message can take before reaching another SMTP server and being labeled as nondeliverable.

➤ **Masquerade Domain** The domain to list the email as being sent from.

➤ **Fully Qualified Domain Name** The FQDN for this SMTP server used for message origin identification.

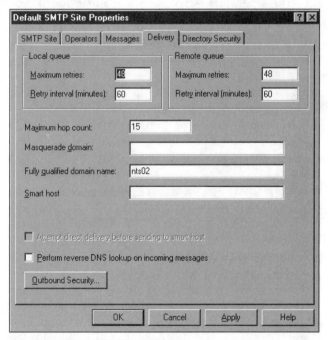

Figure 11.4 The Delivery tab of the SMTP Site Properties dialog.

➤ **Smart Host** Sends all messages to a "smart host" instead of the default delivery route (to another SMTP server).

➤ **Perform Reverse DNS Lookup On Incoming Messages** Performs a reverse DNS lookup on incoming messages to verify their origin.

➤ **Outbound Security** Provides a remote SMTP server with access credentials in the form of a user name and password via clear text or NT Challenge/Response; also, you can turn on Transport Layer Security (TLS) to encrypt messages.

The Directory Security tab is where security for the SMTP service is defined:

➤ **Authentication Methods** The standard control of allowing anonymous access, basic authentication, or NT Challenge/Response to verify users before allowing them to use the SMTP service.

➤ **Secure Communications** The standard control for installing and using certificates. Includes access to the Key Manager.

➤ **IP Address And Domain Name Restrictions** The standard control for granting or denying access to groups, subnets, or individual computers.

➤ **Relay Restrictions** A control similar to IP Address And Domain Name Restrictions, where groups, subnets, or individual computers are allowed or restricted from being allowed to relay email messages through this SMTP server. By default, this privilege is restricted.

NNTP Server: Explored And Explained

IIS 4.0 includes an NNTP service that can be used to host discussion forums. The NNTP service is not a full-featured Usenet newsgroup hosting server—it cannot access Usenet newsfeeds or send messages to Usenet newsfeeds. It's used to host NNTP-compliant discussion forums on a single server that can be accessed by user agents (that is, client software) supporting the NNTP protocol.

The NNTP service is installed as an optional component through the Option Pack setup routine. The setup routine creates an Nntpfile directory under the InetPub directory (C:\InetPub\Nntpfile). This directory stores all the messages handled by the NNTP service.

The NNTP service can be managed through the IIS MMC snap-in or via a Web interface; both tools offer the same controls. The IIS MMC snap-in is accessed by selecting Start|Programs|Windows NT 4.0 Option Pack|Microsoft Internet Information Server|Internet Service Manager. Notice that the node below the IIS computer is named Default NNTP Site. Below this node are the Expiration Policies, Directories, and Current Sessions options. The Expiration Policies option includes rules that define when one or more discussion groups' messages will be automatically deleted. An expiration policy can be based on age in days or size in megabytes. The Directories option is used to spread the storage of discussion group messages across multiple servers. By default, all files are stored within the \InetPub\Nntpfile directory. The Current Sessions option displays the currently active discussion group users.

To access the HTML administration interface for the NNTP service, use a URL with the following construction: http://localhost:port/news/Admin/Default.htm.

Configuration and management of the NNTP service is handled through the service's Properties dialog. This is accessed by selecting the Default NNTP Site node and then issuing the Action|Properties command. The News Site tab (shown in Figure 11.5) is where the following general properties about the NNTP service are set:

➤ Site description, path header, IP address, TCP port (default 119), and SSL port (if secure communications is enabled; default 563)

➤ Number of simultaneous connections (default 5,000) and timeout (600 seconds)

➤ Logging, which records NNTP activity in IIS, NCSA, ODBC, or W3C extended format

The Security Accounts tab (shown in Figure 11.6) is where the NT user account for anonymous access is defined, as well as where the accounts with Administrative access are defined. Both of these settings use the standard Add User dialogs, accessed by clicking the Add button.

The NNTP Settings tab (shown in Figure 11.7) is where NNTP-specific settings are defined:

➤ Enable or disable client posting, with post and connection size limitations

➤ Allow other servers to pull articles from this server

➤ Enable control message processing

➤ Define an SMTP server where all moderated group messages are mailed

➤ Define the aliasing default moderator domain name

➤ Define the administrator's email account

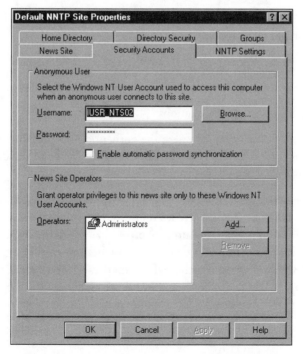

Figure 11.5   The News Site tab of the NNTP Site Properties dialog.

Figure 11.6   The Security Accounts tab of the NNTP Site Properties dialog.

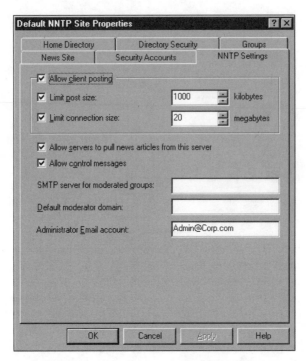

Figure 11.7   The NNTP Settings tab of the NNTP Site Properties dialog.

The Home Directory tab (shown in Figure 11.8) is where the location for message storage is configured:

➤ Define the default storage path locally or to a network share

➤ Restrict posting, restrict visibility, log access, and index new content

➤ Enable SSL-secured transactions

The Directory Security tab is where the authentication methods and IP address and domain name restrictions are defined. These are the standard control interfaces, as seen throughout IIS.

The Groups tab (shown in Figure 11.9) is where newsgroups are created and configured. Newsgroups are created simply by clicking the Create New Newsgroup button. A Newsgroup Properties dialog prompts you for a name and description, and it also asks you to specify whether or not the group is read only and if it's moderated (by the default moderator or by a specified user). Existing group settings can be altered by selecting them in the display list and clicking Edit. This brings up the same Newsgroup Properties dialog box used for new groups.

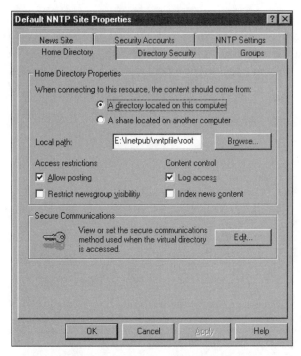

Figure 11.8   The Home Directory tab of the NNTP Site Properties dialog.

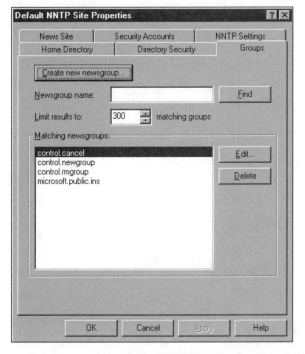

Figure 11.9   The Groups tab of the NNTP Site Properties dialog.

The NNTP service functions automatically, otherwise. Simply point a UA, such as Internet Explorer News and Mail, at the news server (typically by providing the IP address, FQDN, or NetBIOS name). Subscribe to a group; then, read or post messages as you would with any other Internet NNTP server.

Exam Prep Questions

Question 1

> Which IIS component offers programmers the ability to create three-tiered applications for Internet deployment?
>
> ○ a. The NNTP service
>
> ○ b. Transaction Server
>
> ○ c. Certificate Server
>
> ○ d. Index Server

Transaction Server offers programmers the ability to create three-tiered applications for Internet deployment. Therefore, answer b is correct. The NNTP service is used to host discussion groups; Certificate Server allows your site to be a certificate authority; and Index Server offers content indexing and searching. Therefore, answers a, c, and d are incorrect.

Question 2

> Under the SMTP service of IIS, what happens to email messages that cannot be delivered to their intended recipient? [Check all correct answers]
>
> ❑ a. They are sent to a default remote SMTP server.
>
> ❑ b. They are returned to the sender.
>
> ❑ c. They are stored in the local queue.
>
> ❑ d. They are deposited in the Badmail directory.

First, undeliverable email is returned to the sender. If it can't be returned, it's placed in the Badmail directory. Therefore, answers b and d are correct. Undeliverable email is not sent to a remote SMTP server, nor is it stored in the local queue. Therefore, answers a and c are incorrect.

Question 3

> Which of the following measures are used to secure the SMTP
> service of IIS? [Check all correct answers]
>
> ❑ a. SSL identity verification
>
> ❑ b. Windows NT Challenge/Response authentication
>
> ❑ c. Reverse DNS lookup
>
> ❑ d. IP address and domain name restrictions

The SMTP service can be secured using any of these methods. Therefore,
answers a, b, c, and d are correct.

Question 4

> Which directory can serve as a deposit box for email messages
> so that when they're copied or placed in that directory, they are
> automatically processed by the SMTP service?
>
> ○ a. Drop
>
> ○ b. Pickup
>
> ○ c. Queue
>
> ○ d. SortTemp

The Pickup directory serves as an inbox for email messages to be copied. All
files in this directory are automatically processed by the SMTP service. Therefore, answer b is correct. The Drop directory is where all messages directed at
the domains hosted by this SMTP service are stored. Therefore, answer a is
incorrect. Queue is the folder used by the SMTP service that holds all active
messages in the process of being delivered. Therefore, answer c is incorrect.
SortTemp is just a storage folder for temporary files. Therefore, answer d is
incorrect.

Question 5

> By default, email with a remote recipient is automatically forwarded or relayed on to other SMTP servers, no matter where the message originated.
>
> ○ a. True
>
> ○ b. False

False. The SMTP service is configured so that no message relaying to remote SMTP servers occurs. Therefore, answer b is correct. This prevents malicious users from spamming (sending lots of unsolicited, anonymous, untraceable email).

Question 6

> The IIS SMTP service can host multiple user mailboxes, so clients with POP3-compliant user agents (email client software) can retrieve messages.
>
> ○ a. True
>
> ○ b. False

False. The IIS SMTP service does not include POP3 support or the ability to host multiple mailboxes. All mail sent to the SMTP service for the domains hosted by this service is deposited in the Drop folder and must be read with a text editor or a UA that can import text email messages. Therefore, answer b is correct.

Question 7

> The NNTP service of IIS supports which of the following functions or features? [Check all correct answers]
>
> ❑ a. Hosting of multiple discussion groups
>
> ❑ b. Access to standard Usenet newsfeeds
>
> ❑ c. Moderated groups
>
> ❑ d. SSL-secured transmissions

The IIS NNTP service supports multiple discussion groups, moderated groups, and SSL. Therefore, answers a, c, and d are correct. IIS's NNTP service is unable to access Usenet newsfeeds. It's restricted to host discussion groups within a single server. Therefore, answer b is incorrect.

Question 8

Communications over the Web are inherently "sessionless," meaning there is no correlation between one request for a resource and another from the same client. If you want to establish a correlation or at least a tracking mechanism for communications over your Web site for each individual client, which IIS component would you use?

○ a. Microsoft Message Queue Server

○ b. Microsoft Management Console

○ c. Site Server Express

○ d. Microsoft Transaction Server

Microsoft Transaction Server is the IIS component that can enable you to track communications based on the client. Therefore, answer d is correct. MMQS is a distributed application communications system, not a client tracking system. Therefore, answer a is incorrect. MMC is a control interface for all the IIS components. Therefore, answer b is incorrect. Site Server Express is an evaluation and statistics analysis tool for IIS. Therefore, answer c is incorrect.

Question 9

The IIS SMTP and NNTP services can be administered and managed through which utilities or interfaces? [Check all correct answers]

❑ a. Server Manager

❑ b. IIS's MMC snap-in

❑ c. Network Monitor

❑ d. An HTML interface

The IIS SMTP and NNTP services can be administered through the IIS MMC snap-in or through separate HTML interfaces. Therefore, answers b and d are correct. Server Manager and Network Monitor are not used to administer these services. Therefore, answers a and c are incorrect.

Question 10

The IIS NNTP service allows the storage of a discussion group's files on a network share instead of only on the local IIS host computer.

○ a. True

○ b. False

True. Group files can be stored on network shares instead of the local computer to distribute the file storage requirements for large discussion groups across multiple systems in the network. Therefore, answer a is correct.

Need To Know More?

Howell, Nelson, et al. *Using Microsoft Internet Information Server 4.* Que Publishing, Indianapolis, IN, 1997. ISBN 0-7897-1263-6. This book discusses the SMTP service in Chapter 7 and the NNTP service in Chapter 8. There is virtually no mention of Transaction Server in this book.

Very little information about Transaction Server, the SMTP service, and the NNTP service can be found in the Reviewer's Guide for IIS 4.0. This document can be found on the TechNet CD-ROM or online via the IIS Web area (www.microsoft.com/iis/).

IIS's own online documentation, accessed through Start|Programs|Windows NT 4.0 Option Pack|Product Documentation, contains extensive detail on Transaction Server, the SMTP service, and the NNTP service.

Troubleshooting IIS

Terms you'll need to understand:

√ Configuration errors

√ HTTP errors

√ Dependency errors

Techniques you'll need to master:

√ Knowing how to perform systematic troubleshooting

√ Understanding of common configuration errors

√ Understanding of common HTTP errors

√ Knowing how to resolve installation problems

√ Understanding how NT errors can affect IIS

Troubleshooting is a very important aspect of any type of software installation, and Internet Information Server (IIS) 4.0 is certainly no exception. In this chapter, we'll discuss various aspects of troubleshooting the installation, configuration, and operation of IIS 4.0.

General Troubleshooting

Your ability to adapt your knowledge and experience to problems that arise with IIS is a skill that is often innate rather than learned. However, systematic or structured troubleshooting is a reliable method of locating and resolving problems—even if you're not inclined toward technical resolution naturally. A systematic approach to troubleshooting is a philosophy or generalized, step-by-step "how-to" system to aid you in eliminating issues that prevent productive use of your computer system. Here are the standard or minimal steps of this process:

1. Investigate the symptoms.

2. Review previous logs of resolutions.

3. Isolate, identify, and define the problem.

4. Hypothesize resolutions.

5. Test these hypotheses individually.

6. Maintain a log of the resolution process.

Taking the time to understand what is going on and why will often lead you directly to the solution. In addition to intimate knowledge about the setup and configuration of your own system, it's often important to have other documentation and resources available. One such resource that is invaluable to anyone administrating a Microsoft product—especially IIS—is the TechNet CD-ROM. This product is a collection of manuals, resource kits, training materials, technical notes, technical resolution messages, and more, in electronic text format. All this data is combined into a single interface that allows keyword searches across all or part of the text—this single feature makes the TechNet CD-ROM the most valuable resource Microsoft has ever produced. TechNet is a yearly subscription service with a monthly issue/update for about $300 per user. To request a trial issue or to get more information or ordering details, go to www.microsoft.com/technet/.

 You'll need to have a solid understanding of the product, its normal functions, and what can go wrong with it. Know how to use troubleshooting logic and your own knowledge of the product to resolve an issue.

The remainder of this chapter highlights specific problems that you should be aware of and accustomed to resolving. This information is not exhaustive. Your own hands-on experience with the product in an operating (if not production) environment is indispensable. You will benefit by your ability to quickly recognize possible viable solutions from actions that either have no effect or cause further problems.

Configuration Issues

IIS 4.0 has a wide range of configuration options with which you need to be familiar. These options include the installation procedure, default installation directories, default security settings, and locations of most commands and settings (that is, which dialogs or menus contain which items). All the relevant items you should be familiar with are detailed in previous chapters. If you're not confident with your knowledge of these basics, be sure to review each chapter and take mental notes. You should also spend time interacting with IIS directly. This will add tactile experience to the knowledge you've gained from reading.

Web Site Configuration Errors

In the following sections, we review some common configuration errors made with Web sites. These items are grouped by the tabs found on a Web site's Properties dialog.

Web Site

The following items are configuration errors that are possible on the Web Site tab:

➤ **IP Address** Setting this to a specific IP address enables the site to receive all traffic directed at that IP address. Be sure the DNS entry mapping an IP address to a frequently qualified domain name (FQDN) is correct for the hosted Web site and the selected IP address. IP addresses only appear in this pull-down list if they are defined in the TCP/IP properties via the Protocol tab of the Network applet.

➤ **TCP Port** The default port for HTTP is 80. All Web clients automatically attempt to establish communication with the server over port 80. If you change the TCP port, you must specify this in any URL used to access that site.

Operators

The Operators tab is prone to certain configuration errors. Each user who is specifically added or who is a member of an added group is granted operator privileges to a Web site. A site operator does not need to be an NT system administrator. Site operators have the ability to change logging, set server access permissions, change default documents and footers, and alter content expirations, HTTP headers, and content ratings. Granting the wrong users operator status can endanger the vitality of your Web site. Not granting the correct users operator status will prevent them from being able to remotely or locally manage their sites.

Performance

The following items are configuration errors that are possible on the Performance tab:

➤ **Bandwidth Throttling** Setting the bandwidth throttle too low can prevent a Web site from responding quickly if multiple users are accessing the site simultaneously. Also, setting the throttle too high may starve other sites on the same IIS server.

➤ **Keep-Alives** Some Web applications rely on consistent connections with clients to maintain a context stream. If these are disabled, some Web applications may no longer function or respond to users with improper information.

ISAPI Filters

Be aware that configuration errors are possible on the ISAPI Filters tab. ISAPI filters that are either corrupt or not designed/configured for a Web site can cause the Web site to fail or performance to be degraded.

Home Directory

The following items are configuration errors that are possible on the Home Directory tab:

➤ **Location** The top three radio buttons on this page are used to define where the resources used by this Web site are stored—locally, network share, or URL. If this is set incorrectly, visitors will not gain access to the correct resources, if anything at all.

➤ **Path** Based on which radio button is selected, this option defines the location (locally, network share, or URL) where resources are pulled. If this is incorrect, visitors will not see the intended resources.

➤ **Access Permissions** The settings of Read and Write determine if visitors can view documents and upload files. If Read access is not enabled, visitors will receive a 403 HTTP error stating that Read access is forbidden.

➤ **Content Control** If directory browsing is allowed, the list of files within a directory will be displayed in the client browser when a default file is not present within that directory.

Documents

The following items are configuration errors that are possible on the Documents tab:

➤ **Default Document** If Default Document is disabled, each URL used to gain access to the site must contain the name of a document; otherwise, a directory listing will be attempted. If the wrong document name is defined, a directory list will be attempted.

➤ **Document Footer** If the content of the footer file is not properly formatted or if it's saved as a file format other than plain text, it may display incorrectly in a client browser.

Directory Security

The following items are configuration errors that are possible on the Directory Security tab:

➤ **Authentication Methods** If Allow Anonymous Access is not defined, only authenticated users (those with valid names and passwords) can gain access to the site. If Anonymous Access is enabled but fails, double-check that Automatic Password Synchronization is enabled.

➤ **Key Manager** If server certificates not issued for a specific server are installed, clients will receive a message stating that the certificate used does not match the server.

➤ **IP Address and Domain Name Restrictions** Because you must set blanket access permission to either Grant or Restrict, and then further refine the setting with exceptions, it's easy to set these backward. Be sure to double-check the restriction methods used.

HTTP Headers

The following items are configuration errors that are possible on the HTTP Headers tab:

➤ **Content Expiration** Setting expiration dates that expire too soon may cause proxy servers to access resources continually in search of current materials. Also, some client browsers can be set to accept only current data, so expired materials may be restricted from being viewed.

➤ **Custom Headers** Defining a header name or its value incorrectly can result in spurious responses by client browsers and proxy servers. Always double-check custom headers to ensure spelling and relevance.

➤ **Ratings** Defining the content's rating level incorrectly prevents users who should not be restricted from gaining access, or it may fail to warn or restrict those users to whom access should be restricted.

➤ **MIME** If a resource accessed via IIS is not being handled properly by a client's browser (such as not calling the proper helper application, failing to automatically play/use the content, or forcing the user to save the content to disk), check the defined MIME types.

Custom Errors

The Custom Errors tab is also prone to configuration errors. If you define a custom error, make sure the contents of the defined error properly reflect the information the user needs to handle the error. This is more a user-friendly mistake than an actual error. Always give your visitors enough information so they can solve the problem themselves or understand that it is out of their control and should be reported to you.

FTP Site Configuration Errors

In the following sections, we review some common configuration errors made on FTP sites. These items are grouped by the tabs found on an FTP site's Properties dialog.

FTP Site

The following items are configuration errors that are possible on the FTP Site tab:

➤ **IP Address** Setting this to a specific IP address enables a site to receive all traffic directed at that IP address. Be sure the DNS entry mapping an IP address to an FQDN is correct for the hosted FTP site and the selected IP address. IP addresses only appear in this pull-down list if they are defined in the TCP/IP properties via the Protocol tab of the Network applet.

➤ **TCP Port** The default port for FTP is 21. All FTP clients automatically attempt to establish communication with the server over port 21. If you change the TCP port, you must specify this when attempting to access that site.

Security Accounts

The following items are configuration errors that are possible on the Security Accounts tab:

➤ **Allow Anonymous** If Allow Anonymous Access is not defined, only authenticated users (those with valid names and passwords) can gain access to the site. If Anonymous Access is enabled but fails, make sure Automatic Password Synchronization is enabled. If authenticated users are unable to log on, verify that you have not selected to restrict access to anonymous only.

➤ **Adding users** Each user who is specifically added or who is a member of an added group is granted operator privileges to this FTP site. A site operator does not need to be an NT system administrator. Granting the wrong users operator status can endanger the vitality of your FTP site. Not granting the correct users operator status will prevent them from being able to remotely or locally manage their sites.

Messages

There really isn't an error on the Messages tab that will prevent proper functioning. You should provide useful information for your visitors, such as contact information and announcement of prosecution for illegal activities, in this section.

Home Directory

The following items are configuration errors that are possible on the Home Directory tab:

➤ **Location** The top radio button on this page defines where the resource used by this FTP site is stored—locally or network share. If this is set incorrectly, visitors will not gain access to the correct resources, if anything at all.

➤ **Path** Based on which radio button is selected, this option defines the location where resources are pulled. If this is incorrect, visitors will not see the intended resources.

➤ **Read/Write** If Read access is not granted, users can't download files or view directory contents. If Write access is not granted, users can't upload and delete files. This setting is in addition to the NTFS file and folder object-level settings.

Directory Security

The following item is a configuration error that is possible on the Directory Security tab:

➤ **TCP/IP Access Restrictions** Because you must set blanket access permission to Grant or Restrict for FTP site access, which is then further refined by exceptions, it's easy to set this backward. Be sure to double-check the restriction methods used.

IIS HTTP Errors

The HTTP protocol used to transmit Web pages has a standard set of error codes that are reported to clients in the event of an error. These error codes inform users of problems that have occurred and let them know if there is anything they can do to avoid these errors in subsequent communications. These errors are defined in the Custom Error tab of a Web site's Properties dialog. Here are the seven HTTP errors you should be familiar with:

Note: The error messages are pulled from the default documents displayed by IIS.

➤ **400 Bad Request** Due to malformed syntax, the request could not be understood by the server. The client should not repeat the request without modifications.

➤ **401 Unauthorized: Logon Failed** This error indicates that the credentials passed to the server do not match the credentials required to log on to the server. It instructs the user to contact the Web server's administrator to verify that he or she has permission to access the requested resource.

➤ **403 Forbidden: Execute Access Forbidden** This error can be caused if a user tries to execute a CGI, ISAPI, or other executable program from a directory that does not allow programs to be executed. It instructs the user to contact the Web server's administrator if the problem persists.

➤ **404 File Not Found** The Web server cannot find the file or script asked for. The user is instructed to check the URL to ensure that the path is correct and to contact the server's administrator if the problem persists.

➤ **500 Internal Server Error** The Web server is incapable of performing the request. The user is instructed to try the request again later and to contact the Web server's administrator if the problem persists.

➤ **501 Not Implemented** The Web server does not support the functionality required to fulfill the request. The user is instructed to check the URL for errors and to contact the Web server's administrator if the problem persists.

➤ **502 Bad Gateway** The server, while acting as a gateway or proxy, received an invalid response from the upstream server it accessed in attempting to fulfill the request. The user is instructed to contact the Web server's administrator if the problem persists.

 You should take notice that the 400 series HTTP error messages are related to the client, whereas the 500 series HTTP error messages are related to the server.

Installation Issues

Fortunately, IIS is very simple to install. As discussed in Chapter 3, the installation procedure is often painless, especially if you follow a few simple rules:

1. Install Service Pack 3 (if you're within the U.S. and you want to use 128-bit encryption, use the 128-bit version of Service Pack 3).

2. Install Internet Explorer 4.01.

3. Close all applications, especially those using ODBC or those that offer services similar to IIS (Web, FTP, SMTP, and so on).

If the installation of IIS fails, your only course of action is to attempt to uninstall IIS and then reinstall. In extreme cases, the installation failure causes NT to fail. This requires the reinstallation of NT.

 The official version of IIS 4.0 does not upgrade the alpha, beta 1, or beta 2 versions of IIS 4.0. If these are present on your system, you must uninstall them before attempting to install the final version of IIS 4.0. However, the final version of IIS 4.0 does properly upgrade the Beta 3 version of IIS 4.0.

Once IIS is installed, you can test the installation by launching a Web browser and attempting to load the default Web pages from the new installation of IIS (or any document placed in the \InetPub\Wwwroot directory). To do so, use a

URL constructed from the IP address, NetBIOS name, or FQDN (if DNS is present) of IIS in the form http://*address*/. If a document fails to load, first check that files actually exist in the Wwwroot directory. Next, verify that the IIS services are started. Finally, check the IIS set and the NTFS-level access control lists (ACLs) for the resources. If none of these actions enables IIS to function, you may need to reinstall IIS and possibly NT as well.

Windows NT Issues

As discussed earlier in this book, IIS is tightly integrated into the Windows NT Server 4.0 operating system. Therefore, a working knowledge and solid familiarity with NT Server and its management, performance, and administration tools is essential. Due to the integration of IIS and NT Server, it's important to recognize that configuration errors in NT Server can directly affect IIS's ability to operate and function properly.

 Knowledge of NT Server is assumed for the IIS certification exam. If you're not already familiar with NT Server or you have not passed the NT Server certification exam, we strongly recommend you take and pass it before moving on to IIS.

The configuration and administration of Windows NT Server can have a direct and profound impact on IIS in four key areas: security, performance, networking, and name resolution. In the following four sections, we look at each of these NT Server-specific issues. However, you should recognize that due to the tight integration of IIS with NT, it can be difficult to distinguish where a problem lies. Several of these topics have been addressed earlier in this book and in this chapter; therefore, some of them overlap.

NT Security

IIS relies on NT security to provide the underlying control mechanism for user access to resources over the information services (Web, FTP, and so on) offered through IIS. If NT security fails to restrict access or grant access correctly, your information services will either be unable to distribute resources or unable to distribute confidential resources.

The ACLs are what control who can use a resource. For most IIS resources (that is, files and folders), ACLs are limited to controlling who can read, write, execute, and delete a specific object. It's important to review the ACLs for all resources hosted by IIS—and even those supposedly outside the reach of IIS—to ensure that all items have properly defined ACLs. Specifically, the

IUSR_*servername* user should be granted Read access to all IIS resources and Execute access on all script resources; except where public access to a resource should be restricted, in which case the IUSR account should have either No Access specifically defined or not be defined at all. Users and groups that control the content of IIS services should be granted Write and/or Delete access to the subsections of those services. All items outside of the IIS roots should either not have the IUSR included in their ACLs or have No Access specified for that account.

You should also keep in mind how multiple group memberships can affect the resultant access for an individual user. The *resultant access* is the accumulation of all access granted to that user specifically and by all group memberships; except if No Access is specified for that user or for the user's group, then that user is denied access.

In a multidomain environment, in addition to ACLs, you also need to monitor trust relationships. *Trusts* are logical security connections between two domains, where one domain is able to share its resources with the authenticated users from another domain. If either of the domains terminates the trust, access over the trust is canceled. If you suspect user inability to access resources is due to a failed trust, your only course of action is to reestablish the trust.

Another important item to remember is that all user accounts that will be accessing resources over IIS must have the Log On Locally user right. Otherwise, they will not be authenticated on the IIS server and will be prevented from gaining access to retrieve resources. This includes the IUSR_*servername* account and any individual user account that needs direct or special access on the IIS server.

CGI scripts and similar files should be limited, when possible, to only Execute access. This prevents anyone from viewing and modifying them. However, some CGI file types, such as the .IDC and .HTX files for Index Server, require Read access to function properly. In some cases, when a script that only requires Execute access is placed in a directory that offers both Read and Execute access, the client browser will attempt to download the file instead of instruct the server to execute it. In such a case, you should move all Execute-only scripts into one directory and all Execute and Read scripts into another.

 A slightly different but related issue is that of Server-Side Includes (SSI). SSI documents require an .STM, .SHTM, or .SHTML extension to be properly handled by IIS. Plus, SSI documents require Execute permissions.

NT Performance

As you should know, the ability of a system to process resource requests is only as good as its ability to perform the actions required to fulfill the requests. In other words, a slow or poorly tuned system will offer sluggish or interrupted service. Maintaining a watch over how well your system is supporting its processing load is an important preventative measure. Waiting until a service fails or too much activity causes the system to crash results in increased repair costs, extensive downtime, and disgruntled users.

As discussed in Chapter 8, monitoring and tuning is a key aspect of administering IIS. If you don't maintain the performance of the underlying hardware and operating system, it will be unable to adequately support the heavy activity of a growing IIS user base.

When your IIS server is in danger of overrunning its available resources, you can use several tactics to shackle IIS to limit its resource usage:

➤ **User limits** On the Web Site tab of the Web site's Properties dialog via MMC, you can restrict the number of simultaneous users. By restricting access to a specified number of users, you gain better control over the performance offered to that limited user base.

➤ **Remove nonessential services** Any service or application that is active on the same NT Server machine that hosts IIS is fighting IIS for access to the limited resources of that system. For larger IIS sites, especially those in which performance is important and/or those with a large user base, no other services or applications should be installed. IIS and only those services and applications essential to the operation of the Web application should be present on the NT Server machine.

➤ **Add more resources** When money is not an issue and upgrading or expanding your current hardware is possible, adding additional RAM, CPUs, faster network/ISP interfaces, and faster/larger storage devices may directly increase the resource availability.

➤ **Optimizing code** If you're using in-house created scripts, CGI, and other custom applications with IIS, take the time to inspect how these utilities allocate, use, and release resources (especially memory and CPU cycles). It's not uncommon for a single server-side application to consume more than its fair share of resources and bring the rest of the system to a standstill. Code that is not optimized is often a direct culprit of declining resources.

➤ **Bandwidth restrictions** You can control, on a global and site basis, the amount of bandwidth used by a Web or FTP site hosted by IIS. By restricting the traffic of one or more sites, you can effectively grant more bandwidth to others, and vice versa.

NT Networking

NT networking is essential to the operation of IIS because it's through the network interface (either to an intranet or to the Internet) that all communication between the server and clients occurs. If this communication pathway is interrupted, terminated, or clogged with traffic, IIS site performance will suffer accordingly.

In relation to NT networking, three problems can occur:

➤ The IIS machine has no network access

➤ The IIS machine has network access but clients cannot access resources

➤ Clients receive the wrong resources

If the IIS machine loses its network connection or that connection becomes unusable for any reason, it should be obvious that access to IIS is not possible. There are several possible causes of network communication loss.

First, the rest of the network or your ISP has somehow failed. This can range from a cable being disconnected to a server crashing. In such cases, check all physical points of failure and test other servers or clients to see if they still have network access.

Second, the network adapter on the IIS system has stopped functioning. This can occur when hardware burns, is disconnected due to movement, or the driver is corrupt. If the NIC fails, check all connections and attempt to restart the machine to see if communication is reestablished. Then, replace/reinstall the driver and/or replace the NIC itself.

Third, the protocol used by IIS is no longer configured correctly or is not the same as that used by the rest of the network. Typically, TCP/IP is the protocol used to transmit IIS-hosted services, but some proxy applications can transport IIS services over IPX. In any case, an incorrectly configured protocol is most often the cause of protocol networking problems. Both making a change to and installing a protocol can result in a system unable to communicate due to incorrect settings. Be sure to double-check the IP address, subnet mask, and default gateway. In some cases, you may need to verify that the routers and gateways in use on your network or between IIS and the ISP are properly configured and functioning.

NT's TCP/IP includes a handful of tools that you can use to determine if you have lost network connectivity. They include PING and TRACERT. Use **PING**

127.0.0.1 to determine if the protocol is properly installed. Use **PING** *network server IP address* to determine if the subnet is defined properly (where *network server IP address* is the IP address of another server within the same subnet). Use **PING** *external server IP address* to determine that the gateway is defined properly (where *external server IP address* is the IP address of a server outside of the IIS server's subnet or out on the Internet). If you see a list of replies with times for any of these uses of PING, you know that aspect of IP is probably configured correctly. If you see timeouts, this indicates either that IP is configured incorrectly or the object of the PING is not present.

The second tool, TRACERT, can be used to determine where in the logical order of servers the network communication fails. The command **TRACERT** *external server IP address* lists each server or router encountered between your machine and the external server. If the external server's IP address fails to appear as the last item in the TRACERT list, a breakdown in communication at the last server listed has occurred.

If your IIS server has network access but clients are unable to access resources, this may indicate the services that normally serve out these resources are not functioning properly. Often, if a service is not functioning, an error message will be displayed on the client stating that a connection with the server could not be established. Make sure that clients have network access by using PING and TRACERT to test the path between the clients and the IIS server. If this test shows the clients to have network access to the IIS server, you can suspect the IIS services.

Use the Services applet or the IIS MMC snap-in to determine if the IIS-related services are started, paused, or stopped. The relevant services include FTP Publishing, IIS Admin, and World Wide Web Publishing. If they are stopped or paused, restart these services. If this fails, try rebooting the server and testing them again. After a reboot, if the services still fail to function, inspect the Event Viewer logs for dependency failures.

 Remember that a *dependency failure* is when a driver, device, or service fails to load, which then causes other drivers, devices, or services to load or function improperly. Take whatever steps are necessary to resolve any dependency failures. As a last course of action, you can reinstall IIS to attempt to repair or replace the services.

If clients are accessing resources from IIS but the resources requested are not the resources returned, a configuration error exists. This configuration error can be in the binding of an IP address with the incorrect Web site or an IP address being defined improperly with an FQDN in DNS.

NT Name Resolution

Name resolution hosted by NT can cause problems with accessing IIS. Because NT uses a wide variety of name resolution schemes (DNS, HOSTS, WINS, and LMHOSTS), it may be difficult to track down the point of failure. DNS is used to manage static mappings of FQDNs to IP addresses for an entire network. The HOSTS file is used to manage static mappings of FQDNs to IP addresses for a single machine. WINS is used to dynamically manage mappings of NetBIOS names to IP addresses for an entire network. The LMHOSTS file is used to manage static mappings of NetBIOS names to IP addresses for a single machine.

Within an intranet, IIS-hosted sites can be accessed using the NetBIOS name of the server as the domain name in a URL (for example, if the server's NetBIOS name is nts03, a URL could be http://nts03/staff/default.htm). However, on larger networks where DNS is present, FQDN is the address method of choice. This is true because most companies with larger networks grant access to their IIS sites (or parts of them) to Internet-based users.

More often than not, DNS name resolution is associated more with IIS than any of the other methods. You should be aware of and have general troubleshooting knowledge of several issues related to DNS and IIS. These include the following:

➤ **DNS unavailable** If the primary and secondary DNS servers on your local network are unavailable due to system crashes or network communication interruption, clients will be unable to have FQDNs resolved into IP addresses. In other words, they will not be able to reach your site because the address they use will not be directed to IIS.

➤ **Old data** If the IP address has changed but this information has not been altered in DNS, clients will be directed to the old IP address. Therefore, they will not be directed to IIS. If the data has been updated on the primary DNS server, but it is not reflected or synchronized over the other DNS servers on the network, some users will be properly resolved whereas others will not. In this case, you need to investigate the synchronization parameters of your DNS system.

➤ **Incorrect entries** All DNS entries are defined by hand. That means it is easy to introduce errors when alterations or new mappings are performed. An incorrect entry can result in two errors. First, an FQDN can be mapped to an unknown or illegal IP address. Second, an FQDN can be mapped to a wrong IP address that is a valid address within the network.

Exam Prep Questions

Question 1

> When a user opens the URL for an IIS site, he is shown a directory listing of the Wwwroot directory instead of being shown the default document. Why? [Check all correct answers]
>
> ❑ a. The directory has Read access set.
>
> ❑ b. Directory browsing is enabled.
>
> ❑ c. A redirection URL is used.
>
> ❑ d. No default is present or the name of the default document does not match the one known by IIS.

If a user is shown a directory listing, directory browsing is enabled and a default document is not found. Therefore, answers b and d are correct. The directory must have Read access defined; otherwise, the directory listing won't be displayed. Therefore, answer a is incorrect. A redirection URL does not cause a directory listing to be displayed, it simply takes you to the alternate location. Therefore, answer c is incorrect.

Question 2

> Clients are unable to access the IIS-hosted Web site. In fact, an error message appears stating that a connection with the server could not be established. However, the client is able to access other Internet sites without difficulty. Using PING and TRACERT, it has been determined that IIS is not experiencing any network communication difficulties locally or with the Internet. What could be the problem?
>
> ○ a. Anonymous access is restricted.
>
> ○ b. The router between the IIS server and the Internet is offline.
>
> ○ c. The World Wide Web Publishing service is stopped.
>
> ○ d. The client does not have TCP/IP installed.

In this situation, it is most likely that the WWW Publishing service is stopped. Therefore, answer c is correct. If anonymous access is restricted, an error message stating this would be seen on the client machine instead of the "unable to establish a connection" error. Therefore, answer a is incorrect. If the router is offline, IIS would not be able to use PING and TRACERT on the sites on the Internet. Therefore, answer b is incorrect. If the client does not have TCP/IP installed, other Internet sites are not accessible. Therefore, answer d is incorrect.

Question 3

Clients attempting to access a Web site hosted on IIS receive an HTTP error 403. What could cause this error?

○ a. Write access is enabled.

○ b. Read access is not enabled.

○ c. That client's domain is restricted from the Web site.

○ d. Resources are located on a share.

A 403 error occurs if the Web site does not have Read access enabled. Therefore, answer b is correct. Enabling Write access has no effect on Read access. Therefore, answer a is incorrect. If the client was restricted from the Web site, an "access denied" error would be issued instead of a "Read access forbidden" error. Therefore, answer c is incorrect. Pulling resources from a share has no effect on the Read error. Therefore, answer d is incorrect.

Question 4

The password for the IUSR_*servername* account in the User Manager For Domains has been changed, and clients are reporting that they can no longer gain access to the public Web site. Why?

○ a. Automatic password synchronization for the anonymous account has been disabled.

○ b. The new password was less than eight characters long.

○ c. Changing the anonymous account password requires a reinstallation of IIS.

○ d. It takes up to three hours before a new password can be used on NT.

If automatic password synchronization was enabled for the anonymous account, any change made to the password in User Manager For Domains would be reflected in IIS instantly. Therefore, answer a is correct. The length of the password does not matter, unless an NT account policy is in force. Even then, the changed password would be forced to comply with the policy before it would be accepted. Therefore, answer b is incorrect. Changing the anonymous account's password does not require a reinstallation of IIS. Therefore, answer c is incorrect. NT propagates new passwords almost instantly; no waiting period is required. Therefore, answer d is incorrect.

Question 5

Within your company intranet, you have 10 workstations used by temporary employees. You do not want users of these computers to have any access to the Web site hosted on your internal IIS server. Therefore, on the IP Address And Domain Name Restrictions page for the company Web site, you define exceptions for these 10 computers as 10 individual IP addresses. After you make this change, you discover that no clients on the intranet can access the Web site except these 10 computers. What could be the problem?

○ a. Individual computers cannot be exceptions. A subnet must be specified.

○ b. A reboot of IIS is required before this takes effect.

○ c. Anonymous access has been disabled.

○ d. The IP Address Access Restrictions option is set to Denied Access.

If all but the exception computers can no longer gain access, this means that Denied Access was selected instead of Granted Access. Therefore, answer d is correct. Individual computers and a subnet can be used as exceptions. Therefore, answer a is incorrect. A reboot of IIS is not required for a change in access restrictions. Therefore, answer b is incorrect. Disabling anonymous access prevents all clients from accessing anonymously, but it does not prevent authenticated users from accessing. This question does not state if anonymous or authenticated access was affected. Therefore, answer c is incorrect.

Question 6

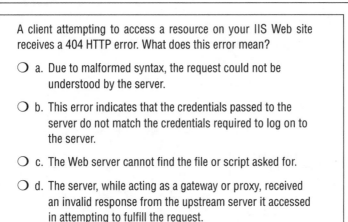

A client attempting to access a resource on your IIS Web site receives a 404 HTTP error. What does this error mean?

○ a. Due to malformed syntax, the request could not be understood by the server.

○ b. This error indicates that the credentials passed to the server do not match the credentials required to log on to the server.

○ c. The Web server cannot find the file or script asked for.

○ d. The server, while acting as a gateway or proxy, received an invalid response from the upstream server it accessed in attempting to fulfill the request.

A 404 HTTP error means the Web server cannot find the file or script asked for. Therefore, answer c is correct. A 400 HTTP error means due to malformed syntax, the request could not be understood by the server. Therefore, answer a is incorrect. A 401 HTTP error means the credentials passed to the server do not match the credentials required to log on to the server. Therefore, answer b is incorrect. A 502 HTTP error means the server, while acting as a gateway or proxy, received an invalid response from the upstream server it accessed in attempting to fulfill the request. Therefore, answer d is incorrect.

Question 7

The Index Server files of IDC and HTX require which permission settings for the IUSR account to function properly? [Check all correct answers]

❑ a. Read

❑ b. Delete

❑ c. Write

❑ d. Execute

The IDC and HTX files require Read and Execute permissions. Therefore, answer a and d are correct.

Question 8

In which ways can you improve the performance of an IIS-hosted Web site without spending more money on hardware or network services? [Check all correct answers]

❏ a. Restrict simultaneous users

❏ b. Remove nonessential services

❏ c. Optimize custom code

❏ d. Impose bandwidth restrictions

All of these actions are useful for improving the performance of an IIS-hosted Web site. Therefore, answers a, b, c, and d are correct.

Question 9

Which Microsoft TCP/IP tools are used to investigate the network communications of IIS? [Check all correct answers]

❏ a. PING

❏ b. ROUTE

❏ c. TRACERT

❏ d. NBTSTAT

PING and TRACERT are TCP/IP utilities that are used to test network communications. Therefore, answers a and c are correct. ROUTE and NBTSTAT are not used to test network communications. Therefore, answers b and d are incorrect.

Question 10

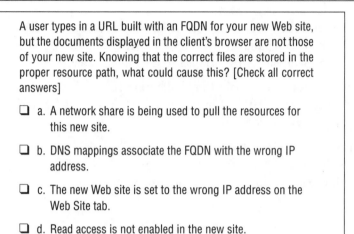

A user types in a URL built with an FQDN for your new Web site, but the documents displayed in the client's browser are not those of your new site. Knowing that the correct files are stored in the proper resource path, what could cause this? [Check all correct answers]

- ❑ a. A network share is being used to pull the resources for this new site.

- ❑ b. DNS mappings associate the FQDN with the wrong IP address.

- ❑ c. The new Web site is set to the wrong IP address on the Web Site tab.

- ❑ d. Read access is not enabled in the new site.

If the wrong Web site appears in a client browser when the correct URL is used, either the DNS mapping is wrong or the site's IP address is wrong. Therefore, answers b and c are correct. Using a network share for resource storage would not cause this problem. Therefore, answer a is incorrect. If the client was directed to the correct Web site and Read access was disabled, an error message stating such would be displayed. Therefore, answer d is incorrect.

Need To Know More?

 Howell, Nelson, et al. *Using Microsoft Internet Information Server 4.* Que Publishing, Indianapolis, IN, 1997. ISBN 0-7897-1263-6. This book discusses IIS troubleshooting in Chapter 18.

 Some information about troubleshooting IIS can be found on the TechNet CD-ROM or online via the Microsoft IIS Web area at www.microsoft.com/iis/.

 IIS's own online documentation, accessed through Start| Programs|Windows NT 4.0 Option Pack|Product Documentation, contains information about troubleshooting IIS.

Sample Test

In this chapter, we provide a number of pointers for developing a successful test-taking strategy, including how to choose proper answers, how to decode ambiguity, how to work within the Microsoft framework, how to decide what to memorize, and how to prepare for the Internet Information Server 4.0 certification exam. Good luck!

Questions, Questions, Questions

There should be no doubt in your mind that you're facing a test full of questions. The exam is comprised of 55 questions, and you're allotted 100 minutes to complete it. Remember that questions are of four basic types:

➤ Multiple choice with a single answer

➤ Multiple choice with multiple answers

➤ Multipart with a single answer

➤ Picking the spot on the graphic

Always take the time to read a question twice before selecting an answer and be sure to look for an Exhibit button. The Exhibit button brings up graphics and charts used to help explain the question, provide additional data, or illustrate layout. You'll find it difficult to answer these questions without looking at the exhibits.

Not every question has a single answer; a lot of questions require more than one answer. In fact, for some questions, all the answers should be marked. Read the question carefully so you know how many answers are necessary and look for additional instructions for marking your answers. These instructions usually appear in brackets.

Picking Proper Answers

Obviously, the only way to pass any exam is by selecting the correct answers. However, the Microsoft exams are not standardized like SAT and GRE exams; they are more diabolical and convoluted. In some cases, questions are strangely worded, and deciphering them is nearly impossible. In such cases, you may need to rely on answer-elimination skills. There's almost always at least one answer out of the possible choices that can be immediately eliminated due to one of the following reasons:

➤ The answer doesn't apply to the situation.

➤ The answer describes a nonexistent issue.

➤ The answer is already eliminated by the question text.

Once obviously wrong answers are eliminated, you must rely on your retained knowledge to eliminate further answers. Look for items that sound correct but refer to actions, commands, or features not present or not available in the described situation.

If, after these phases of elimination, you are still faced with a blind guess between two or more answers, reread the question. Try to picture in your mind's eye the situation and how each of the possible remaining answers would alter the situation.

If you've exhausted your ability to eliminate answers and are still unclear about which of the remaining possible answers is the correct one—guess! An unanswered question offers you no points, but guessing gives you a chance of getting a question right; just don't be too hasty in making a blind guess. Wait until the last round of reviewing marked questions before you start to guess. In other words, guessing should be a last resort.

Decoding Ambiguity

Microsoft exams have a reputation for including questions that are confusing, ambiguous, or, at times, difficult to interpret. In essence, the Microsoft exams are difficult.

The only way to beat Microsoft at its own game is to be prepared. You'll discover that many exam questions test your knowledge of things that are not directly related to the issue raised by the question. This means that the answers offered to you, even the incorrect ones, are just as much a part of the skill assessment as the question itself. If you don't know about all aspects of IIS 4.0 cold, you may not be able to eliminate obviously wrong answers because they relate to a different area of IIS than the one being addressed by the question.

Questions often give away the answer, but you have to be better than Sherlock Holmes to see the clues. Often, subtle hints are included in the text in such a way that they seem like irrelevant information. You must realize that each question is a test in and of itself, and you need to inspect and successfully navigate each question to pass the exam. Look for small clues, such as the mention of times, group names, and configuration settings. Little items such as these can point out the right answer; if missed, they can leave you facing a blind guess.

Another common difficulty with the certification exams is that of vocabulary. Be sure to brush up on all the terms presented at the beginning of each chapter. You may also want to review the Glossary before approaching the test.

Working Within The Framework

The test questions are presented to you in a random order, and many of the elements or issues are repeated in multiple questions. It's not uncommon to find that the correct answer to one question is the wrong answer to another.

Take the time to read each answer, even if you know the correct one immediately. The incorrect answers may spark a memory that helps you on another question.

You can revisit any question as many times as you like. If you're uncertain of the answer to a question, mark the box provided so that you can come back to it later. You should also mark questions you think may offer data you can use to solve other questions. The testing software is designed to help you mark an answer for every question, so use its framework to your advantage. Everything you want to see again should be marked; the software will help you return to marked items.

Deciding What To Memorize

The amount of rote memorization you must do for the exams depends on how well you remember what you've read. If you're a visual learner and can see the drop-down menus and the dialogs in your head, you won't need to memorize as much as someone who is less visually oriented. The tests will stretch your recollection of commands and functions of commands as well as the locations of features of the utilities.

Here are the important types of information to memorize:

➤ The order of steps in setup or configuration

➤ Features or commands found in pull-down menus and configuration dialogs

➤ Applications found by default in the Start menu

➤ Applets in the Control Panel

➤ Names and functions of the five main Registry keys

If you worked your way through this book while sitting at an Internet Information Server system, you should have little or no problem interacting with most of these important items.

Preparing For The Test

The best way to prepare for the test—after you've studied—is to take at least one practice exam. We've included a practice exam in this chapter. Give yourself 100 minutes to take the exam. Keep yourself on the honor system and don't cheat by looking back at the text earlier in the book. Once your time is up or you finish, you can check your answers in Chapter 14.

If you want additional practice exams, visit the Microsoft Training and Certification site (www.microsoft.com/mcp/) and download the Self-Assessment Practice Exam utility. Currently, there is only a practice exam for Internet Information Server 3.0, but an updated version is expected to be released sometime this year.

Taking The Exam

Relax. Once you're sitting in front of the testing computer, there's nothing more you can do to increase your knowledge or preparation. Take a deep breath, stretch, and attack the first question.

Don't rush; there's plenty of time to complete each question and to return to skipped questions. If you read a question twice and are clueless, mark it and move on. Both easy and difficult questions are dispersed throughout the test in a random order. Don't cheat yourself by spending so much time on a difficult question early on that it prevents you from answering numerous easy questions positioned near the end. Move through the entire test, and before returning to the skipped questions, evaluate your time in light of the number of skipped questions. As you answer questions, remove the mark. Continue to review the remaining marked questions until your time expires or you complete the test.

That's it for pointers. Here are some questions for you to practice on.

Sample Test

Question 1

A digital signature performs two functions—it indicates the identity of the sender as well as encrypts the signed message.

○ a. True

○ b. False

Question 2

A user performs a query using an Index Server query form on the office's intranet. The results from his query fail to list the SALES1997.DOC file, which he knows contains the words "April" and "1997". What could be the reason for this? [Check all correct answers]

❏ a. The user was not authenticated.

❏ b. The user does not have Read access to the file.

❏ c. Another user was accessing the document at the time the query was performed.

❏ d. The file is not included in the corpus.

Question 3

As a busy Webmaster, you would like to automate the process of creating regular reports on the popularity of your Web site. However, you're concerned about the performance of your under-powered server. You've already set up the W3C extended log to take the data you need. Which of the following actions can you add to the Scheduler that won't compromise performance on your server?

○ a. Look up HTML titles

○ b. Resolve IP addresses

○ c. Perform Whois organization queries

○ d. All of the above; this is all good information for reports to management

○ e. None of the above; each of these actions is performance-intensive on the server

Question 4

As the Webmaster of the growing company Web site, you're getting a number of complaints from users: pages are too slow to load, text browsers just can't search through your site, and a number of links just end up in space.

You've already used the Verify Links tool. Which types of data can you get on these issues without having to go through the time and trouble of using a Usage Import of a log file? [Check all correct answers]

❏ a. Perform a quick search for all images without HTML **<ALT>** tags.

❏ b. Do a quick search for all pages above 32K.

❏ c. Create a Site Summary report.

❏ d. Check the links and HTML tags on each page one by one. There's no other way to be sure what is and isn't working.

Question 5

By default, email with a remote recipient is forwarded automatically or relayed on to other SMTP servers, no matter where the message originated.

○ a. True

○ b. False

Question 6

Clients attempting to access a Web site hosted on IIS receive HTTP error 403. What could cause this error?

○ a. Write access is enabled.

○ b. Read access is not enabled.

○ c. That client's domain is restricted from the Web site.

○ d. Resources are located on a share.

Question 7

Creating a key certificate request is an integral step of what process?

○ a. Installing IIS 4.0

○ b. Configuring a Web server to offer SSL-based secure communications

○ c. As a client, purchasing a product with a credit card over a secure link

○ d. Applying Service Pack 3 to Windows NT Server

Question 8

For an intranet, if the server name is "marketing", you can reach the Web site's home directory by typing which one of the following URLs within the browser's URL text box?

○ a. http://localhost/marketing

○ b. http://marketing

○ c. http://www.iis.com/marketing

○ d. None of the above

Question 9

For anonymous access, you can configure IIS so Windows NT automatically synchronizes the Windows NT password with the HTTP or FTP password.

○ a. True

○ b. False

Question 10

If you do not have Read access to a file on the FTP server, you cannot perform which of the following operations? [Check all correct answers]

❑ a. Download the file

❑ b. Read the file

❑ c. Write to the file

Question 11

If you need to make modifications to the certificate key mappings for a Web site, which administration utility can you use?

○ a. Internet Service Manager snap-in

○ b. Server Manager

○ c. Internet Service Manager HTML

○ d. Certificate Server

Question 12

IIS can be administered through which interfaces or utilities? [Check all correct answers]

❑ a. Internet Service Manager MMC snap-in

❑ b. Internet Service Manager applet in the Control Panel

❑ c. Internet Service Manager Administrative wizard

❑ d. Internet Service Manager HTMLA via a Web browser

Question 13

IIS is used to host four Web sites, named SITE1, SITE2, SITE3, and SITE4. You enable bandwidth throttling for the server/computer and set it to 4,096K. SITE3 and SITE4 are the most popular sites hosted by your installation of IIS. You want to grant each of them twice the bandwidth of the other sites. Which modification should you perform?

○ a. Set server/computer-level bandwidth throttling to 8,192K.

○ b. Set service/site-level bandwidth throttling to 2,046K for SITE1 and SITE2.

○ c. Set service/site-level bandwidth throttling to 8,192K for SITE3 and SITE4.

○ d. This cannot be done with IIS 4.0.

Question 14

In addition to IIS 4.0 and Windows NT Server, what is another component required to enable 128-bit data encryption?

○ a. An InterNIC-assigned domain name

○ b. Microsoft Transaction Server

○ c. Service Pack 3

○ d. Microsoft Certificate Server

Question 15

> Netscape Navigator is an Active client.
>
> ○ a. True
>
> ○ b. False

Question 16

> One of your users cannot connect to IIS. You have checked every-
> thing on the user's machine, including the TCP/IP configuration
> and IP address. Everything looks fine. How do you verify that IIS
> is installed and up and running on the server properly? [Check all
> correct answers]
>
> ❑ a. Open Internet Explorer 4.01 on the server and verify that
> the connection to the localhost is okay.
>
> ❑ b. Make sure both the network and IIS are running.
>
> ❑ c. Make sure the WWW service is configured properly.
>
> ❑ d. Make sure the TCP/IP protocol stack is installed.

Question 17

> The access permission on one of your server's directories,
> SalesData, is set to No Access. The Microsoft Index Server uses
> this directory within its full-text search.
>
> ○ a. True
>
> ○ b. False

Question 18

> The IIS SMTP and NNTP services can be administered and man-
> aged through which utilities or interfaces? [Check all correct
> answers]
>
> ❑ a. Server Manager
>
> ❑ b. IIS's MMC snap-in
>
> ❑ c. Network Monitor
>
> ❑ d. An HTML interface

Question 19

The Index Server files of IDC and HTX require which permission settings for the IUSR account to function properly? [Check all correct answers]

❑ a. Read

❑ b. Delete

❑ c. Write

❑ d. Execute

Question 20

The NNTP service of IIS supports which of the following functions or features? [Check all correct answers]

❑ a. Hosting of multiple discussion groups

❑ b. Access to standard Usenet newsfeeds

❑ c. Moderated groups

❑ d. SSL-secured transmissions

Question 21

What is a certificate authority (CA)?

○ a. The single worldwide distribution point for client identities

○ b. An Internet standards organization, similar to IETF and IEEE, that sets the requirements for certificates

○ c. A division of the National Security Council (NSC) with the sole purpose of cracking down on computer fraud

○ d. A third-party organization that is trusted to verify the identity of servers and individuals

Question 22

What is the default port for the WWW service?

○ a. 80

○ b. 81

○ c. 82

○ d. 83

Question 23

What tool is included with IIS 4.0 to simplify the troubleshooting process of Active Server Pages?

○ a. Java Virtual Machine

○ b. Script Debugger

○ c. W3C logging

○ d. ODBC drivers

Question 24

When a user opens the URL for an IIS site, he is shown a directory listing of the Wwwroot directory instead of being shown the default document. Why? [Check all correct answers]

❑ a. The directory has Read access set.

❑ b. Directory browsing is enabled.

❑ c. A redirection URL is used.

❑ d. No default is present or the name of the default document does not match the one known by IIS.

Question 25

While trying to install IIS, the installation fails due to insufficient privileges. How do you resolve this problem?

○ a. Reboot the machine.

○ b. Log on the machine as Administrator and reinstall IIS.

○ c. Reinstall IIS with all the components of Windows NT Options Pack.

○ d. Share your root directory.

Question 26

Where are the files that compose the Administrative HTML tools for remotely managing IIS stored by default?

○ a. \Inetpub\Iisadmin

○ b. \Winnt\System32\Inetsrv\Iisadmin

○ c. \Program Files\Inetput\Admin

○ d. \Inetpub\Adminroot

Question 27

Which do you use to monitor the performance of Index Server? [Check all correct answers]

❑ a. Index Server MMC snap-in

❑ b. Performance Monitor

❑ c. Server Manager

❑ d. An IDA script

Question 28

Which IIS component offers programmers the ability to create three-tiered applications for Internet deployment?

○ a. The NNTP service

○ b. Transaction Server

○ c. Certificate Server

○ d. Index Server

Question 29

Which Microsoft TCP/IP tools are used to investigate the network communications of IIS? [Check all correct answers]

❏ a. PING

❏ b. ROUTE

❏ c. TRACERT

❏ d. NBTSTAT

Question 30

Which NT Server 4.0 update installs the password-filtering security component?

○ a. Windows NT Service Pack 3

○ b. Windows NT Options Pack

○ c. Internet Explorer 4.01

○ d. Windows NT Server 4.0

Question 31

Which of the following are needed to install Internet Information Server 4.0? [Check all correct answers]

❑ a. A local network connection

❑ b. An NTFS partition

❑ c. A computer with at least the minimum hardware required to support Windows NT Server 4.0

❑ d. The TCP/IP protocol installed

❑ e. Access to the Option Pack distribution files

Question 32

Which of the following are requirements for the installation of IIS 4.0? [Check all correct answers]

❑ a. Service Pack 3 for Windows NT Server 4.0

❑ b. NetBEUI

❑ c. Internet Explorer 4.01

❑ d. Windows NT 4.0 Workstation

Question 33

Which of the following are true statements about IIS 4.0 and its support services and applications? [Check all correct answers]

❑ a. HTML, text, Microsoft Office, and Adobe PDF documents can be searched.

❑ b. Client identities can be tracked and verified.

❑ c. A single Web server can be copied to three or more other servers simultaneously.

❑ d. Applications can communicate even if network connections are broken.

Question 34

Which of the following do you need before creating a virtual directory?

- ○ a. A physical path
- ○ b. Read and Write permissions
- ○ c. Gopher
- ○ d. An IP address

Question 35

Which of the following Index Server indexes is stored only in memory?

- ○ a. Word lists
- ○ b. Persistent index
- ○ c. Shadow index
- ○ d. Master index

Question 36

Which of the following measures are used to secure the SMTP service of IIS? [Check all correct answers]

- ❑ a. SSL identity verification
- ❑ b. Windows NT Challenge/Response authentication
- ❑ c. Reverse DNS lookup
- ❑ d. IP address and domain name restrictions

Question 37

Which one of the following lines of code should you add to the first line within the following script so that the script runs on the server?

```
<SCRIPT LANGUAGE=VBScript>
<!--
Option Explicit

Dim validCreditCardNumber
Sub Submit_OnClick
    validCreditCardNumber = True
    Call CheckCreditCardNumber
    (CreditCardNumberField.Value,
    "Please enter your credit card number.")
    If validCreditCardNumber then
        MsgBox "Thank you for your order"
    End if
    End Sub
</SCRIPT>
```

○ a. **RUNAT=SERVER**

○ b. **EXECUTEAT=SERVER**

○ c. **PARSEAT=SERVER**

○ d. None of the above

Question 38

Which technology is used most often to establish secure communications over networks where data interception is possible?

○ a. CRC

○ b. Encryption

○ c. TCP/IP

○ d. DHCP

Question 39

Which views are available in the Site Server Express Content Analyzer? [Check all correct answers]

❑ a. Orthogonal

❑ b. Tree

❑ c. Cyberbolic

❑ d. Visual

❑ e. Web

Question 40

Why must you install Internet Explorer 4.01 before installing IIS 4.0?

○ a. To browse the Web.

○ b. Because Internet Explorer 4.01 installs various system DLLs on the server that provide functionality for the Microsoft Management Console, the Microsoft Java VM, and so on.

○ c. Because HTMLA works only with Internet Explorer 4.01.

○ d. None of the above.

Question 41

Windows NT Challenge/Response is a built-in Windows NT security feature. What technology can you use to implement similar functionality independent of the operating system? [Check all correct answers]

❑ a. CGI scripts

❑ b. Active Server Pages with ActiveX controls

❑ c. Visual Basic

❑ d. Visual C++

❑ e. Perl

Question 42

Which of the following actions is not performed with Windows NT's basic authentication scheme?

○ a. Password encryption

○ b. User name encryption

○ c. Both user name and password encryption

○ d. None of the above

Question 43

With MMC, you have the ability to add or remove an individual snap-in; however, once it's added, you cannot save the configuration for future sessions.

○ a. True

○ b. False

Question 44

Within your company intranet, you have 10 workstations used by temporary employees. You do not want users of these computers to have any access to the Web site hosted on your internal IIS. Therefore, on the IP Address And Domain Name Restrictions page for the company Web site, you define exceptions for these 10 computers as 10 individual IP addresses. After you make this change, you discover that no clients on the intranet can access the Web site except these 10 computers. What could be the problem?

○ a. Individual computers cannot be exceptions. A subnet must be specified.

○ b. A reboot of IIS is required before this takes effect.

○ c. Anonymous access has been disabled.

○ d. The IP Address Access Restrictions option is set to Denied Access.

Question 45

You're running a Web site for a winery in the state of Washington. There's a steady stream of users from all over the country who go to your Web site to purchase wines and to get advice on wine making. You're looking to customize the site to provide the best possible experience for your users. You're even considering the use of a mirror site in Delaware if you can show sufficient demand from the East Coast. Which of the following preformatted Report Writer reports could help you meet this need? [Check all correct answers]

❑ a. IP Server

❑ b. Geography

❑ c. Browser And Operating System

❑ d. Referrer

❑ e. Path

Question 46

You're the Webmaster within an organization. You have set the default document for your Web site to DEFAULT.ASP. However, whenever a user tries reaching your Web site, he gets the error message "Directory listing not allowed." What is the problem?

○ a. The .HTM extension should be used instead of the .ASP extension for the default page.

○ b. You cannot use an ASP as your Web site's default page.

○ c. Execute rights need to be allowed on the directory where the DEFAULT.ASP page physically resides on your Web server.

○ d. The directory listing style needs to be set to Unix.

Question 47

You can configure IIS to block specific IP addresses from accessing and using which of the following services? [Check all correct answers]

❑ a. Web

❑ b. FTP

❑ c. Gopher

❑ d. Telnet

Question 48

You format your machine and then install Windows NT under NTFS. There's no partition on the machine. Assume your Windows NT installation was not successful and NT crashes every time you load it. Which of the following approaches would you take to resolve this problem? [Check all correct answers]

❑ a. Use the emergency repair disk (ERD) to repair NT.

❑ b. Use Service Pack 3 to repair NT.

❑ c. Use the DOS **FORMAT** command to reformat the hard disk and then reinstall NT.

❑ d. Use FDISK to delete NTFS and create a primary DOS (FAT) partition.

Question 49

You have been the IIS administrator for your company for more than a year. The Internet content for your company's Web site has grown, and you are asked to create a proprietary authentication program for the site. As the Web site administrator, you are asked to choose the design technique. What technique would you choose? [Check all correct answers]

❑ a. Create an ISAPI filter to authenticate all the users.

❑ b. Create a CGI script to authenticate all the users.

❑ c. Create a user account on Windows NT for all the users.

Question 50

You must manually start a virtual Web or FTP server.

○ a. True

○ b. False

Question 51

You want to create a new Index Server catalog for a Web site. The corpus of the Web site is 500MB. How much space will be required by the catalog?

○ a. 100MB

○ b. 200MB

○ c. 500MB

○ d. 800MB

Question 52

You would like to design an HTML form that accepts data from the user, processes the data on IIS, and returns results to the browser. Choose the IIS extensions for this type of implementation. [Check all correct answers]

❑ a. JScript

❑ b. VBScript

❑ c. CGI

❑ d. ASP

Question 53

Your public Web server also hosts a private data area. You have configured Index Server to index every document stored on the server in both the Web root and the data directory. All the files in the data directory are set so that only internal users have Read access. If an external user performs a search using a word that exists in one or more files from both the Web root and the data directory, how will items from the data directory appear in the results lists?

○ a. They will appear without hyperlinks.

○ b. They will appear with authentication fields to gain access.

○ c. They will appear just as any item from the Web root.

○ d. They will not appear, and the external user will be unaware of their presence.

Question 54

Your supervisor has just read an article that mentioned the power of inference algorithms. She asks you to explain to her what an inference algorithm is and what it has to do with measuring the performance of the Web server. Which of the following would be an accurate description?

- ○ a. An inference algorithm is a program that uses fuzzy logic to perform tasks such as HTML title lookups and IP address resolution. Because it simplifies the lookup of things such as DNS files, it improves performance of these otherwise high-intensity tasks.

- ○ b. An inference algorithm is a set of calculations that improves logging speed in IIS. Without it, ODBC logging would be a process that would overcome all but the fastest processors with at least 64MB of memory.

- ○ c. An inference algorithm works like a statistical correction factor for things such as request data in an ODBC-compliant log file. Without it, Web pages with 100 thumbnail images would appear to be many times more popular than they really are.

- ○ d. An inference algorithm works like a set of statistical correction factors for things such as IP address resolution and database caching. Without it, database references to cached data would not be possible.

- ○ e. An inference algorithm is a set of calculations that improves the speed of Site Server Express Report Writer.

Question 55

You're working for an accounting firm that has 26 Web administrators. The firm has one Windows NT Server to service all its needs. The firm has a mission-critical application developed with SQL Server as the database back end running on the Windows NT Server. The client front end is in Visual Basic, and it resides on each user's machine. Recently, the firm also installed IIS and created an intranet. The intranet is yet within its nascent stage, where the firm posts all its notices, policies, procedures, and more. After deploying IIS, the network administrator began to complain that the network is becoming increasingly slower. This, in turn, affects the mission-critical application. How do you resolve this problem?

○ a. Stop the FTP service on IIS.

○ b. Disable the keep-alive HTTP connection.

○ c. Tune your Web site's performance for fewer than 10,000 hits per day.

○ d. Enable bandwidth throttling.

14

Answer Key
To Sample Test

1. b
2. a, b, d
3. e
4. a, b, c
5. b
6. b
7. b
8. b
9. a
10. a, b
11. a
12. a, d
13. c
14. c
15. b
16. a, b, c, d
17. b
18. b, d
19. a, d

20. a, c, d
21. d
22. a
23. b
24. b, d
25. b
26. b
27. b, d
28. b
29. a, c
30. a
31. c, d, e
32. a, c
33. a, b, d
34. a
35. a
36. a, b, c, d
37. a
38. b

39. b, c
40. b
41. a, c, d, e
42. d
43. b
44. d
45. b, c, e
46. c
47. a, b
48. a, d
49. a, b
50. a
51. b
52. a, b, c, d
53. d
54. c
55. d

Question 1

False, a digital signature is only used to indicate the identity of the sender; it's not used to encrypt data. Therefore, answer b is correct.

Question 2

The nonappearance of a known file in a results list can be due to a user not being authenticated, a user not having at least Read access, or the file not being part of the corpus. Therefore, answers a, b, and d are correct. Because a query is performed against an index and not the original file, it's not affected by the status of the document. Therefore, answer c is incorrect.

Question 3

The best answer to this question is e. HTML title lookup, IP address resolution, and Whois organization queries are all resource-intensive operations and should be avoided whenever possible when performance is an issue. However, if you can find a time of day when demand on this server is low, it's certainly possible to schedule these operations for specific times. It would be helpful to find out when these times are through the appropriate report; however, you don't know what these times are right now. Therefore, answers a, b, c, and d are incorrect.

Question 4

The correct answers to this question are a, b, and c. Not everyone has a browser that shows images. When a text-based browser gets to an image without HTML <ALT> tags, the browser stops. For test purposes, all pages with more than 32K are too slow to load for all modem users. A Site Summary report is a useful overview of the status of key quick search items on the Web site. Because you've already used the Verify Links tool, broken links will be reported. It isn't necessary to go into a Web page to check all the links. Therefore, answer d is incorrect.

Question 5

False, the SMTP service is configured so that no message relaying to remote SMTP servers occurs. Therefore, answer b is correct. This prevents users from spamming (sending lots of unsolicited, anonymous, and untraceable email).

Question 6

A 403 error occurs if the Web site does not have Read access enabled. Therefore, answer b is correct. Enabling Write access has no effect on Read access. Therefore, answer a is incorrect. If the client was restricted from the Web site, an "access denied" error would be issued instead of a "Read access forbidden" error. Therefore, answer c is incorrect. Pulling resources from a share has no effect on the read error. Therefore, answer d is incorrect.

Question 7

Creating a key certificate request is an integral part of configuring a Web server to offer SSL-based secure communications. Therefore, answer b is correct. Installing IIS and applying Service Pack 3 do not require a key request. Therefore, answers a and d are incorrect. As a client, purchasing a product with a credit card over a secure link does not require a key request to be generated, but it does rely on the Web server to have installed a certificate already. Therefore, answer c is incorrect.

Question 8

The correct answer to this question is b. For an intranet, the Web site's home directory is mapped to the server name; "http://marketing" represents a direct mapping between the Web site's home directory and the server name. None of the other options represents this direct mapping. Therefore, answers a, c, and d are incorrect.

Question 9

The correct answer to this question is a, True. Synchronizing the Windows NT password with the HTTP or FTP password is IIS's default configuration.

Question 10

The correct answers to this question are a and b. Downloading a file is equivalent to a Read operation. Because there's no Read access on the file, you can neither read nor download the file. To be able to write to the file, you must have Write access to the file, which is a separate permission from read and does not rely on Read access. Therefore, answer c is incorrect.

Question 11

Only the locally accessible ISM snap-in can be used to manage certificate mappings. Therefore, answer a is correct. The Server Manager is not involved with certificate management. Therefore, answer b is incorrect. ISM HTML does not have the ability to manage certificate mappings. Therefore, answer c is incorrect. The Certificate Server is only used to issue certificates if you want to be a certificate authority—it's not used to map certificates to Web sites. Therefore, answer d is incorrect.

Question 12

IIS is administered through an MMC snap-in and HTMLA. Therefore, answers a and d are correct. IIS does not have an applet or an Administrative wizard. Therefore, answers b and c are incorrect.

Question 13

The correct modification is to set service/site-level bandwidth throttling to 8,192K for SITE3 and SITE4. This will grant twice the bandwidth granted to SITE1 and SITE2 for both SITE3 and SITE4. Therefore, answer c is correct. Setting server/computer-level bandwidth throttling to 8,192K will not specifically grant twice the bandwidth to SITE3 and SITE4; instead, it will just double the total bandwidth shared by all four sites. Therefore, answer a is incorrect. Setting service/site-level bandwidth throttling to 2,046K for SITE1 and SITE2 will not double the available bandwidth to SITE3 and SITE4 but will only force SITE3 and SITE4 to compete for the 4,096K server/computer throttle limit. Therefore, answer b is incorrect. Throttling by site and by computer is possible with IIS. Therefore, answer d is incorrect.

Question 14

Service Pack 3 is the component required for 128-bit data encryption. Therefore, answer c is correct. IIS does not need a true Internet domain name assigned by the InterNIC, Microsoft Transaction Server, or Microsoft Certificate Server to use 128-bit encryption. Therefore, answers a, b, and d are incorrect.

Question 15

The correct answer to this question is b, False. Netscape Navigator does not include built-in support for Microsoft's ActiveX technology. Therefore, answer a is incorrect.

Question 16

All of these answers are correct. First, you want to check whether both the network and IIS are running. Next, you want to check whether the TCP/IP protocol stack is installed. Then, check whether the WWW service is configured properly. Finally, to test if everything is working right, open Internet Explorer on the server and verify the connection to the localhost.

Question 17

The correct answer to this question is b, False. An important point to understand about the Microsoft BackOffice products is that they are tightly integrated with each other. As such, if you set the access permission on a server directory to No Access, the Microsoft Index Server recognizes the access permission and does not use the directory within its full-text search.

Question 18

The IIS SMTP and NNTP services can be administered through the IIS MMC snap-in or through separate HTML interfaces. Therefore, answers b and d are correct. Server Manager and Network Monitor are not used to administer these services. Therefore, answers a and c are incorrect.

Question 19

The IDC and HTX files require Read and Execute permissions. Therefore, answers a and d are correct.

Question 20

The IIS NNTP service supports multiple discussion groups, moderated groups, and SSL. Therefore, answers a, c, and d are correct. IIS's NNTP service is unable to access Usenet newsfeeds. It's restricted to host discussion groups within a single server. Therefore, answer b is incorrect.

Question 21

A certificate authority (CA) is a third-party organization that is trusted to verify the identity of servers and individuals. Therefore, answer d is correct. A CA is not a single worldwide distribution point for client identities. This type of entity does not currently exist. Therefore, answer a is incorrect. A CA is not an Internet standards organization similar to IETF and IEEE that sets the requirements for certificates. Therefore, answer b is incorrect. A CA is not part of the NSC. Therefore, answer c is incorrect.

Question 22

The correct answer to this question is a. The default port for the WWW service is 80. Therefore, answers b, c, and d are incorrect.

Question 23

The Script Debugger is the tool included with IIS 4.0 that simplifies the troubleshooting process of Active Server Pages. Therefore, answer b is correct. The Java Virtual Machine is not a troubleshooting tool for ASPs. Therefore, answer a is incorrect. W3C logging is a troubleshooting tool for the Web server as a whole. Therefore, answer c is incorrect. ODBC drivers are not troubleshooting tools; they enable database application communications. Therefore, answer d is incorrect.

Question 24

If a user is shown a directory listing, directory browsing is enabled and a default document is not found. Therefore, answers b and d are correct. The directory must have Read access defined; otherwise, the directory listing won't be displayed. Therefore, answer a is incorrect. A redirection URL does not cause a directory listing to be displayed, it simply takes you to the alternate location. Therefore, answer c is incorrect.

Question 25

The correct answer to this question is b. While you're installing IIS, Setup needs to create some directories as well as give share access to others. Only an

NT administrator can do this. None of the other options will resolve this problem. Therefore, answers a, c, and d are incorrect.

Question 26

The IIS Administration HTML tool files are stored in \Winnt\System32\Inetsrv\Iisadmin, by default. Therefore, answer b is correct. The other listed folders are incorrect. Therefore, answers a, c, and d are incorrect.

Question 27

You can monitor Index Server's performance via the Performance Monitor or an IDA script. Therefore, answers b and d are correct. The Index Server MMC snap-in is not used to monitor Index Server's performance, but instead, it's used to manage indexed directories and indexes. Therefore, answer a is incorrect. Server Manager is not used in any way with Index Server. Therefore, answer c is incorrect.

Question 28

Transaction Server offers programmers the ability to create three-tiered applications for Internet deployment. Therefore, answer b is correct. The NNTP service is used to host discussion groups; Certificate Server allows your site to be a certificate authority; and Index Server offers content indexing and searching. Therefore, answers a, c, and d are incorrect.

Question 29

PING and TRACERT are TCP/IP utilities that are used to test network communications. Therefore, answers a and c are correct. ROUTE and NBTSTAT are not used to test network communications. Therefore, answers b and d are incorrect.

Question 30

The correct answer to this question is a. Windows NT Service Pack 3 installs a number of new security components and application programming interfaces, including the password-filtering security component. Windows NT Options Pack installs IIS 4.0. Therefore, answer b is incorrect. Internet Explorer 4.01 installs various system DLLs, thus providing functionality for the Microsoft Management Console, the Microsoft Java VM, and so on. Therefore, answer c is incorrect. Windows NT Server 4.0 installs Windows NT. Therefore, answer d is incorrect.

Question 31

The correct answers to this question are c, d, and e. You need a machine that supports the minimum hardware requirements to install Windows NT Server

4.0. The TCP/IP protocol is also required for IIS. Access to the Option Pack distribution files can be via an Internet connection to the Microsoft Web site or on a CD-ROM. You don't need a local network connection (because IIS can be an isolated or standalone machine) or an NTFS partition for installing Windows NT or IIS. Therefore, answers a and b are incorrect.

Question 32

Service Pack 3 and Internet Explorer 4.01 are installation requirements for IIS 4.0. Therefore, answers a and c are correct. NetBEUI is not a requirement of IIS 4.0. Therefore, answer b is incorrect. Windows NT 4.0 Workstation is not a requirement of IIS 4.0. In fact, Workstation cannot host IIS; it can only host Peer Web Services. Therefore, answer d is incorrect.

Question 33

The statements in answers a, b, and d are all correct. Answer a refers to Index Server, answer b refers to Certificate Server, and answer d refers to Message Queue Server. The statement in answer c is incorrect. Site Server Express can only replicate one server to one server. Only the full Enterprise version of Site Server can replicate one server to multiple servers.

Question 34

The correct answer to this question is a. When creating the virtual directory, you need to provide the directory's physical path. If you do not grant the Read and Write permissions for the directory, the client browser may not be able to browse the virtual directory; however, you can grant these permissions at a later stage. IIS 4.0 does not support Gopher. Also, you need an IP address for a virtual server, not for a virtual directory. Therefore, answers b, c, and d are incorrect.

Question 35

Only word lists are stored only in memory. Therefore, answer a is correct. Persistent, shadow, and master indexes are stored on a hard drive. Therefore, answers b, c, and d are incorrect.

Question 36

The SMTP service can be secured using any of these methods. Therefore, answers a, b, c, and d are correct.

Question 37

The correct answer to this question is a. **RUNAT=SERVER** is the keyword. The others answers (b, c, and d) are incorrect.

Question 38

Encryption is the technology used to establish secure communications over insecure networks. Therefore, answer b is correct. CRC is a technology used to verify the integrity of transmitted data; it's not associated with security. Therefore, answer a is incorrect. TCP/IP is a network protocol. Secure communications can occur over it, but TCP/IP does not directly provide for security. Therefore, answer c is incorrect. DHCP is a technology used to dynamically configure clients. Therefore, answer d is incorrect.

Question 39

The correct answers to this question are b and c. The tree and cyberbolic views are the two views available in Site Server Express Content Analyzer. The other answers are not options in Content Analyzer. Therefore, answers a, d, and e are incorrect.

Question 40

The correct answer to this question is b. IIS 4.0 uses the system DLLs that Internet Explorer 4.01 installs. You don't need to use Internet Explorer to browse the Web—you can use any other browser. Therefore, answer a is incorrect. The HTMLA works with many other browsers, not just IE 4.01. Therefore, answer c is incorrect. Because b is correct, answer d is incorrect.

Question 41

The correct answers to this question are a, c, d, and e. You can use Visual Basic, Visual C++, and Perl to create CGI programs. A CGI program runs independent of the operating system, as long as the program does not use or call any functions specific to the operating system. Active Server Pages with ActiveX controls is Windows platform specific. Therefore, answer b is incorrect.

Question 42

The correct answer to this question is d. The basic authentication scheme is just that, basic. The scheme does not encrypt anything involved in the authentication process. Therefore, answers a, b, and c are incorrect.

Question 43

False, MMC has the ability to save the configuration of each console as an MSC file for use in subsequent sessions. Therefore, answer b is correct.

Question 44

If all but the exception computers can no longer gain access, this means that Denied Access was selected instead of Granted Access. Therefore, answer d is correct. Individual computers and a subnet can be used as exceptions. Therefore, answer a is incorrect. A reboot of IIS is not required for a change in access restrictions. Therefore, answer b is incorrect. Disabling anonymous access prevents all clients from accessing anonymously, but it does not prevent authenticated users from accessing. This question does not state if anonymous or authenticated access was affected. Therefore, answer c is incorrect.

Question 45

The correct answers to this question are b, c, and e. A Geography report will help you determine the distribution of where your users are coming from. Knowing the browser of most of your users will help determine the type of add-ons that are more important for your site (for example, ActiveX for MSIE or Java for Netscape). The Path report shows how your users are navigating through the site and therefore helps determine whether you need to change the locations and sizes of some pages, images, and other objects to make navigation easier. There is no IP Server report. Therefore, answer a is incorrect. The Referrer report provides data on where users are coming from, meaning what ISP they log in to to gain Internet access. Although this can provide useful data on where your advertising is working best on the Web, this does not address the user experience once he or she has reached your site. Therefore, answer d is incorrect.

Question 46

The correct answer to this question is c. You must enable execute rights on the directory where the DEFAULT.ASP page physically resides on the server. It doesn't matter whether you use an HTML or Active Server Page as your Web server's default page. You can, of course, use an Active Server Page as your site's default page. Setting the directory listing style to MS-DOS or Unix is not relevant. Therefore, answers a, b, and d are incorrect.

Question 47

The correct answers to this question are a and b. You can configure both Web and FTP services to block specific IP addresses. IIS 4.0 does not support Gopher or Telnet. Therefore, answers c and d are incorrect.

Question 48

The correct answers to this question are a and d. Using the ERD should be your first option. Chances are the ERD will fix the problem. If not, because there's no partition on the machine, you must use FDISK to delete NTFS and create a primary DOS (FAT) partition. Then, you can reinstall Windows NT. Typically, it's recommended you create a partition on your machine and then install NT. The Service Pack 3 cannot repair NT—that's not its purpose. Therefore, answer b is incorrect. The DOS **FORMAT** command does not work because there's no partition on the machine, and the **FORMAT** command cannot recognize NTFS. Therefore, answer c is incorrect.

Question 49

The correct answers to this question are a and b. Answer a is the most efficient technique because the approach uses an ISAPI filter. ISAPI implementation consumes fewer server resources compared to a CGI implementation. Answer b is less efficient (but still correct) because an ISAPI solution is faster than a CGI solution. Answer c is not an option because you do not want to create a Windows NT user account for each user. Therefore, answer c is incorrect.

Question 50

The correct answer to this question is a, True. When you first create a virtual Web or FTP server, the server's default state is Stopped. Therefore, answer b is incorrect.

Question 51

The index catalog is typically 40 percent of the corpus, so 200MB is required in this scenario. Therefore, answer b is correct.

Question 52

The correct answers to this question are a, b, c, and d. Both JScript and VBScript are scripting languages you can use with ASP. ASP is an alternative to CGI, and CGI is the standard Web mechanism for transmitting data between the client and server.

Question 53

Items from an ACL-restricted directory will not appear in the results list for a user without proper access privileges. That user will be unaware of the existence of those documents because Index Server will not even show the file name of restricted items to unauthorized users. Therefore, answer d is correct. Because Index Server will not display restricted items to unauthorized users in any way, answers a, b, and c are incorrect. The fact that even when items are included in the index files used by a search to which the current user does not have valid access, these items are not displayed in the results.

Question 54

The correct answer to this question is c. Without inference algorithms, a Web page with 100 thumbnail images would get 101 hits each time a user links to it, which would make the page seem much more popular than a text-only page that gets only one hit for each time a user links to it. Inference algorithms correct for this discrepancy. However, they only address the data related to hits, requests, visits, users, and organizations. Although IP address resolution is loosely related to organizations, database caching is not an inference algorithm function. Therefore, answer d is incorrect. None of the other answers is related to the function of inference algorithms. Therefore, answers a, b, and e are incorrect.

Question 55

The correct answer to this question is d. By enabling bandwidth throttling, you can limit the bandwidth your Web site uses. Stopping the FTP service on IIS is not a solution. You do not want to disable the FTP service. Therefore, answer a is incorrect. Disabling the keep-alive HTTP connection is no solution, either. In fact, keeping the HTTP connection alive helps improve the performance. Therefore, answer b is incorrect. Again, tuning your Web site's performance to fewer than 10,000 hits per day does not help. Although this may improve performance, your site will not be able to handle a larger volume traffic. Therefore, answer c is incorrect.

Glossary

.HTM (HTML form document)—The extension applied to all standard HTML 3.0 and later documents.

.HTX (HTML extension file)—One of the files involved in the resolution of a query. The .HTX file is used to format the query results for presentation back to the user.

.IDQ (Internet data query file)—One of the files involved in the resolution of a query. The .IDQ file specifies how the query from the form is to be processed.

AATP (Authorized Academic Training Program)—A program that authorizes accredited academic institutions of higher learning to offer Microsoft Certified Professional testing and training to their students. The institutions also are allowed to use the Microsoft Education course materials and Microsoft Certified Trainers.

ACL (access control list)—A list of users and computers that controls who can use a resource and who cannot.

Active client—An application that includes built-in support for ActiveX technology and supports client-side scripting (for example, Internet Explorer).

Active platform—The foundation of designing and developing Internet and intranet business solutions using Microsoft tools and technologies. As three-tier client/server model, the Active platform is an extensible component-based architecture.

Active Server—A Web server or similar application that supports server-side scripting (also known as *Active Server Pages*).

Active Server components—A collection of IIS prepackaged components that allow you to build your ASP applications quickly and efficiently.

Active Server objects—Five core server objects that constitute the core functionality of ASP. These server objects contain methods and properties that you can configure to meet your application requirements.

ActiveX—A suite of technologies you can use to deliver business solutions over the Internet and intranets.

ActiveX controls—A stripped-down version of OLE controls with their size and speed optimized for use over the Internet.

ADO (Active Data Object)—Probably the most important and popular ASP component, the ADO is used to build data-driven dynamic Web applications.

alias—A short name for a directory that is easy to use and remember.

anonymous account—The IUSR_*servername* account created by IIS for Web and FTP services that can only access the files and applications for which the system administrator grants permission.

ARP (Address Resolution Protocol)—A Network layer protocol that associates logical (IP) addresses to physical (MAC) addresses.

ASP (Active Server Pages)—A Web programming technique that enriches commerce and business communications by improving script management. ASPs can execute with a transaction. Therefore, if the script fails, the transaction is aborted.

ASP script—The Active Server Page script that executes on the server and takes advantage of the server's processing power as well as delivers client-side HTML. ASP scripts end with .ASP.

assessment exam—Similar to the certification exam, this type of exam gives you the opportunity to answer questions at your own pace. This type of exam also uses the same tools as the certification exam.

ATEC (Authorized Technical Education Center)—The location where you can take a Microsoft Official Curriculum course taught by Microsoft Certified Trainers.

automatic password synchronization—When the server automatically synchronizes the FTP site password with the Windows NT password for anonymous users.

bandwidth—The range of frequencies that a communications medium can carry. For baseband networking media, the bandwidth also indicates the theoretical maximum amount of data that the medium can transfer. For broadband networking media, the bandwidth is measured by the variations that any single carrier frequency can carry.

bandwidth throttling—Limits the total bandwidth used by all IIS sites to the kilobytes per second defined in the associated field.

BDC (Backup Domain Controller)—A backup server that protects the integrity and availability of the SAM database. BDCs are not able to make changes or modifications, but they can use the database to authenticate users.

Boolean—A form of algebraic logic that is diminished to either on or off, yes or no, or true or false.

bottleneck—The component of a computer or network that is preventing at least one other component from operating at its maximum efficiency.

CA (certificate authority)—A third party that issues certificates and claims to have verified the identity of a server or an individual.

cache—A temporary storage area that holds current information and is able to provide that information faster than other methods.

catalog—The highest level of content organization within Index Server.

CATALOG.WCI—The default catalog folder created by Index Server.

certificate—A digital signature issued by a third party (called a certificate authority or CA) that claims to have verified the identity of a server or an individual.

Certificate Server—A component installed with IIS's Web and FTP services that gives individual Web servers the ability to issue, revoke, and renew X.509 digital certificates to clients.

chunked transfers—A method of data transmission that greatly increases the efficiency of delivering Active Server Pages (ASPs).

chunking—The process of breaking a transmission into multiple pieces of different sizes, each with its own header and size indicator.

client software—See *UA (user agent)*.

COM (Component Object Model)—Microsoft's groundwork of the ActiveX platform. Used to support interprocess communications and designed to promote software interoperability.

computer name—The name of a computer on a LAN that is specific to an individual workstation or server.

configuration error—An error that occurs in the installation procedure, default installation directories, default security settings, or locations of most commands and settings.

connection timeout—The maximum time a client connection can exist without any activity.

Content Analyzer—A Site Server Express tool that is used to visualize what is and is not working on a Web site.

content filters—The file format-specific add-ons that enable Index Server to index the contents of non-Microsoft documents.

cookie—A marker downloaded to a PC that identifies a specific user to a Web site.

corpus—The collection of all documents that Index Server is configured to monitor and index.

CRL (certificate revocation list)—Maintained by the CA, the list of all invalid certificates.

CryptoAPI—This application programming interface (API) allows programmers to create applications that can use or even rely upon cryptography without requiring knowledge of the encryption system. The CryptoAPI separates applications from encryption, thus enabling an application without modification to use different types or new technologies of encryption.

custom error—A customized error message.

cut score—On the Microsoft Certified Professional exam, the lowest score a person can receive and still pass.

database—A collection of information arranged and stored so that data can be accessed quickly and accurately.

decryption—The necessary flip-side of encryption. Decryption is the process of unscrambling data.

decryption key—The mathematical inverse of the encryption key. The decryption key unscrambles encrypted data to extract the original.

dependency error—When a driver, device, or service fails to load, which then causes other drivers, devices, or services to load or function improperly.

DHCP server—A service used in a TCP/IP environment to dynamically assign IP address and other IP settings to clients upon bootup.

digital certificate—An electronic identification and verification tool used to secure online commerce and other transactions.

digital signatures—The private key of the sender.

directory browsing—An IIS content control that allows users to navigate through the directory structure on the IIS server. To prevent this, uncheck Directory Browsing Allowed. By default, IIS lets the users browse through the directory structure.

directory security—An IIS setting used to secure the directories on your FTP server. You can choose to grant or deny access to all or specific directories on your FTP server.

DNA (Distributed interNet Applications)—A Windows platform architectural framework that enables the deployment of scalable, multitier, distributed computing solutions over any type of network.

DNS (Domain Name Service)—A service that resolves host names (such as microsoft.com) into IP addresses (such as 207.68.145.42).

drop directory—Where all messages directed at the domains hosted by an SMTP service are stored.

encryption—The process of scrambling data (message, streaming multimedia, data files, and so on) into a form that is unusable and unreadable by anyone except the intended recipient.

encryption key—An electronic mathematical formula used to scramble data.

ERD (Emergency Repair Disk)—The disk that contains files and other resources that can be used to repair the system partition of a Windows NT computer.

event auditing—The security activity of recording a log of events or occurrences on a computer system.

Exam Preparation Guides—Guides that provide information specific to the material covered on Microsoft Certified Professional exams to help students prepare for the exams.

Exam Study Guide—Short for Microsoft Certified Professional Program Exam Study Guide. Contains information about the topics covered on more than one of the Microsoft Certified Professional exams.

firewall—A piece of equipment that is used to secure an Internet connection.

FTP (File Transfer Protocol)—An application protocol that is used for file transfer, file manipulation, and directory manipulation.

Gopher—A large database that provides search capabilities.

host headers—A delivery and communication mechanism used by IIS to distribute multiple sites using transferred session information.

HTMLA—The HTML administration tool (also known as *ISM*).

HTTP (Hypertext Transfer Protocol)—The World Wide Web protocol that allows for the transfer of HTML documents over the Internet or intranets.

HTTP 1.1—A version of the HTTP protocol that supports several improvements to the Web communication process.

HTTP errors—A standard set of error codes that are reported to clients in the event of an error.

HTTP headers—An IIS setting that lets you configure information such as content expiration, content rating, custom headers, and MIME maps.

HTTP keep-alives—A request that the Web server keeps a communication connection open across multiple requests.

ICS (Internet Connection Services)—An extension and upgrade module for Windows NT Server's Remote Access Service (RAS). ICS adds several enhancements to RAS, including customizable client dialers, centrally controlled network phonebooks, new RADIUS authentication support, and improved administration and management tools.

IDC (Internet Database Connector)— Tool that lets you connect IIS to 32-bit relational databases, including Microsoft SQL Server, Microsoft Access, Microsoft FoxPro, Sybase SQL Server, dBASE, and so on. The IDC is an ISAPI DLL (HTTPODBC.DLL) server extension.

IIS (Internet Information Server)—Web server software by Microsoft; included and implemented with Windows NT Server.

IIS directory—The location on IIS in which you store files, including ASP scripts and other programs.

index—The database of all remaining words extracted from the corpus after it has been handled by the content filters, word breakers, normalizers, and noise word filters.

Index Server—A component of IIS that brings site content indexing and searching to IIS-hosted Web sites.

inference algorithm—A statistical correction factor for situations, such as hits, that are not recorded due to Proxy Server caching.

Internet—The collection of TCP/IP-based networks around the world. Information on nearly every subject is available in some form somewhere on the Internet.

intranet—An internal, private network that uses the same protocols and standards as the Internet.

IP (Internet Protocol)—A Network layer protocol that provides source and destination addressing and routing.

IP address—Four sets of numbers, separated by decimal points, that represent the numeric address of a computer attached to a TCP/IP network, such as the Internet.

IPX/SPX (Internet Packet Exchange/Sequenced Packet Exchange)—Novell's NetWare protocol, reinvented by Microsoft and implemented in Windows NT under the name NWLink. It's fully compatible with Novell's version and, in many cases, is a better implementation than the original.

ISAPI filter—A program, typically an executable and always resident within the server's memory, that responds to the events during an HTTP request's processing.

ISDN (Integrated Services Digital Network)—A form of digital communication that has a bandwidth of 128Kbps.

ISM (Internet Service Manager)—In older versions, this was the tool used to manage IIS. Internet Service Manager has been replaced in IIS 4.0 by the MMC and the Web-based administration tool.

ISP (Internet Service Provider)—A service company that sells network access to the Internet. An ISP purchases bandwidth in bulk and, in turn, resells it in smaller packages.

job function expert—A person with extensive knowledge about a particular job function and the software products/technologies related to that job. Typically, a job function expert is currently performing the job, has recently performed the job, or is training people to do the job.

LAN (local area network)—A network that is confined to a single building or geographic area and comprised of servers, workstations, peripheral devices, a network operating system, and a communications link.

mailroot directory—The directory in which all the messages handled by the SMTP service are stored.

master index—Created when all current shadow indexes and the current master index are integrated into a new master index. There is always only one master index (also called a *catalog*).

maximum connections message—The warning message users see when they connect to the FTP site and it has already reached the maximum number of connections.

MCP (Microsoft Certified Professional)—An individual who has taken and passed at least one certification exam.

MCSD (Microsoft Certified Solution Developer)—An individual who is qualified to create and develop solutions for businesses using the Microsoft development tools, technologies, and platforms.

MCSE (Microsoft Certified Systems Engineer)—An individual who is an expert on Windows NT and the Microsoft BackOffice integrated family of server software. This individual also can plan, implement, maintain, and support information systems associated with these products.

MCT (Microsoft Certified Trainer)—An individual who is qualified by Microsoft to teach Microsoft Education courses at sites authorized by Microsoft.

Message Queue Server—A component of the Windows NT Server 4.0 Option Pack that enables applications to communicate via a message queue system, even when remote systems are offline.

metabase—A high-speed, memory-resident, hierarchical system used as a storage device for most of the configuration parameters used by IIS.

Microsoft Certificate Server—This application is used to organize, issue, renew, and revoke private certificates without relying on a third-party external CA.

Microsoft Certification Exam—A test created by Microsoft to verify a test-taker's mastery of a software product, technology, or computing topic.

Microsoft Certified Professional Certification Update—A newsletter for Microsoft Certified Professional candidates and Microsoft Certified Professionals.

Microsoft official curriculum—Microsoft education courses that support the certification exam process and are created by the Microsoft product groups.

Microsoft Proxy Server 2.0—Acts as an IPX-to-IP gateway for LAN clients, as a firewall to protect the internal network from the external network, and as a cache area for Internet objects that allows faster response time when a client requests an Internet object, such as a URL.

Microsoft Roadmap To Education And Certification—An application, based on Microsoft Windows, that takes you through the process of deciding what your certification goals are and informs you of the best way to achieve them.

Microsoft Sales Fax Service—A service through which you can obtain Exam Preparation Guides, fact sheets, and additional information about the Microsoft Certified Professional Program.

Microsoft Script Debugger—A utility used to debug application scripts. It can only be invoked from within Internet Explorer.

Microsoft Solution Provider—An organization, not directly related to Microsoft, that provides integration, consulting, technical support, and other services related to Microsoft products.

Microsoft TechNet—A service provided by Microsoft that gives helpful information via a monthly CD-ROM. TechNet is the primary source of technical information for people who support and/or educate end users, create automated solutions, or administer networks and/or databases.

MMC (Microsoft Management Console)—A Windows-based tool that provides users with total management of all services and applications within a single utility.

MMC snap-in—The primary means by which IIS is configured locally.

MOLI (Microsoft Online Institute)—An organization that makes training materials, online forums and user groups, and online classes available.

MRI (multiple-rating item)—An item that gives you a task and a proposed solution. Every time the task is set, an alternate solution is given, and the candidate must choose the answer that gives the best results produced by one solution.

MSDN (Microsoft Developer Network)—The official source for Software Development Kits (SDKs), Device Driver Kits (DDKs), operating systems, and programming information associated with creating applications for Microsoft Windows and Windows NT.

MTS (Microsoft Transaction Server)—An IIS component that allows distributed transaction applications to be developed for IIS.

NDA (nondisclosure agreement)—A legal agreement signed both by Microsoft and by a vendor, rendering certain rights and limitations.

NetBEUI—A simple Network layer transport protocol developed to support NetBIOS networks.

NetBIOS interface—The networking service used by Windows NT to communicate NetBIOS-level (typically name space) information to other network members.

network—A collection of server and client computers that communicates to share wire-based resources.

network adapter card—A synonym for "network interface card." Refers to the hardware device that mediates communication between a computer and one or more types of networking media.

NNTP (Network News Transfer Protocol)—The protocol used to distribute, retrieve, inquire about, and post Network News articles.

NNTP service—A service designed to host private discussion forums. Does not support news feeds or message replication from the global USENET NNTP news services.

node—An object that can be managed through MMC by means of an installed snap-in.

noise word—A language-specific word that offers no useful content and is not stored in the index.

NOISE.ENU—The location of the noise word list.

normalizer—A software tool that standardizes words emitted by a word breaker. Standardization includes removing capitalization, plurality, and punctuation. Plus, the normalizer identifies and removes noise words from the index.

NTFS (New Technology File System)—A file system used in Windows NT that supports file-level security, fault tolerance, and file-level compression.

NTLM (NT LAN Manager) authentication—An authentication technique the browser uses to encrypt and send a password across the network.

ODBC (Open Database Connectivity)—A standard API (Application Programming Interface) used to construct platform/application-independent databases.

Option Pack—The Microsoft Windows NT Server 4.0 product distribution that contains IIS 4.0 (and its subcomponents), Service Pack 3, Internet Explorer 4.01, Transaction Server 2.0, Message Queue Server Standard Edition, Site Server Express, and Connection Services for Microsoft RAS.

OS (operating system)—A software program that controls the operations on a computer system.

packet filter—An Internet Service Manager (ISM) option that controls inbound access to a network on a packet level. By utilizing this option, users can accept or deny traffic based on packet types, datagrams, or packet fragments.

PCT (Private Communication Technology)—An encryption technology similar to SSL.

performance tuning—The process or task of improving the performance of a computer by locating and eliminating bottlenecks.

permissions—A level of access assigned to files or folders. Permissions determine who has access rights to those files or folders.

persistent connections—A communication mechanism used to send multiple objects over fewer connections. This reduces communication overhead and improves performance.

persistent index—The combination of one or more word lists into a file stored on hard drive. Also called a *shadow index*.

pickup directory—An inbox for email messages to be copied. All files in this directory are automatically processed by the SMTP service.

PICS (Platform for Internet Content Selection) rating—A rating given to a Web site that provides control over what content can be accessed by which audiences.

pipelining—Used by HTTP 1.1 to allow clients to send multiple requests without waiting for a server's response. Pipelining improves response time and Web display performance.

policies—The evaluation of requests and assignment of new certificates is governed through the use of policies. Policies are installed by an administrator and instruct the Certificate Server to accept, deny, or delay a request based on the contents of the request. Policies are written in Java, Visual Basic, or C/C++.

proxy server—A software product that acts as a moderator or go-between for a client and a remote host. Most proxy servers also offer content caching and firewall capabilities.

public key encryption—The form of cryptology used by IIS. In this system, both the server and the client use two keys—a private key and a public key.

PWS (Personal Web Server)—A scaled-down version of IIS that works only on Intel-based Windows 95 systems.

query—Another word for *search*. More specifically, the term used to describe the data sent from an Index Server Web page to the server-side script that attempts to locate matches within the corpus.

queue—The folder used by the SMTP service for storage of messages actively being delivered.

RDS (Remote Data Service)—A database connection tool that enables client-side data caching in Web applications to reduce server traffic and overhead.

rebar—The MMC command bar that lists node- and object-specific commands.

Registry—A database that stores all the configuration information for Windows NT.

Report Writer—A Site Server Express tool that is used to mine information from the Usage Import Database.

Resource Kit—The additional documentation and software utilities distributed by Microsoft to provide information and instruction on the proper operation and modification of its software products.

resultant access—The accumulation of all types of access granted to a user specifically and by all group memberships, except if No Access is specified for that user or for a group to which that user is a member, in which case the user is denied access.

Results pane—The right pane of the MMC console. It displays the contents of the selected node.

robot—Also called a *spider*. It's an automated tool used to explore links.

Robot protocol—A protocol or behavioral control language used to define how a robot (crawler, spider, and so on) interacts with a specific Web site.

RPC (Remote Procedure Call)—A programming interface that allows software applications running on separate computers on different networks to use each other's services.

Scope pane—The left pane of the MMC console. It displays the namespace tree where all items to be managed, called *nodes*, are listed.

secure communication—An IIS security feature that directs the client browser to establish an encrypted link to a directory or file on the system, which enables a secure communication link between the browser and the server.

secure envelopes—The public key encryption of the sender.

security—The protection of data by restricting access to only authorized users.

server-centric—A term that implies that most of the actual execution or work of the application occurs on the server instead of on the client.

server-side scripting—Another name for Active Server Pages.

Service Pack—A component of the Windows NT Server 4.0 Option Pack. It's a requirement for IIS 4.0 and its related components.

SGC (Server Gated Crypto)—An extension to SSL that grants IIS the ability to use 128-bit encryption.

shadow index—The combination of one or more word lists into a file stored on a hard drive. Also called a *persistent index*.

Site Server Express—An express version of the Microsoft Site Server that is included with the IIS 4.0 Option Pack. This application gives you a wide variety of analysis tools to keep tabs on your Web sites as well as several publishing utilities to ease content issuance.

SMTP (Simple Mail Transport Protocol)—Another upper-layer protocol. SMTP is used by messaging programs such as email.

SMTP Service—A client service that allows Web applications to send and receive email messages.

snap-ins—A product or service specific to COM or DCOM object management utilities.

SortTemp—A storage folder for temporary files.

spamming—The act of sending a lot of unsolicited, anonymous, untraceable email.

spider—See *robot*.

SQL Server—A Microsoft product that supports a network-enabled relational database system.

SSL (Secure Sockets Layer)—An industry-standard protocol used to establish secure communications between a Web server (or other information service server) and a client.

SSL Client Authentication (SSLCA)—Another and more secure authentication scheme (added to the existing set of three—anonymous, basic/clear text, and Microsoft Challenge/Response).

SSL Handshake protocol—The higher layer of the SSL protocol that is used to coordinate between a client and server on an encryption algorithm to use for further secured communications.

SSL Record protocol—The lower-layer SSL protocol that operates just above the Transmission Layer Protocol (TCP). It encapsulates higher-level protocols; therefore, it's a security scheme that is flexible and application protocol-independent.

subnet—A portion or segment of a network.

subnet mask—A 32-bit address that indicates how many bits in an address are being used for the network ID.

TCP (Transmission Control Protocol)—A connection-oriented Transport layer protocol that accepts messages of any length from the upper layers and provides transportation to another computer. TCP is responsible for packet fragmentation as well as reassembly and sequencing.

TCP port—A representation of a data stream.

TCP/IP (Transmission Control Protocol/Internet Protocol)—The most commonly used network protocol and the central protocol of the Internet.

Three-tiered programming architecture—A system in which the components of an application are positioned in three distinct locations.

trusts—Logical security connections between two domains in which one domain is able to share its resources with the authenticated users from another domain.

UA (user agent)—A standard email client utility. Also called *client software*.

Unicode—A 16-bit system used to encode characters and letters from many different languages.

Unix—An interactive time-sharing operating system developed in 1969 by a hacker to play games. This system developed into the most widely used industrial-strength computer operating system in the world, and ultimately supported the birth of the Internet.

URL (Universal Resource Locator)—The addressing scheme used to identify resources on the Internet.

Usage Import—A Site Server Express tool that brings Web site logs into a database, which then can be refined by Report Writer into any number of formats.

user authentication and authorization—An IIS security feature that simplifies the logon process because the user only provides the logon information once rather than logging on to both IIS and NT.

virtual directory—Any directory that is not the home directory and not contained within IIS's home directory.

virtual server—Additional Web and FTP sites hosted on the same IIS server.

W3C extended log file format—A standardized log file format created by the W3C.

WAN (wide area network)—A network that spans geographically distant segments. Often, the distance of two miles or more is used to define a WAN; however, Microsoft equates any RAS connection as establishing a WAN.

word breaker—A software tool that takes the stream of characters emitted by a content filter and breaks it into words based on known language-dependent syntax and structure rules.

word list—The list of non-noise words and relevant properties extracted from a document. This list only exists in memory.

WSH (Windows Scripting Host)—A language-independent scripting host for 32-bit Windows platforms.

Index

Bold page numbers indicate sample exam questions.

Numbers and Symbols

- (hyphen), in anonymous user IDs, 88, **103**
32-bit databases, connecting to, 154-156
400 Bad Request message, 258
401 Unauthorized: Logon Failed message, 258
403 Forbidden: Execute Access Forbidden message, 258, **267**
404 File Not Found message, 8-9, 258, **269**
500 Internal Server Error message, 259
501 Not Implemented message, 259
502 Bad Gateway message, 259

A

Access permissions. *See* Permissions.
Active Client, 147
Active Server Components, 151-152
Active server objects, 150
Active Server Pages (ASPs). *See* ASPs (Active Server Pages).
Active Server pages object, 174
ActiveX, 147-148
ActiveX controls, 147
ActiveX Data Object (ADO), 19, 151
ActiveX scripting, 148
Activity logs, file system differences, 34. *See also* Event log files.
Administrator account, 85
ADO (ActiveX Data Objects), 19, 151
Advertisement Rotator, 151
Aliases, virtual directory, 135
<ALT> tags, searching for missing, 212

Analysis tools, 17
Anonymous access, **100**
- (hyphen), in user names, 88, **103**
configuring, 61
enabling, 95
FTP service, 67-68
overview, 82
security, 82, 94-95
troubleshooting, 257
Anonymous accounts, Windows NT, 85-86
Application object, 150
ASP scripts, 148-151, **159**, **160**, **161**
ASPs (Active Server Pages), **162**
Active Client, 147
ActiveX, 147-148
vs. CGI, 148
chunked transfers, 13
debugging, 19, **29**
definition, 148
JavaScript, 147, **160**
JScript, 147-148
server-side scripting, 148
VBScript, 147-148
Auditing events, 83-84, 87-88, **100**
Authentication. *See also* Encryption; Microsoft Certificate Server 1.0; Security.
CAs (certificate authorities), 109-110
Certificate Server 1.0, 17
certificates, 109-110, 121-122
certificates and identities, 23, **28**
CRL (certificate revocation list), 110, 121-122
digital certificates, 83
digital signatures and secure envelopes, 108-109

X

Order Practice Tests From The
Authors Of The *Exam Cram* Series

. . . .

LANWrights offers diskette copies of practice tests for these MCSE exams:

70-058 Networking Essentials   70-059 TCP/IP for NT 4
70-064 Windows 95   70-081 Exchange Server 5.5
70-067 NT Server 4   70-087 IIS 4
70-073 NT Workstation 4   70-088 Proxy Server 2
70-068 NT Server 4 in the Enterprise   70-098 Windows 98

Each diskette includes the following:

√ Two practice exams consisting of 50-70 questions, designed to help you prepare for the certification test. One test automates the test that appears in each *Exam Cram* book; the other is new material.

√ Feedback on answers, to help you prepare more thoroughly.

√ Access to the LANWrights Question Exchange, an online set of threaded discussion forums aimed at the topics for each of these books, where you can ask for help and get answers within 72 hours.

Note: These tests are written in HTML and use Java and JavaScript tools, so you must use Navigator 3.02 or Internet Explorer 3.02 or higher. (IE 4.01 is recommended.)

Fees for practice exam diskettes:

$ 25 for single diskette $115 for any six
$ 45 for any two $130 for any seven
$ 65 for any three $145 for any eight
$ 85 for any four $160 for any nine
$100 for any five $175 for all ten

All amounts are US$

To order, please send a check or money order drawn on a U.S. bank. Please include complete delivery information with your order: Name, Company, Street Address, City, State, Postal Code, Country. Send all orders to LANWrights Exams, P.O. Box 26261, Austin, TX, USA 78755-0261. For orders from Mexico or Canada, please add US$5; for orders outside North America, please add US$10. For expedited delivery, online orders, or other information, please visit www.lanw.com/examcram/order.htm.

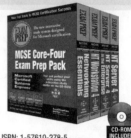